Praise for Lydia Cacho and Sla

'Cacho is a woman of great strength and courage, who is deeply committed to ethical journalism and the advancement of human rights'   —MARIANNE PEARL

'Cacho has brought to light information that was previously unavailable and she has exposed herself to enormous risk... The importance of her evidence is universal'
                    —ROBERTO SAVIANO, AUTHOR OF *GOMORRAH*

'Cacho inspires, encourages, protects, empowers. She has modelled what investigative journalism should be for generations to come'
                    —AGNES CALLAMARD, DIRECTOR, ARTICLE 19

'The work that Lydia Cacho does is as indispensable as the air we breathe'
                    —ENGLISH PEN

'Cacho uncovers some of the most harrowing tales from kidnapped sex trafficking victims, those who save and protect m, as well as traffickers themselves'
                    —*NORTHERN ECHO*

SLAVERY INC.

The Untold Story of
International Sex Trafficking

Lydia Cacho

Foreword by Roberto Saviano

SOFT SKULL PRESS
An imprint of COUNTERPOINT
BERKELEY

Cover design by Faceout Studio

Typeset in Bembo by Avon DataSet, Warwickshire

Library of Congress Cataloging-in-Publication Data is available.

ISBN 978-1-61902-296-6

SOFT SKULL PRESS

An imprint of COUNTERPOINT

1919 Fifth Street

Berkeley, CA 94710

www.softskull.com

Printed in the United States of America

Distributed by Publishers Group West

10 9 8 7 6 5 4 3 2 1

To my brothers Oscar, José and Alfredo, who have shown that masculinity can be loving, pro-equality and non violent.

Violence is not good because it hurts and it makes me cry.

—Yeana, sex-trafficking victim survivor,
ten years old

Contents

Foreword

The Power of Ethics

Roberto Saviano

Lydia Cacho is a model for anyone who wishes to become a journalist. She is a woman of great courage who has endured prison and torture to defend a minority that nobody listened to, to draw people's attention to the wrongs that women and children are subject to in Mexico and in the poorest parts of the world. She has uncovered hitherto unknown information and she has exposed herself to enormous danger by informing against important businessmen and politicians.

I, too, have made accusations against organized crime. I have opened windows that revealed collaboration between organized crime and politics, but I have not explicitly attacked the government of my country. I am threatened by the Camorra but I am defended by the Italian state.

Lydia Cacho has had to serve an unjust term of imprisonment, she has been threatened and tortured to frighten her off, yet it was later discovered that all her accusations were well-founded. The importance of her evidence has universal validity. Wherever government is weak, wherever society accepts criminality, women and children are the first victims. The trafficking and exploitation of human beings is the most primitive of crimes that, in contrast to the trafficking of arms and drugs, provides sky-high profit margins but limited risks.

Roberto Saviano is an eminent Italian journalist best known for his investigative reporting on the Camorra, the Italian mafia, which he exposed in his book and movie entitled Gomorrah.

Introduction

When I was seven years old, every time my sister Sonia and I went out on the street, our mother warned us to stay away from the "child-snatcher," an old woman, well known in our neighborhood, who stole girls. She would entice girls by offering them candy and then she would kidnap them and sell them off to strangers. Of course, the word "kidnapper" refers to the snatching of people of all ages, not just children. Forty years later, I discovered that the lesson of my childhood, which could have been taken from Charles Dickens, has now become one of the most serious problems of the twenty-first century. Society in general tends to consider trafficking in women and children as a throwback to a time when the "white slave trade" was a small-time business run by pirates who kidnapped women to sell them to brothels in faraway countries. We thought that modernization and strong global markets would eradicate this type of slavery and that the abuse of children in the darkest corners of the "underdeveloped" world would simply disappear through contact with Western laws and market economies. My research for this book shows the exact opposite. There is a world-wide explosion in organized-crime syndicates that kidnap, buy, and enslave women and children; the same forces that were supposed to eradicate slavery have strengthened it on an unprecedented scale. All over the planet, we are witnessing a culture that considers the kidnapping, disappearance, trade and corruption of young girls and adolescents as normal. They become sexual objects for rent and sale, and our global culture celebrates this objectification as an act of freedom and progress. In a dehumanizing market economy, millions of people assume that prostitution is a minor evil. They choose to ignore the fact that what underlies prostitution is exploitation, abuse, and the tremendous power of organized crime, exercised on a small and large scale around the world.

For centuries, mafiosi, politicians, military officers, businessmen, industrialists, religious leaders, bankers, police officers, judges, priests, and ordinary men have participated in global organized-crime networks. The difference between individual offenders or small local gangs and the global criminal syndicates lies in their strategies, codes, and marketing practices. Without a doubt, corruption is what gives the mafia economic and political power in every city where they do business. The search for pleasure is universal and provides a vital link in the chain: while some create the market for human slavery, others protect it, promote it, and feed it, or are in charge of renewing the demand for raw materials.

Organized crime includes mafias, syndicates or cartels that run illegal businesses to generate profits. The individuals who participate in these illegal activities are called gangsters, mafiosi, mobsters, or narcos, and they belong to the so-called "black economy." They do not pay taxes to legitimate governments but they must negotiate with such governments in order to operate. The deals between organized criminals and governments contribute to the trade in arms, drugs, and human beings. This trade involves crimes such as robbery, fraud, and the illegal transport of goods and people.

In the twenty-first century organized-crime groups have become more professional. The capitalist rules of free trade have provided the mafia with countless opportunities to create new routes for the trafficking of goods and services between countries and continents. Violence and protection are their main businesses; money, pleasure, and power are their primary goals.

Trafficking in persons, as defined in the Glossary at the end of this book, has been documented in 175 nations. It shows the weakness of global capitalism and the disparity created by the most powerful countries' economic rules. Above all, it reveals the normalization of human cruelty and the culture that has encouraged it. Each year, 1.39 million people around the world—mostly women and girls—are subjected to sexual slavery. They are bought, sold, and re-sold like raw materials in any given industry, like social waste, like trophies and gifts.

Over a period of five years I set out to track the small and large international mafia operations by listening to the stories of survivors of sexual exploitation. I found men, women, and children who were victims of labor trafficking or forced marriages. But my main focus was to follow the trail of a criminal phenomenon born in the twentieth century: the sexual trafficking of women and children. The sophistication of the global sex industry has created a market for sex slaves that may soon outnumber the African slaves sold from the 1500s to the 1800s.

Sex has always played a central role in the history of every mafia. Mafias buy, sell, give, kidnap, rent, loan, rape, torture, and kill women and girls. The notion of women as objects of pleasure is always present in the stories of the criminal groups around the world—the Japanese Yakuza, the Chinese Triads, the Italian, Russian, and Albanian mafias, and the Latin American drug cartels. Sexual pleasure feeds economic and political power. According to macho codes, women are valued as objects, not as people; and even the women who participate in criminal organizations adopt attitudes of misogyny and contempt.

Access to sexual pleasure is a great tool of cohesion and negotiation among groups of males in the military and business worlds, to such an extent that the sex trade is the most profitable in the world, even more so than the arms and drug trades. The products are adult women, adolescents, and young girls, regardless of age, as long as they can be controlled, used, and dominated by their owners.

This book explores the male mentality towards women and sexuality. We learn about the so-called "feminist boomerang," which pushes many men to seek younger and younger women from countries where the culture of feminine submission still prevails. The book also lends a voice to women who work as street prostitutes as well as to those who call themselves "free prostitutes" and create associations to defend prostitution as "just another job" in a capitalist and exploitive world. Without them, we would not be able to explain the complex global debate on sexual slavery and prostitution.

Traveling around the world and investigating the trafficking rings radically changed my perspective on how the mafias are connected. The impunity with which these groups run their businesses is alarming and suspicious, especially at a time when the most powerful countries have put the battle against human trafficking near the top of their national and international agendas. Why are there so many contradictions in migration policies and free-trade agreements? Why are more women than men now becoming migrants? How many countries legally protect labor exploitation in an effort to improve their economies? Why is it that in wealthy countries there is a lack of transparency in the temporary detention of migrants from poor countries? How do border factories operate? How do businesses and governments choose a territory for labor exploitation?

On an emotional level, having to confront the fact that I am a female journalist made this investigation much more complex. The challenge was monumental. Even though I speak four languages, I had to trust interpreters and native stringers who knew the ins and outs of every city and the local mafias' rules.

Several international correspondents, all men, recommended chauffeurs, informants and guides to me. None of my colleagues had followed the trail of human traffickers, although some of them had covered the issue as part of other investigations into corruption or organized crime. Without arousing suspicion, many of them were able to enter the brothels and karaoke bars where young girls and women are trafficked in about twenty countries. They are men, and this is their passport to the crime scene.

In Cambodia, Thailand, Burma, and central Asia, I had to adopt various strategies to avoid danger. I encountered enormous frustrations, such as when I had to flee a Cambodian casino run by the Chinese Triads, where girls under the age of ten were being bought and sold.

There were many obstacles. Throughout the tourist destinations of the world, there are taxi drivers, concierges and chauffeurs who provide services to promote prostitution and participate in trafficking rings, which makes it difficult to gauge whether they will betray you. It is highly likely that the person driving you through the streets of Sri Lanka, Miami, or Cuba is also reporting to local crime syndicates that a woman journalist is asking about their services or to be taken to specific neighborhoods where pimps and trafficking victims live.

The ever-present fear I felt was heightened by the fact that I am a woman. It made me take precautions, but it also pushed me to look harder at my sources and be more suspicious of them. It also made me more empathetic with the victims who dared to share their stories, and it reminded me how dangerous it is to be a woman in any patriarchal society.

I interviewed various survivors and experts, but I also had to approach those operating inside the networks and still live to tell the tale. In order to do so, I put into practice the lessons of Gunter Wallraff, a German journalist and author of *The Lowest of the Low*. I met Gunter when he visited Mexico and we had the chance to share our experiences. Following his advice, during my trip from Mexico to central Asia I disguised myself and assumed false identities. As a result, I was able to sit down and have coffee with a Filipino trafficker in Cambodia; dance in a Mexican nightclub with Cuban, Brazilian, and Colombian dancers; enter a brothel of young women in Tokyo where everyone looked like a manga character; and, dressed as a nun, I was able to walk through La Merced, one of the most dangerous neighborhoods, controlled by powerful traffickers, in Mexico City.

Although all forms of human trafficking are rooted in the search for economic power, sex trafficking encourages, creates, and strengthens a culture in which slavery is normalized and considered to be a viable answer for the millions of women, girls, and boys who live in poverty and lack education. The power of the international sex trade lies in turning the human body into a commodity, to be exploited, bought, and sold without the owner's permission. During the 2009 World Sex Fair, I had the opportunity to interview several of the best-known marketers and promoters of the sex trade, and most of them repeated the same phrase as if it were their mantra: "This is all about money, not people." This is the slogan they use to train sex entrepreneurs. The millions that these people invest annually in political lobbying to normalize slavery could save an entire country from starvation.

Before embarking on this journey, a retired Mexican army general told me that an illegal cargo of AK-47s did not need anything more than proper packaging, a buyer, a corrupt government intermediary, and a seller. A human slave, however, must be convinced that her life has no value except to her buyer and seller. The trafficker's power is sustained by eliminating the potential victims' chances of dignity and freedom. Poverty is not only the fertile ground, but the machine that plants the seeds of slavery in the world. Governments' complicity is undeniable.

This book features the full cast of characters who appear in this tragedy: the traffickers; the victims who became victimizers, and those who healed their bodies and minds and transformed their lives; the intermediaries, clients, madams, military officers, public servants—more or less honest or corrupt—in various countries; mothers who offered to sell me their babies; mothers desperately searching for their daughters who were kidnapped by traffickers; and those who participated in local sex tourism rings. Their voices, threats, and hopes are in these pages.

We cannot understand this criminal business unless we follow the money trail. How do they launder their money and where? The banks and stock-market investors play their part. To understand this phenomenon I had to analyze various countries' stance on human trafficking and prostitution, to examine how governments profit from its legalization or regulation, and the cultural value that men and women give to commercial sex. I found profoundly religious nations, such as Turkey, where prostitution is legal and the government runs brothels. Sweden, on the other hand, has criminalized the consumption of commercial sex and has legally protected women who are victims of commercial sexual slavery.

Finally, this work would not be complete without the millions of people who have devoted their lives to rescuing and healing victims of trafficking, from China to Brazil, from India to Los Angeles, from Guatemala to Canada and Japan.

This is a map of contemporary slavery; an investigation that answers the essential journalistic questions of who, how, when, where, and why, in the twenty-first century, more people, more arms, and more drugs are being sold. The means to fight this crime lie in the hands of the world's citizens. I hope that every human being can find his or her own path to freedom and hope, regardless of the moral panic that this issue has generated in recent years.

I

Turkey and the Golden Crescent

I check my passport, ticket, and Turkish visa. I am ready to begin my trip to central Asia. As I study the map, memories of my previous trip come back to me.

Some years ago, I traveled to Finland, and then to St Petersburg, Moscow, and Kiev. Later, I flew to Tbilisi, Georgia, where I came to know and respect the journalist Anna Politkóvskaya, who helped me understand the complexities of the region. I traveled through Azerbaijan and Armenia. I visited Tashkent and Samarkand, once one of the most beautiful cities of the Persian empire. From Uzbekistan, I went to Ashgabat in Turkmenistan. It was October, and I suffered the winter as only a woman from the tropics can, incapable of stoically tolerating temperatures of ten degrees below zero.

This time, it is February, and the cold will not be as cruel. I return to the map and trace my route, following the path of the slave traffickers. I will fly from London to Turkey and visit Ankara and Istanbul, the principal cities of that beautiful country.

I have mixed emotions. How many times as a young girl did I dream about traveling the world, admiring civilizations and cultures that were new to me? I imagined myself walking through the underground cities of Cappadocia, an underworld whose giant stones might whisper their secret stories to me. I also remember my mother telling me how much it meant to her to visit the church of Santa Sofia in Istanbul.

I am going to a country that represents a bridge between civilizations. Before leaving Mexico, I re-read Orhan Pamuk. This time I will not be chasing the voices of the past. I will be visiting a secular republic that plays the important role of connecting Asia and Europe. The country's borders are porous, and I can imagine the surveillance challenges faced by the authorities. In the northeast, Turkey is bordered by Georgia; in the east, by Armenia and Azerbaijan; in the southeast, by Iran; in the north, by the Black Sea; and in the west, by Greece, the Aegean Sea, and Bulgaria. Iraq, Syria, and, of course, the Mediterranean Sea lie to the south. The ancient trade routes have not changed much, but my goal is to discover how the pattern of smuggling has evolved to operate in the globalized world of organized crime.

Turkey is a country of seventy-five million inhabitants. Since signing a free-trade agreement with its European neighbors in 1996, Turkey, like the majority of other countries that have opened their borders, has faced the paradox of fostering the growth of the free market while also experiencing the growth of an illicit one. Turkey is an associate member of the European Union, but it has not yet met EU requirements for admission as a full member.

The plane lands in Turkey at night. The beauty of the starry sky painted with violet brushstrokes takes my breath away. Sitting in a taxi, on my way to the hotel, I roll down the window. The smells of Istanbul reach me: the diesel, the spices, and the salty breeze from the sea. Every city has its unique aroma.

The taxi driver, proud of his country, decides to give me a tour. He explains that we are in the area that separates Anatolia and Thrace, encompassing the Sea of Marmara, the Bosporus and the Dardanelles—the area known as the Turkish Straits, which form a boundary between Asia and Europe. "We are about to be recognized as a member of the European Union," he informs me in a friendly tone, using touristy English that hints at various accents. "Here everything is good," he assures me. "Muslims, Jews, Christians, Agnostics, Protestants all live together," he adds. He speaks as though he is repeating a slogan. I smile and think about the reports coming out of PEN International, an organization that defends freedom of expression, citing the persecution and incarceration of Turkish journalists. However, I remain silent because I know that the world is not black and white and that all countries, just like the people who inhabit them, are diverse, complex, and magnificent at the same time.

The kindness of the people, their smiles, the warmth of the bellhop's eyes as he greets me at the hotel, and the sweet voice of a receptionist who speaks perfect English, make me feel welcome. These things remind me that one cannot see the darkness without also seeing the light, and that kindness exists everywhere. I suppose that some of the 200,000 women and girls who have been trafficked to this country over the last five years have at one point experienced the kindness of someone who saw them as human beings, someone who made them smile, helping them to feel less alone.

I contact Eugene Schoulgin, an extraordinary writer, novelist, and journalist, born in 1941 of Russian-Norwegian descent. Eugene has lived in Afghanistan and Iraq, and he is now in Istanbul, serving as director of PEN International. He helps me to schedule some meetings with political analysts and direct sources. This dear friend affectionately takes care of me, and I intend to keep him informed as to my whereabouts and the people I meet, just in case something happens and he needs to know how and where to find me. I would not have been as successful at getting information on this trip without his security advice.

The Informant

It is Friday in Maslak, a neighborhood known as the "Manhattan of Istanbul." The skyscrapers in this modern financial district

embody the cosmopolitan mix of this jewel of a city, half
European and half Asian. The February chill invites people to
seek refuge in the bars and cafés that smell of dark tobacco,
strong coffee, and, in some cases, of recently cooked lamb.
Slim young women, fashionably dressed in Italian or French
styles in mini-skirts, leggings, and tall boots, enter the bars as
though they own the world. Others walk absorbed in their own
thoughts, with their heads covered with fine silk scarves and
wearing modest dresses. Young men wear cologne and look
very polished in their Hugo Boss suits—some authentic, some
fake. They greet each other with a hug and a firm touch of
the cheeks—the masculine form of the double kiss, as learned
from their grandfathers. The voice of a Turkish pop singer who
sounds like Britney Spears fills the air.

I am standing at the bar drinking a beer and waiting for my
contact to arrive. After a little while, a tall, handsome, dark-
skinned man with close-cropped hair and bushy eyebrows,
wearing a brown leather jacket, stops beside me. His nose still
red from the icy air outside, he removes his wool scarf, and,
without even giving me a glance, he says my name and asks for
a drink.

He looks at me from the corner of his eye and in halting
French mumbles that we cannot speak here: "In five-star hotel.
We can meet tomorrow in five-star hotel." I reach into my
purse and retrieve a card from my hotel and give it to him. He
looks at it, observes me, and then returns his gaze to the card.
"That is the Taya Hatun neighborhood," he says. "Yes, it's a
small hotel, only tourists," I insist. "At nine in the morning.
Only you, madam," he adds. He pays for the drink without
having touched it. He leaves the bar and jumps on a streetcar,
looking over his shoulder.

Mahmut is a police officer—one of the good ones, according
to a colleague who is a foreign correspondent. He was trained
by the International Organization for Migration (IOM), an

inter-governmental agency based in Geneva, as part of a special group to combat human trafficking in Turkey. The US Department of State has invested seven million dollars in Turkey to fight trafficking. The Norwegians have also invested the same amount. Mahmut is a secular Turk, a remarkably well-educated man. He believes that the fight against the sexual exploitation of women in Turkey and on the Silk Road, which Marco Polo once traveled, is a farce and this is why, after months of negotiations with contacts, he has decided to tell me his story.

I am waiting for him at the small boutique hotel and drinking a delicious, fragrant Turkish coffee. A group of Spanish tourists chat happily in the restaurant. Their tour guide arrives and, as they stand up, they ask me if I will be joining them. "No," I answer. A woman from Seville warns me that I will regret not taking this tour. "Absolutely," I reply. I say goodbye, and I think about these tourists going down the avenue that runs parallel to where the Turkish brothels are, unaware that the darkened windows hide slaves from other countries.

I take a seat at the bar. It is an elegant place with a luxurious atmosphere, straight out of a novel. It is furnished with honey-colored armchairs with velvet scatter cushions embroidered in different styles. The place is bright, and soft music is playing. Nothing suggests that someone might have a conversation about the sale and purchase of human beings here. The policeman arrives and the young receptionist barely looks at him as he enters.

He approaches me with such stiffness that the tension between us remains unbroken. I invite him to sit down. He looks around and in a low voice he says, "If they find out that I was the one who gave you the information, I will rot in jail. That is, if they don't kill me first for violation of Article 301 and for treason against my country and against the police code. According to the state, the media is our enemy; we are never to trust it." I know. On the basis of the penal code of this country, thousands of writers and journalists have been prosecuted for daring to give their opinions on the Turkish government. The legal case against Orhan Pamuk, banning his freedom of expression, is perhaps the best known in the West. The authorities maintain that the law has been changed, as required by the European Union, but judges in Turkish courts continue to hear such cases. Pamuk provided evidence of the killing of one million Armenians and 30,000 Kurds in Turkey in 1915. According to the Turkish government, Pamuk's statements insulted Turkish identity and warranted a three-year jail sentence.

We order a large pitcher of an exquisite, fragrant cardamom tea. We smile politely. Suddenly, silently, he points out the cameras on the bar's ceiling. I tell him that we can go up to my room, and he accepts.

He is cautious. The room is small, but it has an armchair and a desk chair. I offer him the armchair. Little by little, he loosens up. He asks me if I know about Turkish corruption and trafficking in women. While I speak, he pays close attention to every word. He asks permission to remove his jacket. I agree with a nod. I freeze at the sight of a gun in his shoulder holster and for a second I lose the thread of my thoughts. With a pen in my hand and a notebook open on my lap, I realize that I am in Turkey, in a hotel room with an armed man, and that we are the only two people who know this. He intuits my anxiety and begins to speak about his wife and about the admirable women he has met at the IOM. With a sigh, we make a silent pact of trust. Without such pacts, we reporters could never survive.

A surprising statistic in Turkey has puzzled experts. Despite an increase in the number of trafficking cases involving women worldwide, the Turkish police have reported a decrease in the number of women trafficked to Turkey from Russia, Moldavia, Georgia and Kyrgyzstan. How is it possible that in a few years the Turkish police force has been able to lower the incidence of women trafficked from these countries by 50 percent?* Why are there no statistics on domestic trafficking?

Mahmut delicately picks up the small crystal glass of tea and takes a few sips. He studies his shoes and explains to me that the Turkish government's new strategy to gain EU membership consists of signing all international agreements and accepting a dialogue on human rights. At the same time, the government has strengthened the army and the police force dedicated to national security. However, Mahmut warns me that the police and army bosses see prostitution as a business, and they are customers themselves.

> They believe that North Americans and some Nordic Europeans are the ones who call it sexual slavery, but that's someone else's problem, not ours. It's a question of approach, madam. For example, a lot of Norwegians and Swedes come to Turkey for sex tourism. In their countries, they don't do it, and here they do, because it is legal and nobody recognizes them . . . Today, more than ever, the Albanian and Russian mafias collaborate with the local mafias to transport women who end up in the prostitution business. It has always worked this way. The difference now is that so-called "civilized" countries have decided to fight this crime, making it a better business for everyone: the traffickers, those who make pornography, and those who simply sell a false dream to women. The wars in Iraq and Afghanistan, with all their black-market opportunities, have fueled the smuggling of drugs, weapons, and women. Nobody speaks of this. You will see that in a few years the media will be surprised to learn how much money

---

* The Turkish government's inter-agency task force reported this to the US research team on human trafficking: *Trafficking in Persons (TIP) Report,* 2009, US Department of State, www.state.gov/j/tip/rls/tiprpt/. During an interview conducted by the author with members of the task force, this official data was confirmed.

the terrorists and North American mercenaries have earned from the sale of women in the region. The Yakuza buy amphetamines processed in Iran and take them to Japan, Italy, the United States, and they also buy girls all over the world.

As I write these lines, I stop to look at the photographs I took and to listen to the recordings I made a month after my trip to Turkey. I interviewed a North American and a Colombian woman who were sold to the Yakuza in Tokyo and in Osaka. I also recall the story of a Mexican girl who was murdered by the Yakuza. I realize that the information is there for anyone who chooses to see it. The problem is what governments choose to address or ignore once they become aware of these tales of globalized slavery.

I decide to tell Mahmut about an interview I had with Dr Muhtar Cokar, founder and director of the Human Resource Development Foundation, a Turkish NGO that runs a shelter for female victims of human trafficking. I interviewed him in his office in downtown Istanbul. Cokar, a calm man incapable of looking me straight in the eye, confirmed that many young women from Moldavia, Russia, and other neighboring territories are first forced into prostitution in their own countries before they are brought to Turkey with promises of better work and more money. However, once they arrive in Turkey, they find themselves alone, without work. There is a preconceived notion that Turkish men go crazy for Eastern European women, who are known as *natashas*, especially blondes and redheads with pale skin and long legs. According to Dr Cokar, there are few Turkish prostitutes; Istanbul is a city with solid morals, and it is impossible for a religious family, regardless of their faith, to accept a daughter becoming a prostitute. The current law, which dates back to the 1930s, prohibits prostitutes from marrying or having children.

Foreign women make perfect prostitutes for Turkish and

foreign men alike. According to rescued women, 40 percent of Turkey's sex tourists come from Russia. According to Dr Cokar, many prostitutes work independently. They save money and when the police start harassing or extorting money from them, they usually end up being extradited or, to put it in politically correct terms, repatriated. On average they spend two weeks in a shelter in Istanbul (although some have stayed up to six months). After that they are sent back to their countries, to their families and children and to a life of poverty and hunger. Some attempt to return to Turkey, paying $15 for a visa at the border; from there they can make their way to Greece or Italy, where the Albanian mafia will take them to England or France. They have to pay for the journey, but, according to the doctor, many of them will do anything in order to send money home.

I was surprised by his calm, clear conviction; the way he spoke of the *natashas* disturbed me—it was almost condescending. When he noticed the surprise in my eyes, he made a strange observation: "Look, Lydia, sometimes foreigners do not understand our customs and they judge without thinking . . ." He stood up and lit a cigarette, blowing the smoke out of the window. "For example, now there are discussions about whether women should wear the veil in Turkey. You may call it sexist [I never said anything on the subject], but in reality it is a good thing because it allows orthodox women to leave their houses. It is a feminist measure," he assured me. "These are customs that, if not understood, can never be appreciated properly," he said to me, as he threw his cigarette out of the window. "There are 3,000 registered sex workers in Turkey. In the government brothel, divided into three buildings, there are 131 adult sex workers. There are foreigners hidden in private houses that operate as illegal brothels." Dr Cokar described how sex tourism adopts the same rules as in the rest of the world: there are five-star hotels where wealthy clients obtain high-priced "call girls." Regions with a lot of tourists or military groups always attract and foster prostitution. He said that, according to reliable sources, there are about 100,000 illegal prostitutes in Turkey, although he could not corroborate that figure.

In 2010, Dr Cokar's shelter assisted 100 women victims of trafficking. According to the doctor, none of them showed signs of "severe physical violence," but there was evidence of psychological and sexual violence. Traffickers inject the prostitutes with antibiotics once a month to protect clients who, for the most part, refuse to use condoms. This practice, he added, leads to terrible medical problems for the prostitutes, because they build up resistance to stronger antibiotics. "Fifty percent of immigrant women who enter Turkey end up in prostitution rings," states a report by Dr Cokar. The IOM further reveals that adolescents trafficked from China, the Philippines, and Sri Lanka have been rescued in five regions in Turkey.

The country's double standard is remarkable. For example, Turkey is notorious for transvestite and transsexual prostitution, which draws its own tourism, but the state considers transvestites and transsexuals to be "sinners," and any homosexual behaviour in public places is strictly prohibited. However, there are illegal brothels specializing in sex tourism that have 2,000 transvestites; they are so well organized that they even accept credit cards.

I asked Dr Cokar about the fact that prostitution is legal and he told me he did not believe that abolishing prostitution was an option for Turkey. "Our organization considers prostitution a form of sexual violence against women, but conditions are such that it becomes an issue of survival. We support them as human beings, but we do not support the business of prostitution." Furthermore, Dr Cokar considered that trafficking would increase if prostitution were abolished. He remained silent when I asked him whether he believed that owning and trading in women was culturally acceptable in his country. As an answer, he handed me the brochures of his institution and spoke of a project to prevent AIDS.

Dr Cokar insisted that the women who come to Turkey travel voluntarily, but Mahmut believes the opposite. He says that very few women seek to become prostitutes. Most of them want dignified jobs as waitresses or domestic employees. Mahmut confirms that in reality almost no foreigner operates independently in Turkey, unless she has become the lover of a married man who can financially support her, and such men abound. Local sources maintain that in Turkey, as in most Muslim countries, a double standard on sexuality favors prostitution and infidelity.

According to *The Protection Project Review of The Trafficking in Persons Report* (2009), Turkey is home to 200 identified groups that traffic women and girls. According to the IOM, from 1999 to 2009, 250,000 people have been trafficked through Turkey. The majority are women who came from Azerbaijan, Georgia, Armenia, Russia, the Ukraine, Montenegro, Uzbekistan, and Moldavia. It should be pointed out that the IOM is the most successful organization at rescuing and identifying victims. However, Turkish authorities claim that between 2003 and 2008 only 994 people were identified as victims of trafficking.

Twelve Turkish non-governmental organizations (NGOs) have recorded a large number of cases of girls who were kidnapped from Romanian orphanages and sold in Turkey. Having been told that a company will send them from Turkey to Germany or the United Kingdom, most women are tricked into traveling to Turkey with a fake employment contract as waitresses, nannies, secretaries, models, dancers, or domestic employees. Hundreds of young women are taken by ferry across the Black Sea to Trebizond in Turkey, or from the Albanian port of Vlore to San Foca, Italy.

Mahmut insists that the Turkish government has taken measures to prevent trafficking. For example, the Turkish police have worked with the governments of Moldavia and the Ukraine to produce educational films that warn women and children against the ploys of sex traffickers. On the other hand, he asserts that the problem is that the Turkish government has also legalized prostitution and that the government itself runs brothels. He is well aware of the statistics: 79 percent of trafficking victims are bought and sold for commercial sexual exploitation. Mahmut is vehement as he explains this to me:

> Most clients are Turkish and the traffickers are locals and for-eigners. The prostitution business is lucrative; it brings in a lot of money, madam. Thousands of tourists come to the coast and to Istanbul looking for pleasure. Of course, they also tour our country's many beautiful historical sites. Unfortunately, there are some who take advantage of young girls. We have found sixteen-year-old girls that were brought here when they were fourteen. They were in the brothels with false papers, and the government looked the other way. When traffickers grow tired of these girls, they simply call the police and turn them in. Or when the raids take place, the traffickers are nowhere to be found. The majority of young prostitutes have real papers but they are here illegally.

This is something I have also seen in the rest of the world: government officials, consular officers, and even some ambassadors are willing to issue authentic passports based on false documents.

Mahmut mentions the difficulties of identifying a sexual slave when immigration documents are legal: if border agents were to decide whether or not to grant entrance to a country based on mere appearance or on suspicion, the borders would become chaotic and diplomatic relations would be irreparably harmed. "This is why, rather than risking making a mistake, officers decide to ignore their suspicions. Furthermore, there are women of certain races that look more like girls, such as Mongols or Cambodians. I have seen Philippine women who look sixteen when they are really twenty-five. It's simply hard to tell," Mahmut adds, as though he is thinking aloud.

According to the organization End Child Pornography and Trafficking of Children for Sexual Purposes (ECPAT), 16 percent of trafficking victims rescued in Turkey are minors sold for commercial sexual exploitation. Mahmut agrees with me when I quote this statistic. He repeats that sex in this sense is considered to be an industry and not criminal activity. He also agrees with the Save the Children reports stating that many pedophiles seek asylum in areas where prostitution is legalized, thus becoming loyal clients and boosting the market for child sexual exploitation.

Despite the Turkish foreign ministry's major public awareness efforts on this issue, their own statistics do not lie. In 2006, there were 422 recorded arrests; in 2007, there were 308; and in 2008, only 255 men were arrested, mostly clients and, in some cases, victims considered to be accomplices of trafficking. This seems to indicate that the Turkish government, like many others, has partially criminalized sexual exploitation to quiet the demands of countries such as the United States and Sweden, which favor the abolition of prostitution, even though a little in-depth investigation reveals that illegal brothels operate and flourish with the government's permission. Meanwhile, the authorities give fewer permits for legal prostitution in an effort to make the international community believe they are enforcing the law.

According to some CIA reports, Turkey is taking the same approach with drugs. US agency reports confirm that Turkey continues to be pivotal to the heroin route between Europe and Asia. Forty-one percent of the heroin in the world, produced in Afghanistan and Pakistan, enters Europe through Turkey. Highways and airports are used to transport Afghan morphine to Turkey, where it is converted into heroin in labs in Istanbul or Kyrgyzstan and then distributed in Europe and Russia. The legal cultivation of opium for medicinal purposes in Turkey (but also in India, Australia, France, the United States and the United Kingdom) encourages lax police controls.

The IOM persuaded the Turkish government to set up a telephone hotline (toll free 157) for victims of sex trafficking. Between May 2009 and June 2011, 209 victims were rescued. The task of rescuing and tending to the victims' needs are in the hands of a couple of NGOs and the IOM. But when I speak to some young women from Moldavia and Croatia, the statistics no longer seem so positive. These young women assure me that repatriation is a farce and that all it entails is the deportation of women who have already spent too much time on the job. Only the newest women and girls can be controlled because they cannot yet speak the language. Tourism earns Turkey 21 billion US dollars a year, and one of the most alluring attractions for Europeans is the sex. In this country the increase in male and female sex tourism is obvious. In contrast to female prostitution, the majority of male prostitutes do not have handlers; they just pay a fee for police protection. Young boys—often the preferred choice of pedophiles—are subjected to the same rules, secrecy, and threats faced by sexually enslaved girls.

Matilde's Girls

Matilde Manukyan, of Armenian descent, was born into an aristocratic family in Turkey in 1914. She was educated in the country's best school run by French nuns. She married but later became a widow, inheriting a beautiful building in the "red light" district of Karakoy. In time, she became known as the queen of the brothels, controlling thirty-two brothels and owning fourteen buildings that housed legal prostitution rings. On various occasions, she was suspected of sexually exploiting minors but her relationship with the government gave her protection throughout her life. Indeed, the Turkish government gave her an award for being the citizen who paid the most taxes during a five-year period (1990–95), even though her earnings came from the sex trade. In 1975 she survived a bomb attack on her car, and she underwent reconstructive surgery twelve times. Matilde had many enemies among the new mafia traffickers. After 1990 the international mafias began to put pressure on Turkish prostitution syndicates and Matilde, who was accustomed to being the queen bee, refused to pay fees for protection from the criminals, who were in collusion with the police.

In 1996, the public was shown evidence that under-age girls were being sexually exploited in her brothels, and the high society that frequented her establishments stopped doing so. When she was exposed as a sex trafficker, Matilde announced that she had converted to Islam. According to the prophet Mohammed, a person's sins are forgiven upon conversion to Islam. She subsequently built a beautiful mosque using the money she earned from trafficking and even got support from the government, despite the public outcry. Although Allah supposedly pardoned her, a large segment of the Turkish population continues to refer to her as the "trafficker of women and girls." It is widely known that Matilde kept a cozy relationship with the Turkish police until in 2001, when she died and was absolved of her sins due to her religious conversion.

In London, I had the opportunity to interview Ulla, a Syrian woman aged thirty-nine who had been kidnapped and sold to a man in Istanbul who took her to Matilde. Ulla worked in two brothels from the age of sixteen until she was twenty. She is now married and works in a convenience store. She hides her past from most of her friends and she volunteers as a translator for a London-based organization that defends women's rights. This is an excerpt from Ulla's testimony:

> Back then we thought we were being treated right. We heard about other young women who were taken to horrible

places and treated like real slaves. The stories terrified us, we were told that the men there were savages and that they paid only a few cents for young girls. We heard that the men had strange diseases and that the women weren't allowed to wash themselves or clean themselves up. Our handlers kept us clean and presentable. They paid us little and sometimes punished us. Some clients were obscene and violent, but that was part of the job. A client bought me—at twenty, I was already considered old—and he took me to London. There I was illegal for some years, and on top of it all I was also an addict. Later on I managed to find help from other women, and I changed my life. Now, I look back and I realize that I was a sex slave, but back then I didn't really understand it. When you have no way out and you're all alone, it is better not to see reality; you just live it and try not to think much. I thought: "What's wrong with selling my body when it's the only thing I have to sell?"

I could not escape, since brothels are legal in Turkey. The police and the politicians were our best clients. They loved the owner so much that they sent their nurses to check on us—we were presumably the most obedient and healthy prostitutes in Turkey.

Ulla admitted that she became addicted to opium after one of the women at the brothel gave her a taste of the drug. It was thanks to the addiction that she was able to withstand the terror of being locked up, used, and raped ten or twelve times a day: "The opium allowed me to fly, not feel, not be me," says Ulla.

For other women, living in the brothels is no great tragedy. Sonya, from Montenegro, arrived in Turkey when she was twenty-four years old, and she is now thirty-five. When she was taken to Turkey, she already knew that she would work as a prostitute. In three years she had paid off her debt and could go out on the streets without being bothered. Sonya recalls:

I lived in terror that someone in the system might get annoyed or tired of me and that I would be swept up in one of the police raids that happened every time new girls were brought in. I was terrified that they would take me and return me to my country. They told us that the police had our photographs on file and that, if we did something bad, we would be deported. I did not want to return to the hunger, the violence; I have nothing in my country . . . I no longer have a country. Being a prostitute was not the best, but it was something to live on for the time being.

The story of Matilde Manukyan, the great Turkish madam, shows how some pimps or madams turn into traffickers of sex slaves. Not only do they work within the system, turning the police and the government into their allies, they also operate legal businesses that are recognized and valued by certain social groups, such as the aristocracy and politicians. Once she was legitimately operating within the legalized system of prostitution, Manukyan began trafficking minors. Next, she invested the profits from trafficking in women and girls in real estate. Before her death, she owned three five-star hotels, more than 120 apartments in many tourist areas of Turkey, an export company and a business of more than 300 luxury taxis. She had a collection of Rolls-Royces, Mercedes, and BMWs. She built a hotel in Germany and had a luxurious mega-yacht that she used to entertain her powerful friends.

Matilde's case fills me with moral panic, but it also allows me to see the complexity of this debate and the difference between prostitution and commercial sexual exploitation. At what point does a woman involved in legal prostitution decide to enslave adolescents and children? How many madams like Matilde are there in the world right now deciding on the future of a girl under the assumption that "What is good for me is good for all?" What happens when prostitution and trafficking are combined?

When the person who handles the prostitutes has economic and political power, the legal system can do nothing to break up the slavery syndicate.

The Golden Crescent

Mahmut goes on to explain the complicated relationship between Turkey and the Golden Crescent, the opium-producing region of Afghanistan, Pakistan and Iran:

> When the heroin problem in Turkey was beginning to be tackled, in 1998, it was easier for the Turkish government to remain silent, as the Turkish, Albanian, and Kosovar mafias were operating in this country. Turkey has the blessing and curse of belonging to both Europe and Asia, to be the stepping-stone between both worlds. The Balkans route has always been complex. We cannot say that the Turkish authorities are not corrupt; all over the world police officers and politicians can be bought with dollars or euros.
>
> In Turkey, we have the IOM so that the Europeans and the North Americans see us as equals. Nobody speaks of how the agreements among the mafias have adapted. When some countries decide to crack down on arms trafficking, they do so immediately if it poses a threat to national or economic interests. However, trafficking in women, which is now simply called "trafficking," has been a profitable business for the last twenty years for the Russian and Albanian mafias that operate in Macedonia and trade with the Turkish mafia.

While some commentators on international affairs, such as the columnist Moisés Naím, refuse to believe that the most powerful mafias in the world have joined forces, labeling the idea as merely a police fantasy, the experts who work on the streets confirm that the globalization of mafia operations is part of international business. A few months after my interview with Mahmut, I came to understand the full significance of his comments when I heard the following news: in Istanbul, the Turkish police department specializing in organized crime arrested four Japanese members of an arm of the Yakuza operating in the region. A group of Iranian drug traffickers who had sold methamphetamines to the Yakuza was also arrested. Two of the Yakuza were arrested with 150,000 pills and their accomplices were detained with 200,000 pills on two different occasions. The drug trafficking routes from Iran to Istanbul are the same as those used for the sale of slaves in the region. Mahmut explained that the traffickers who carry the drugs and those who transport the women and girls are not necessarily the same, but those who control the routes are. He says that he knows Turkish and Iranian colleagues who get angry about drug trafficking, but they accept trafficking in women and girls because they believe that this involves prostitutes exercising their free will.

Mahmut speaks about the big police raids on Albanian and Kosovar mafias in Scandinavia in the 1990s. On February 23, 1993, the Norwegian police dealing with heroin trafficking arrested the so-called "godfather," Princ Dobroshi, a Kosovar born in 1964 who was also wanted in Sweden and Denmark on similar charges. He was sentenced to fourteen years, but he escaped from the Ullersmo prison in 1997. Even though he underwent plastic surgery several times, the Czech police were able to arrest him in Prague in 1998. According to official reports, Dobroshi admitted that the transport of heroin to European countries had funded the purchase of arms that were later used in the Kosovo war. The investigations revealed, without giving it much importance, that Dobroshi also ran minor businesses involving trafficking in women and selling protection to brothels. Most of the Dobroshi cartel members ended up in Swiss and Czech prisons.

On December 10, 1998, *The Independent* newspaper revealed

that the Albanian mafia controlled 70 percent of the heroin market in Eurasia. Mahmut, as well as other sources, states that the new generation of mafia bosses are younger and more sophisticated and that they continue to oversee the business of human trafficking and forced prostitution in the region. Organized-crime syndicates now have better technology and, just like governments, they enter into regional and international agreements. Another significant difference, evident in many countries, is the active participation of women in the trafficking syndicates. Many women who have been victims of trafficking are chosen by syndicate leaders to recruit and train other women and girls. The market and its operators, affirms my Turkish informant, are as sophisticated as the times require.

People in high places do not seem to learn their lesson. In January 2005 Princ Dobroshi, considered a terrorist and one of the cruelest mafiosi in the region, was released on parole by the Norwegians, having been handed over to them by the Czechs. According to NATO, he was released on "good behavior."

Mahmut looks at his watch. Speaking in French, searching for the words to express his concerns over mafia operations, has been exhausting. A Turkish–French dictionary has become our ally.

The man before me has already drunk five cups of black tea. He looks toward the window and falls silent every time he hears voices in the corridor. He suddenly pulls his cell phone out of his pocket and shows me a video of a beautiful, three-year-old girl dancing to some music playing in the background. He speaks aloud, as though to himself: "The people at the IOM asked us during our training: 'What would you do if your daughter were sold for sexual exploitation?' This is why I am here," he says as he puts his cell phone away and clears his throat. Perhaps regretting what could be seen as a sign of male weakness, he simply says that his father educated him to put his moral principles above everything. His French ancestry left him with a desire to learn this language at a time in his life when he was able to study more than the average Turkish policeman. His wife, like the majority of Turkish women, can barely read or write. He wants his daughter to feel safe.

In what I judge to be an unusual confession, he admits that he was once "carnally tempted by the *natashas*," but he adds that he is not one to go to brothels.

"You told me that you went to England," he mumbles, lowering his head, looking at me from below those black eyebrows. "What did they tell you about the arrival of women from Turkey and about the famous Albanian-Turkish pimps? Did you see how they get to Italy? You know that we have maritime borders [the Anatolian Peninsula has 8,000 kilometers of coastline]. Go and find out what is inside the containers on those cargo boats."

Geopolitically, Turkey is a strategic area. It is linked to the Caucasus, central Asia, and the Balkans. Its economic liberalization has led to trade agreements with Japan and South Korea. Its automobile, iron and steel, and construction industries are growing, as is the manufacture of electrical household appliances. But experts say the growing market for military hardware is critical. It is no secret that Turkey has the second most powerfully armed force in NATO, trailing only the United States. This nation has 1,043,550 soldiers ready to go to war, and at Incirlik air base there are ninety B-61 nuclear bombs.

Trafficking victims I spoke to told me that soldiers are their best clients in the thousands of legal and illegal brothels in Turkey. The production, sale and re-sale of nuclear and military weapons has also made Turkey an ideal country for organized-crime groups that traffic in arms.

"What would be easier for me to buy, an Asian girl or an AK-47?" I ask Mahmut. He looks at me, smiles, and answers: "An AK-47 is old news. You could buy one tomorrow for $250, but since you're a woman," he says, almost playfully, "it would be better to get an AKM [a much lighter version], which you could buy for $400. It would cost you about the same to buy a weapon or a 'new' woman to exploit. Drugs probably wouldn't be a good idea . . . Of the three, it's the only one you cannot use and re-sell." His no-nonsense tone makes me nervous, but I write his words down just as they are uttered. He realizes that he has made his point and concludes with some information about legal and illegal trade and the difficulty of differentiating between the two.

"Is it the same for women?" I ask. "The business of slavery requires the existence of legal prostitution to make it more difficult to distinguish which is which."

"Exactly, madam," he assures me, "this is why there are so many people interested in encouraging the legalization of prostitution."

With its buoyant economy, Turkey is among the top four countries in the world for the number of boats, yachts and mega-yachts built and sold. In 2008 alone, Turkey imported $141,800,000 worth of goods and services, while $204,800,000 worth of products were exported that same year.

"Check out the charters and how the authorities turn a blind eye at the airports. And be careful," Mahmut says, before bidding me farewell, placing his hand on his heart and bowing slightly.

"Don't worry," I respond, inclining my head. "I come from Mexico. Things aren't so different there for journalists." Even though he is not religious, Mahmut says goodbye, wishing me Allah's protection.

2

Israel and Palestine: What the War Hides

I am sitting facing a woman with huge eyes and poetic wisdom. Her name is Rim Banna, a figure who symbolizes the occupied Palestinian territories, which lie within the state of Israel and comprise the West Bank and the Gaza Strip.

Rim lives in Nazareth, where she was born in 1966. She is a Palestinian poet and women's rights advocate. She uses music to reveal the reality behind political and media manipulation of events. She has composed and recorded eleven albums, each better than the one before. She and her partner, Leonid, also a musician, have a son and a daughter and together they work to promote freedom and peace.

We are seated in a small sitting room with two wooden chairs. I set up my camera and take out my pen. We begin to talk about life and about the safety of women and girls in the occupied territories of Palestine. After a few minutes, her cell phone rings. Excusing herself, Rim reads a text message, smiles, and her face lights up. She shows me the screen: it is a message from her young daughter, Baylasan, telling her mother she has got to school safely. The small girl has even sent a photo of herself smiling. This moves me. Rim proceeds to explain that this is not a game between a mother and her six-year-old daughter. This is how they cope with the bombings, the presence of military forces, the kidnappings, and the illegal arrests. This is how they keep each other calm and informed that they are still alive and free. At least for today.

This singer possesses an emotional intelligence that I have seldom seen in those who risk their lives on a daily basis. She asks me to tell her stories about women and girls from Mexico. Afterwards, Rim says to me that trafficking in women and girls is similar to the occupation of a town.

> The outside world will never understand the real story until it understands that a conflict cannot be resolved when there are such vast inequalities of power, money, arms, and ideas; when one side acts as the patriarchs; when one side gives the orders and the other side is forced to obey, to submit, to prostitute its spirit and accept colonization because they are "the other." I do not support violence; I don't believe in it. This is why my music shows the human side of Palestine, the history of its people, of women and girls, like my daughter. I sing to celebrate the children's strength and their ability to play ball and laugh together, despite knowing that Israeli soldiers are watching them. I sing for the women and girls who maintain and support the whole community, who work, who lose their parents, their spouses, and siblings. I sing for their children who continue to work, believing in life, dreaming of the future and the freedom that will one day dawn . . . Maybe with the morning light, freedom, peace, and understanding will come.

During her concerts, she has sometimes been threatened and called a Muslim extremist. Few people know that Rim is a Christian. "It is difficult to have a dialogue with those who don't want to listen and who reject any sort of criticism. Investigating violence in these circumstances is very difficult," she says. This is why feminist groups that rescue women do their work almost entirely in secret. Resources are for war, not for peace.

Palestine is, in many ways, a mined territory. The Israelis posted at the checkpoints are not their only enemies. There is the ongoing dispute with Lebanon, as well as the deep-rooted conflicts among Muslims, Christians, and Jews. The level of contempt, intolerance, and racism among nations that appear to be sister countries is almost incomprehensible.

I ask Rim if she believes that women and girls are at greater risk of being kidnapped and sold as long as there is no peace in the region. She answers, "Yes, exactly, the war opens the door to all sorts of evil. This is why I sing about hope; we can't lose hope."

Rim tells me about the years since 1967, when the Israeli army occupied the Palestinian territories of Gaza, the eastern part of Jerusalem, and the West Bank. The occupation policy is to control movement within the territories as well as outside, along the borders. Palestine has been fragmented. The occupation, violence, and oppression create a war-like environment in which human rights are not respected.

Roads are surrounded by trenches and checkpoints, which change depending on the Israeli government's needs and strategies. There is a destroyed building here, the remains of a school there. Suddenly checkpoints appear on the highways or on the streets to control people's comings and goings. When children come upon a roadblock on their way to school, they turn around without saying anything and look for another path that will take them there. These children remain silent because they know that speaking out may cost them their lives. Children and their mothers have learned to save their energies and choose their battles; they joke quietly to break the tension and ease the fear they feel when they see a new military checkpoint outside a relative's house.

A young child lifts a tree branch. His twenty-year-old aunt sees this and walks over to him, almost furious, and she breaks the branch into small pieces. Not until this moment do we realize that, from a distance, the branch could appear to be a rifle. This reminds me of the Chiapas massacre in southern Mexico in 1994, when the Mexican army attacked hundreds of people who were carrying wooden sticks during the Zapatista uprising. When photos of the event were later released, the army stated that, from a distance, the sticks looked like rifles.

The United Nations Children's Fund (UNICEF) has reported that in the occupied Palestinian territories dozens of boys and girls continue to die due to armed conflicts. Poverty levels have risen substantially since the year 2000. Security controls and roadblocks have made it more difficult for the population to get to their workplaces, schools, and medical facilities. Considering that half of the population of Gaza is under the age of eighteen, the need to defend children is particularly urgent.

Unlike in other countries, prostitution in Palestine and Israel is illegal. The authorities of both countries consider prostitution a highly immoral activity, from both a social and a religious perspective. This does not mean that prostitution does not exist; it is simply more difficult to investigate due to its illicit status. This is very similar to what happens in Iraq and Iran, where religious precepts support the orthodox belief that men own women and their destinies.

In Palestine, even the human-rights organizations deny the existence of trafficking and the sexual exploitation of women and girls. Only one organization recognizes these problems, and it keeps a low profile in order to avoid harassment. Sexism and misogyny are major obstacles to attempts to investigate, especially for women, like me, who need to interview police and military officials; they are not willing to speak of these "immoral" issues with someone who does not work for the media owned and protected by their faction.

In the growing global market of human trafficking and slavery, the vulnerability of children in Palestine needs to be taken into account, just as much as in African and Latin American countries where law and order do not serve the people or protect children. According to UNICEF, in the occupied Palestinian territories almost 10 percent of children under five years of age suffer from chronic malnutrition. The situation is especially critical in Gaza, where the number of malnourished children reaches 50,000 (out of a population of 800,000 minors). Half of the children under two are anemic and 70 percent have a vitamin A deficiency. Around 10 percent of girls between the ages of fifteen and eighteen are pregnant or have already had children. The high percentage of teenage and child pregnancies points to sexual violence against women and girls. This is the first clue. The next question is: who are the aggressors and where do they live?

Thanks to UNICEF's efforts, more than 50,000 children have received counseling to help them cope with the violence. Hundreds of children under the age of ten have already suffered anxiety attacks and depression. Their faces give me a greater understanding of Rim Banna's work. Fifty percent of students have witnessed the takeover of their schools by Israeli forces and more than 10 percent have seen the death of a schoolteacher. UNICEF's monumental fieldwork required the training of thousands of adults to provide assistance to children, including courses on how to avoid stepping on landmines.

Zaide is a Palestinian woman who rescues abused women from male-dominated homes and reports the disappearance of girls. She states that a growing number of young people are victims of trafficking for sexual exploitation and, on a smaller scale, for the sale of organs. The ability to assess the danger of certain situations—such as the ones I am about to analyze—is infinitely lower in someone who has lived with post-traumatic-stress syndrome since childhood.

All the Women Together Today and Tomorrow (SAWA), a women's organization that protects victims of domestic violence, undertook the first and only formal study on human trafficking in the region. Thanks to the United Nations Development

Fund for Women, SAWA succeeded in publishing a report in June 2008, entitled "Trafficking and Forced Prostitution of Palestinian Women and Girls: Forms of Modern Day Slavery."

I followed the routes used for trafficking in women analyzed by SAWA, which are practically the only access routes for the movement of people: from the West Bank toward Jerusalem, from Gaza toward Jerusalem, and within the West Bank itself. At the time this book was being written, the occupied Palestinian territories had 156 military checkpoints that restricted the movement of 2.4 million Palestinians, which means that the communities are fragmented. Jericho is encircled by a ditch on three sides and there is only one exit that does not face what the local women call "the cliff." Moving among the enclaves of Nablus, Ramala, and Hebron, as well as Jericho, requires passing under strict Israeli military surveillance.

The SAWA report revealed what occurred in a small hotel in the Old City of Jerusalem. After the hotel faced serious economic problems, the owner decided to turn it into a brothel. The majority of clients were locals and some were government officials. (The report does not specify whether they were police, politicians, or army officers.) Fourteen girls and women between the ages of fourteen and twenty-eight were illegally brought from the Gaza Strip and the West Bank to Jerusalem. During the day they were sent out to work as beggars and by night they were forced to prostitute themselves. The madam charged 200 shekels (approximately $54) for the use of a room. The client would pay the girl or woman what he believed she was worth, usually between 30 and 200 shekels, depending on her "experience" and "beauty." The Israeli police arrested the owner, who was accused and convicted of running a brothel. Eight hours later, the investigation was closed and the authorities deported the women and the girls for being in Jerusalem illegally, without the Israeli government's permission. The case was never tried as one involving human trafficking.

A hotel owner in Jerusalem, who prefers to remain anonymous, was infuriated by the news of this sexual exploitation. He told the SAWA investigators the story of how one of these young women lived:

> A while ago, a girl from Nablus stayed in my hotel for a month. She said that she was a nurse working in a hospital in Jerusalem and her shift was always at night. But eventually we found out that she had been working as a prostitute in an Israeli settlement in Jerusalem. I hear of many cases of Palestinian women from the West Bank who work as prostitutes in East Jerusalem. I can assure you that the Old City of Jerusalem is full of brothels.

The recruitment tactics are the same as those employed in most countries. Often a family member or a person known in the community sells the young girls. The brothel is run by a woman, and the traffickers threaten the girls that pornographic photographs of them being raped for the first time will be made public. Talk of the family's and the victim's "honor" is effectively used to gain their submission. The victims know that exposure to their communities, especially to the most religious and conservative groups, would mean brutal punishment, which often includes ostracism.

In the occupied Palestinian territories, traffickers form small, local networks that are generally protected by the military or police authorities. There is no evidence that international networks or mafias are involved in the trafficking of women and girls in the occupied Palestinian territories. However, armed conflicts, as UNICEF has repeatedly reported, provide the perfect opportunity for violent acts to be carried out against children, from turning them into child soldiers to forcing groups of girls into prostitution in order to satisfy soldiers' "biological needs."

It is difficult to investigate adult female prostitution and to quantify the number of girls forced into prostitution by small groups of traffickers. Sexuality and a person's freedom to exercise it are not easy subjects to broach in Palestine, and the occupation makes it almost impossible to investigate how many women are being prostituted in the region, although the feminist writer Cristina del Valle confirms that the presence of soldiers sets a demand for commercial sex.

As I have already mentioned, Palestinian girls are taught how to avoid stepping on mines; how to lower their gaze and stay quiet when faced with the country's patriarchs; and how to behave when they come to a military checkpoint that requires them to find another path to get to school. However, they are not taught how to avoid being recruited and sold. Sexism, inequality, and the war keep them in a state of extreme defenselessness.

The SAWA report also shows that some of the young women involved in prostitution escaped unbearable domestic violence. Just as in Mexico, Afghanistan, Vietnam, the Philippines and Colombia, among other places, violence pushes adolescents out of their homes. Once on the streets, in a sexist and unequal society, they have few options other than prostitution if they are to survive. The traffickers know this, and they make the most of the sexist mechanisms that run the world.

According to the OIM, in Tulkarem in the north-west of the West Bank, on June 16, 2007, a Palestinian man sold his two daughters, aged thirteen and fourteen, to two brothers, aged seventeen, from the refugee camp of Quadura. The young men paid 1,150 Jordanian dinars ($1,600). A year later, the younger girl went to a hospital with profuse vaginal bleeding. She showed signs of abuse, and a medical examination showed that she was pregnant. The police intervened at the request of one of the doctors, and the two brothers were arrested for sexual exploitation of the minors. The judge decided that since the father had sold the girls and the girls were no longer honorable (because they had lost their virginity), they should marry the young men. The trial took place in the presence of the young men, but the victims were not allowed to enter the courtroom or offer their opinions. The case was closed, and the girls were married to their purchasers. This is how the institutional machine vindicates the enslavement of women as well as men's right to exploit and trade them legally. The number of girls aged twelve and thirteen who rebel after being sold into marriages with older men is increasing. Many brave girls in Iran and Afghanistan, as well as in Palestine, have spoken out about how child brides are treated like sexual objects and domestic slaves.

Since the Israeli military checkpoints and the Palestinian National Authority's outposts are considered border crossings, the trafficking of women and girls across these lines is considered an international crime. All the sources I spoke with—Palestinians, Jordanians, Lebanese, and Israelis—confirmed that most of the exploitation and violence against women and girls takes place in the refugee camps, where there is no control whatsoever. This was a complicated issue to investigate, and proving it, at least on this occasion, was impossible. However, the case of the adolescent girls of Tulkarem is a typical example.

Israel's Rosy Statistics: The Other Side of the Coin

In 2000, the Knesset (the Israeli parliament) approved a law against trafficking in women and girls. Like many other countries, Israel has bundled together prostitution and the crime of human trafficking for sexual exploitation. By doing so, it faces the same problems as those countries that criticize prostitution on moral and religious grounds, and yet issue licenses for the opening of bars and brothels where adult prostitution conceals the sexual exploitation of adolescents.

On November 11, 2009, Yitzhak Aharonovich, Israel's internal security minister, testified before the Knesset that the government was reviewing a law that would increase the sentence for pimps and clients of prostitution to a sixteen-year prison term. Before the Parliamentary Subcommittee on Trafficking in Women, the minister stated that his office would re-examine those businesses running brothels with a state license and that he would "try" to cancel their licenses. The chair of the subcommittee, Orit Zuaretz, supported Yitzhak Aharonovich's position:

> We must raise the level of punishment for those convicted of trading in women's bodies. I call upon the police and the other law enforcement authorities to act to try offenders under the existing law that forbids human trafficking and employment under conditions of slavery for the purpose of sex, which includes a sentence of sixteen years.

During the meeting, police representatives took their turn to testify. The police officers reported that since 2007 they had noted a significant decline in organized prostitution in Israel, including a decline in the number of victims of illegal trafficking for the purposes of trade.

While researching this book, I heard such claims that prostitution and trafficking have decreased on only two occasions. The first time was in Cambodia, where flagrant police corruption endorses, conceals, and permits the sexual exploitation of women and girls. The second time was in Israel, where none of the members of parliament requested concrete data from the police officers who testified. In contrast, institutions such as Interpol, Europol, and Great Britain's National Crime Agency—one of the most renowned in the world—have stated that the global phenomenon of trafficking for sexual purposes has increased.

Although Israel claims that it is getting forced prostitution under control and has almost wiped it out, statements made by the police chiefs during my interviews with them, and the local organizations that work to protect trafficking victims, provide alarming statistics. From 1990 to 2004, between 3,000 and 3,500 women were brought to Israel for forced prostitution; the majority of them crossed the border from Egypt. In 2009, the Maagan Shelter for Women Victims of Trafficking, the only shelter of its kind in Israel, rescued seventy-five women and nine girls under the age of fifteen. Government authorities reported that in 2011 the police rescued seven victims of forced labor and took them to the shelter.* The Israeli government refused to admit that the problem even existed until local NGOs, as well as the United States and the United Nations, began to apply pressure. Israel has its own contradictions: prostitution is not illegal, but it is illegal to run a brothel or to work as a pimp. A walk through the neighborhood of Neve Shaanan in Tel Aviv reveals that, as in the rest of the world, there are brothels masquerading as spas, massage parlors, public baths and even a couple of Internet cafés.

While the police state in interviews and in testimony before the Knesset that there are no more than 2,000 registered prostitutes, NGOs such as the Israel Crisis Management Center, which defend women's rights in this country, report that there are more than 20,000 prostitutes and that a large percentage of them arrived in Israel under coercion or were indebted to their traffickers, who confiscate their official documents in order to stop them from leaving the country. In 2007 the anti-trafficking police chief, Raanan Caspi, told *BBC News* that women forced into prostitution are "in better conditions, much more humane than before." In contrast, Yedida Wolfe, a member of the Working Group Against the Trafficking of Women, has pointed out that the police measures are not working: even though there have been arrests and significant legal rulings, prostitution rates remain the same, which means that supply has not decreased.

---

* *Trafficking in Persons Report*, 2011, US Department of State: www.state. gov/j/tip/rls/tiprpt/.

Now the traffickers open more up-market businesses, such as escort agencies and call-girl services, sending the prostitutes directly to the clients at their hotels: as in most parts of the world, the business of supply and demand has diversified and become more sophisticated.

Israel provides the "rosiest" statistics in the world. If the Israeli government could provide concrete evidence for them, its tactics to reduce trafficking should be shared with the rest of the world. The Israeli law against trafficking in women was approved in 2000 and, according to the police report submitted to the Knesset in 2009, the results are impressive: "When we first started working to identify trafficking victims, they numbered approximately 3,000. We now believe that this number does not exceed a few dozen victims."

However, something does not add up with these figures. According to official documents reviewed by feminist organizations in Jerusalem, in 2007 alone the police began twenty-one investigations of cases involving trafficking of women for the purpose of sexual exploitation. In 2008 and 2009, they opened ten more investigations. In 2009, the police filed 331 reports for crimes related to prostitution, the majority of them involving pimping or the running of brothels, almost double the number of similar cases investigated during 2008.

It should be noted that in 2006, Israel's judiciary approved the inclusion of slavery for labor purposes as a trafficking crime. Following the UN Protocol to Prevent, Suppress, and Punish Trafficking in Persons, the police do not require the victim to prove the way in which she was trafficked. In other countries, such as Mexico, the burden of proof is placed on the victim.

Refugees
The Maagan Shelter for Women Victims of Trafficking opened its doors in Israel in 2004 and has assisted over 200 women rescued from traffickers. It is located in a redbrick building

surrounded by beautiful gardens that make its walls seem alive. There is space to house forty women at any one time. Although the Department of Social Rehabilitation of the Ministry of Social Welfare funded the shelter under Israel's anti-trafficking law, victims are cared for in collaboration with the Keshet NGO. Other organizations that work with victims of sexual violence are Sha-le-Isha, the Foreign Workers Help Center, and the Todaha Institution. The law provides that victims who agree to testify against their traffickers will be provided with shelter. This is similar to what occurs in the United States and Mexico, where, if the victim asks for help but refuses, possibly out of fear, to participate in a criminal trial against the traffickers, she is deported.

I flip through my notebook, looking for the notes from my interviews with agents of the IOM during my trip to central Asia. I find the reports on young Kyrgyzstanis and Kazakhstanis who were kidnapped by traffickers to be sold as nurses to care for elderly people in Israel, particularly in Tel Aviv. What the traffickers never told them was that they would live as slaves and that their documents would be confiscated; they would never have a chance to live a normal life or to come and go as they please.

The government wants the best for Israeli women: education, progress, and freedom. For this reason, foreign women are allowed to enter and do the work that no Israeli woman, who has other options available to her, would voluntarily choose to do. The majority of these foreign women are from Uzbekistan, Moldavia, Russia, and the Ukraine. Others come from Lithuania, Kazakhstan, China, and Belorussia. Almost all of them are under the age of twenty-seven. Fifty percent of them leave behind a son or daughter in their country of origin. The need to offer their children a better life is the driving force behind their search for work and it also becomes a tool used by traffickers to remind the women that the sacrifice is worth it. In some cases, traffickers even threaten to murder their children if they do not pay their debts. All the women trafficked from Uzbekistan are Muslims.

Organs for Israelis from Latin America and Asia

The United Nations identified five cases of women under the age of twenty-five who were trafficked to Israel; four were Muslims from Uzbekistan and one was Chinese. All of them had been contacted and promised that they would be taken to Israel, paid a large sum of money, and given legal work in exchange for donating a kidney.

During the many years I have investigated human trafficking, I have interviewed hundreds of public servants and experts around the world. Most police chiefs insisted that trafficking in organs is a myth invented by tabloid journalists: an exception, not a rule. "There are a few cases, but they are very isolated occurrences," authorities from various countries assured me.

Israel is one of the few countries where various cases of trafficking from poor countries for organ extraction have been clearly identified. The Israeli government has even admitted to being a recipient territory for trafficked organs.

In November 2009, the head of the Jerusalem police publicly announced the arrest of two men with connections to a group that trafficked people for organ extraction. Gilad Behat, the head of the police, stated that Sammy Shem-Tov and Dimitri Orenstein were accomplices in the crime of trafficking in persons and organs. Shem-Tov, aged sixty-seven, had worked in the Hadassah University Hospital, where both the perpetrators were able to make contact with various families whose relatives were on a long waiting list for organ transplants. Most of the patients needed a kidney, but a few of them required a liver transplant—a very common operation throughout the world, according to hospital authorities.

A healthy liver is usually obtained from a donor who has recently died with no liver damage. The healthy liver is transported in a saline solution and refrigerated as a way to conserve it for up to eight hours. This allows time to carry out the necessary tests to determine compatibility between the donor and the recipient. The unhealthy liver is removed through a surgical incision in the upper part of the abdomen. The donor's liver is put in its place and the patient's blood vessels and bile ducts are connected. The whole operation may last up to twelve hours and the patient must receive a large blood transfusion. In some cases, a live donor may give part of his liver for a transplant to someone in his family or another healthy person. The donor runs some risk due to the nature of the operation; however, the liver may regenerate itself up to a certain point. Normally, the livers of both people function well after a successful transplant.

The Israeli police opened an investigation after several newspaper advertisements appeared seeking healthy people willing to donate organs in exchange for substantial financial compensation. The ads were published in several languages, including Russian and Spanish. Second Lieutenant Behat said that all the operations to extract the organs—which were later taken to Israel—were carried out in Latin America and the Philippines, although they suspected that other countries were also involved.

Each operation costs at least $200,000. The contact fee is around $2,000 or $3,000, and the victim receives no more than $1,000, depending on the agreement. The rest is divided among surgeons, hospital administrators, and organ-handling experts, and "tips" are paid to corrupt officials in order to transport the organs from one country to another, or from one city to another, in adequate conditions.

In 2008 Israel passed the Law on Organ Transplants, prohibiting the sale of organs. In an exceptional case, the police unit that specializes in combating fraud was able to interrogate ten people who had signed contracts for the sale of their organs.

None of them were from Israel. The investigation is ongoing and has uncovered evidence that hundreds of organs have been taken from Latin America to Israel to be transplanted into very ill patients.

I was able to interview three doctors from the Hadassah University Hospital and the Dana Children's Hospital in Tel Aviv. They agreed that a desperate family is capable of doing anything to save the life of a loved one: if they have to pay for a healthy organ, they'll do it. What is clear is that the complexities of an effective organ transplant require the participation of real experts in order to evaluate the organ's compatibility and to ensure that it is extracted and transported in a viable way. Yet in the case exposed to the public by Gilad Behat, nobody besides the two men—no doctor or public servant—has been arrested. Some were interrogated, but they were released within a couple of hours.

Who gets the organs? Who performs the surgeries? Who transports the organs? These are the questions that nobody could or would answer.

The Legal Gap in the Sale of Organs

The Israeli police found itself in a serious predicament when it received a phone call from a woman in Tel Aviv, saying that she had been taken to the Ukraine by a group of organ traffickers to extract a kidney in exchange for $35,000. The Israelis could make the arrests in collaboration with the Ukrainian police, but most likely, despite evidence, the perpetrators would have to be released because Ukrainian law does not *explicitly* prohibit organ trafficking. The Russian mafia, like the Mexican and Chinese mafias, has managed to control the market for organs. When it comes to saving the life of a loved one, many people are capable of buying organs without asking any questions; they simply make sure that their money goes toward paying for adequate medical care.

Alex Kaganski, the Israeli police spokesperson, admits that the challenge is monumental: the government enforces its laws against organ trafficking, but people travel to nearby countries for transplants. Attorney Lizzy Troend confirms that buying or selling organs is illegal; however, the law does not prohibit a person from allowing an organ to be extracted from his or her body. This debate has arisen in various developing countries: in India, Pakistan, the Philippines, Mexico, El Salvador, and various African nations, people ask why the government believes it has rights over people's bodies. In an interview, several young Pakistanis who had sold their kidneys argued it was their right to do so—if selling a kidney could deliver them from poverty for six months, then it was their prerogative. But what lies behind the sale of organs? The answer is this: networks of criminals, terrorists, guerrillas, and traffickers who enslave women and minors. Are they all the same? No, not at all. The complexities of organ trafficking are exactly the same as those involved in human trafficking for sexual purposes. We are dealing with a chain of people whose activities require specialized protection of the local or international mafias. These criminal syndicates function like a clock that marks not the passing of minutes and hours but the flow of millions of US dollars through the legal gaps that exist between one country and another.

There is no simple explanation. It is difficult to determine where the line is crossed between illicit and legal activities in a global economy. The boundaries of criminal activities, as with political activities, are invisible and porous.

The *Christian Science Monitor* magazine did an extraordinary job of explaining how nations are connected in the organ trade.* Here is a brief summary of the main findings:

---

* "The rise and fall of the South African organ-trafficking ring," *Christian Science Monitor*, June 4, 2004: http://www.csmonitor.com/2004/0609/p12s01-wogi.html

- 2001: Ian Perry meets Roderick Kimberly in Durban, South Africa. They join an organ-trafficking ring and in two years they organize 107 transplants. The surgeries are performed in Saint Augustine Hospital in Durban. The donors are from Brazil, Romania, and, probably, Russia. All of the recipients are Israeli.

- 2002: Hernani Gomes da Silva is contacted for the first time by the organ-trafficking mafia in Recife, Brazil. He later flies to Durban. His left kidney is extracted and he is registered as a "live donor." Amiram Aharoni, from Israel, receives Hernani's kidney.

- 2003: In Israel, Ari Pach, who has severe kidney problems, refuses to live with dialysis. He flies to Durban to receive a new kidney taken from a Brazilian. Meanwhile, in Durban, Health Department authorities contact investigator Johan Wessels to obtain information about an organ-trafficking ring.

- An Israeli donor, called S. Zohr, undergoes surgery in Saint Augustine and confirms the existence of an international mafia that is buying and selling kidneys.

- The Durban police raid Saint Augustine Hospital. A week later, the Brazilian and South African police arrest fourteen people involved in the trafficking syndicate in both countries.

- Aganina Robel, from Israel, pays a fine ($770) to the Israeli authorities for having traveled to Durban to receive a kidney transplant in violation of the laws of the Jewish State.

- 2004: Kimberly, the Durban trafficker, pleads guilty to creating the ring and asks for clemency. He is sentenced to six years in jail, but this sentence is forgiven when he pays a $38,000 fine. He reveals the names of the doctors at the clinic and accuses them of performing 107 kidney operations. Meanwhile, Hernani testifies in Pernambuco,

Brazil, and says that he has received death threats. Four mafia members are arrested in South Africa and more rings are discovered in Cape Town and Johannesburg. Of all the people implicated, three go to prison; one has his sentence forgiven in exchange for testifying.

• Almost all patients from Israel paid between $150,000 and $200,000 to receive an organ on the requested dates. In Pakistan, buyers paid $1,000 to people selling their kidneys and resold their organs for up to $150,000 to European and North American clients.

3

Japan: Mafia of Geishas

Sarah Against the Dragons

Sarah is a beautiful woman with alabaster skin and blonde hair that no artificial color could ever match. As she speaks, her large green eyes blink to the rhythm of her intense words. She visits me in my Cancún office. She is willing to tell me her story, and she has also brought a donation for the women's and girls' shelter I direct. Her capacity to feel compassion seems boundless. It wasn't until I immersed myself in her story and traveled to Japan that I could fully comprehend why this North American dedicates her life and work to the cause of justice. This is how she tells me about her encounter with Japanese culture:

> Freedom, without limits, can be destructive and dangerous. I had just turned eighteen when I left my parents' home. I felt so alive, so excited at my newly acquired freedom: for a long time, I had been waiting for this day. All my life, I had been in a glass box. My box contained my family and religion. That was it; I didn't know anything outside that box: Christian schooling; church attendance three times a week, daily Bible stories; the weekly study of the Holy Scriptures . . . My life was about good and evil, but I knew absolutely nothing about real evil. I had the mentality of a five-year-old girl, without the maturity to understand the real world. What I lacked was an education beyond religious precepts and television

fantasies to help me face the outside world. I was never given the knowledge or the tools to protect myself from violence. My freedom awakened in me a need to travel, an urgent, irrepressible desire.

When I was seventeen, I decided that when I turned eighteen, I would travel to Japan with a contract to become a singer. I had been discovered as a musician, and I knew that I needed to take advantage of this opportunity. Against my family's wishes, I packed my suitcases and prepared to explore Asia with my voice and my music. My parents were frightened. At first, they refused, but later my father reviewed the contract and made certain that it did not require that I wear mini-skirts or provocative clothing when performing. My first trip was a dream. I was fascinated by Japanese culture and customs, even though later on I would discover that fake smiles and kind ways were part of a social hypocrisy. The Japanese see North Americans as a people without pride. They think we are unable to contain our emotions. For this reason, they don't appreciate us, but I learned this much later on. My first trip made me believe that everything was beautiful and that I could succeed.

I returned home to my town in the southern United States. I saw a newspaper ad for singers and waitresses in Japan. The agency was different from the first one, but I liked it because it offered a lot more money.

The nightclub where Sarah ended up working was very elegant. Seated beside a wealthy Japanese businessman, drinking a whiskey and Coke, she tried to answer the question he had asked her, assuring him that, yes, all the hair on her body was as blonde as her beautiful locks. Later she was called to another table where she continued to chat with other distinguished clients. Several days had gone by, yet she still hadn't been allowed to sing. They told her to wait. A week later, the mafiosi began to arrive. The air of mystery and luxury that surrounds the elite Yakuza mafia impresses many young girls who come close to them. Sarah tells it like this:

> I was stunned: "The real mafia!" I said to myself, "Like in
> the movies!" The idea that the "real mafia" was linked to the
> cruelest human evil did not register in my adolescent mind.
> Later, much too late, I found out that the club was used for
> the sale of high-class sex slaves and that I was being offered to
> the buyers that night.

Sarah had signed a contract to sing and possibly record an album. To begin with, she only worked as a waitress, but she was thrilled: the drinks were free and the club was upscale. At the age of eighteen, Sarah believed she was embarking on her adult life. However, after a while, she began to feel angry and anxious, and she demanded that they take her to the club where she would sing, like the first time she had been in Japan. She complained that her employers were not fulfilling their end of the employment contract. Slowly, the nightmare began to unfold. Their lawyer had kept her visa and return plane ticket, arguing that he needed them in order to get a work permit for her. Furthermore, instead of providing her with an apartment, as stated in the contract, they had put her up in a closet-sized hotel room. If this were not enough, there was not one American with whom she could talk: she was alone.

Late one night, as the clients were leaving, an adolescent geisha named Miko invited Sarah to dance in another club:

> This surprised me. The geishas are mean and hostile towards
> foreigners. Miko hardly ever spoke to me, so the invitation
> confused me, but I felt flattered. I thought, "Maybe she likes
> me now and we can be friends!" So I went with her, be-
> lieving that when the other Japanese girls saw me with the

geisha, they would want to meet me. Most of the waitresses were Japanese. Besides them, there was a beautiful Chinese girl, a Filipino, and myself. The club was on the sixth floor of a building. When I entered with Miko, it seemed strange that nobody was dancing. In fact, there was only a group of ten businessmen, and they were all Japanese. I noticed that the men, who acted as though they were expecting us, were sitting at round tables. I recognized a few of them who had been in "our" club before. I was absolutely transfixed by these elegant mafiosi. I looked at them as though they were a novelty, and in fact for me they were, with their mutilated pinkies. [To ask the mafia boss for forgiveness after making a mistake, the Yakuza cut off their little finger and give it to him as a sign of loyalty. This is the only way they can be forgiven.] In my immature mind, I couldn't see them for what they really were. The power and wealth of the Yakuza is impressive; and, like other adolescent girls, I let myself get swept away by it. Instead of giving a slight bow as a greeting, as is the Japanese custom, people greet the Yakuza by practically kissing their feet . . .

Miko and I were sitting down, surrounded by gangsters, and I felt impressed that these men, like in the movies, would want to party with me. "What an adventure!" I thought. They asked me to sing a karaoke song, and I sang the only one I knew in Japanese. Their applause thrilled me. Later, I sat down to have the drink they had ordered for me.

Fifteen minutes after having the drink, I felt very heavy. I had never felt this way from drinking alcohol. Something was wrong. Suddenly, I felt as though cement had been injected into my veins. A couple of Yakuza picked me up by the arms and took me to the elevator. I couldn't understand what was happening. I spoke to them in English, and they didn't answer. Where was Miko? Why was the building spinning? By the time I was in the elevator, I could no longer feel my legs; my knees folded and one of the Yakuza picked me up as though I was a little girl.

Sarah was conscious but her body was paralyzed. As she was leaving the building, she spotted a long line of Mercedes, and then she lost consciousness. Terrified, she let go; in her mind, she knew that something was very, very wrong. Later, she discovered that she had been drugged in order to take part in a sexual ceremony.

I woke up in a mental fog. I was completely dressed and seated on a couch. I looked around. The suite was amazing, the most luxurious I had ever seen. An enormous round bed was in the center of the room. There were sofas, a hot tub, and what looked like a steam room. I was overcome by a sense of calm: maybe the alcohol had caused me to get dizzy, and these men had taken me to their suite so I could rest a little.

Next, several Yakuza appeared before me. They were naked, except for white towels wrapped around their waists. [In brothels and massage parlors in Japan, men bathe themselves before having sex with prostitutes.] Their bodies were completely covered with tattoos. Sitting on the couch, I became overwhelmed by fear; absolute terror consumed me. My uncle Jim's words came back to me. He did not want my parents to allow me to travel to Japan. He insisted that in Japan, young girls are made into sex slaves. "Sex trafficking!" he'd said. Panicked, I jumped to my feet and ran for the door. Before I knew it, three Yakuza stopped me. One of them banged my head against the wall, and I heard the "crack" of my skull. I passed out.

When Sarah woke up, she was lying on the bed, blindfolded and naked. Needless to say, the men who had raped her did not want to be identified. The two FBI agents I interviewed

about this case told me that from Sarah's story and the fact
that the details coincided with the stories of the few other US
victims rescued from the Yakuza, they had enough information
to understand the degree of cruelty with which these mafiosi
operate. They select a woman to serve as the ritual object in a
ceremony meant to unite them.

> I am sure that the first one to rape me was the boss of the
> Yamaguchi-gumi, called 0293845 0934. He was the boss of
> about 38,000 members of that Yakuza sect at the time. During
> the night, the blindfold fell from my eyes, which of course
> wasn't supposed to happen. I was honestly a very good girl.
> In high school, I had won contests as "most sensitive" and
> "most artistically talented." I remember crying almost silently
> as they took their turns. I said to myself, "Mommy, Mommy,
> please" but all I could hear was male laughter. Finally, when
> I couldn't take it any more, I started screaming Jesus's name.
> They looked at each other, trying to understand my words.
> "Dear God, please help me!" I continued to scream. I guess
> God's name made one of them very angry, because he hit me
> hard. My screams were more like whispers, from the fear,
> exhaustion, and the drugs.

Sarah has courageously told her story hundreds of times; she
is one of the few survivors of the Yakuza who has been able
to speak out publicly and to help the authorities by providing
exact information, names, and descriptions of places and people.
However, she exhibits clear post-traumatic-stress symptoms.
A victim cannot recall the details of her story, over and over
again, without it taking a toll. She must seek a way to heal.
Sarah understands this, and she nurtures her strength with her
religious faith. She is convinced that God allowed her to leave
Japan alive so she could help other young women like her. After
our meeting, she wrote me a letter:

I died that night. It was April 21, 1989. Who have I become since then? I don't know. The only thing that I do know is that I am a creature of God.

In the span of twenty-four hours about forty men raped me in every possible way. One of them had a fixation with little girls. He held me and rocked me like I was a baby. He put me in the hot tub and gently bathed me while singing softly, like a psychopath. He was bald and muscular, with the typical Yakuza tattoos all over his body. It was terrifying. I grew up in a religious and protective home, and there I was in the hands of these men! He was missing two fingers. He could have never imagined that this would cost him another finger. I was not willing to let them get away with it. The things that were done to me during the following three days in that suite are beyond words and inconceivable to most human beings. Every one of those men had his perversions. Some stuck objects into me in such a way that I suffered serious hemorrhaging. To this day, the genital scars they left have kept me from becoming a mother.

Three days later, while two Yakuza slept in the suite, Sarah got up and ran out on to the street, naked. She started beating on the neighbors' doors, and the only thing she could think to scream was: "Yakuza, Yakuza!" Finally, a girl opened her apartment door, and Sarah ran inside. The girl called the police and covered Sarah's injured body with a small kimono-style robe.

Sarah's story about how the Japanese policemen treated her is practically identical to the stories I have heard about the police in Mexico, Colombia, Guatemala, Thailand, and Russia: they are insensitive, they lack empathy towards the victims, and they imply that victims are prostitutes who have no rights. The Japanese police usually publicly humiliate young women who have been trafficked for sexual purposes. What is truly amazing about Sarah's case is that after leaving the hospital, she was taken to the place where she had been raped in order to reconstruct her "version of the facts." Beaten up, terrified, dressed in only slippers and the robe given to her by the girl who had rescued her, she had to testify:

> I remember climbing the stairs where I had escaped. This time, the police accompanied me. When I arrived at the floor of the suite, there was a group of reporters and cameramen. In very simple English, sticking their cameras and microphones in my face, they asked me a thousand questions, and I could only stare at them. My mind was blank and I couldn't speak. I was in a state of shock, and I stayed like that for a year.
>
> That night, half-naked, wearing only the kimono, I murmured a few answers, but I don't remember what I said. I didn't understand how the reporters had gotten there. The police opened the door to the suite and took evidence: the bloody sheets, objects from the trash, etc.

The following three weeks were frantic. The authorities took Sarah to a safe house two hours outside the city. She spent days giving her statement in the police station. They made her lie down on a table and explain to the officers every detail of what had happened to her. She reviewed hundreds of mug shots and succeeded in identifying some of the Yakuza members. Once she had overcome the initial shock, she called her parents: "I waited more than two weeks to call my mother and father to tell them everything, in part because I was in shock and in part because I felt so ashamed about what had happened to me. Throughout this ordeal, nobody bothered to tell me that there was a US embassy where people spoke my language," Sarah says, sadly. However, her courage has not been in vain. Because of her, many international organizations, including many Japanese ones, have focused on the Yakuza's operational tactics.

After hearing Sarah's story, I followed in her footsteps to

the bars and places in Japan where the Yakuza were operating. I wanted to confirm what Sarah had so vividly described to me. When I was ready for my trip to Japan, I sent her an e-mail to say goodbye. Affectionately and emotionally, she gave me tips and clues on where to find the traffickers.

It was nine at night. I was walking through Ginza, a Tokyo neighborhood that is the equivalent of Fifth Avenue in New York. I knew what I was looking for. I walked slowly with my small camera and a camcorder. I suddenly saw three young geishas stepping out of an alley. I approached them. Two men in black suits followed. They emerged from an unmarked door where a tall, impeccably dressed bodyguard was standing. I decided to film the scene and the bodyguard immediately addressed me in an angry tone. I told him that I was a tourist filming my trip. "*Nihongo wakaranai*," I said, meaning, "I don't speak Japanese." Next, looking naïve, I asked him in English, "Why does it bother you?" He simply grabbed my arm and told me to get lost.

I walked two blocks and entered a small restaurant to look over my material, grab a bite, and catch my breath. Later, when I asked a police officer if that was a Yakuza bar, he told me that it probably was, but that they could not prove it because the mafia "doesn't break the law."

I can corroborate that the Yakuza are very well organized and they are stronger and more powerful than ever. Their principal business is the sex trade. As of January 2012, Sarah's case is still open in both the United States and Japan, with no results.

4

Cambodia: Europe's Hideout

At daybreak in Phnom Penh, from the window of my hotel room, I observe an idyllic scene: round tables draped in white tablecloths, metal chairs on a wooden terrace, tourists break-fasting under a clear blue sky, the sun shining on their damp white skin. With cameras around their necks and straw hats on their heads, most of them have purchased tickets for a tour that will take them from Mekong to Vietnam and remind them of the films that inspired them to visit this corner of Indochina. These men and women are looking for adventure and the enlightenment of a new culture. I, on the other hand, have come here to explore the dark underworld of slavery.

I take a photo on the shore of the Tonle Sap, an arm of the Mekong River framed by lush tropical plants. A small traditional Cambodian pagoda with gold, red, and yellow baroque sculptures catches my eye. I go to Preah Sisovath Avenue and climb into the tuk-tuk waiting for me. Jaz is the Americanized name of a young driver who was recommended to me. I show him our first stop: Western Union, to request a money transfer from Mexico. I decided to corroborate that some money transactions, from one bank to another and from one country to another, are untraceable. I will soon discover how small amounts of dirty money can be laundered in this way.

Riding in a tuk-tuk is a singular experience. Cars are for foreigners, the rich, and the mafia. The rest of the population and most tourists get around by using these typical, brightly painted, miniature metal cabins attached to motorcycles. "Three dollars" or "Hello, madam," yell the tuk-tuk drivers in English. Whether you are going two blocks or twenty, the initial charge is always $3. The tuk-tuk drivers do not like riel, the local currency. As in all tourist destinations in the less-developed world, they want money with real value. That means the US dollar. I carry a backpack with a recorder, notebooks, a digital camera, and a small video camera.

Clear skies, a temperature of 34°C, humid air, the palm trees swaying in the soft breeze, the Buddhist monasteries, and the royal palace—imposing and mystical at first sight—make this tourist area of Phnom Penh an earthly paradise. As we leave the resort area behind and make our way inland, the city starts to reveal itself in its noisy, colorful splendor. Amidst the waves of motorcycles speeding by, I flinch twice in anticipation of an imminent crash. The scooters buzz through the streets like bumblebees flying inside a honeycomb. They carry entire families: a man, a woman, and two girls, one of them barely two or three years old, riding up front—a balancing act worthy of even the most experienced trapeze artist. The rule for driving is that there are no rules. Large groups of motorcycles and tuk-tuks move in unison with a loud purr that you get used to after a week. The vehicular hierarchy is clear: everyone yields for cars; motorcycles yield for tuk-tuks; and pedestrians stop for motorcycles. Pedestrians cross in large groups. Buddhist monks and novices beg for food and medicine; with wooden bowls in their hands they brighten the streets with their orange and gold tunics. They are the only people that all drivers respect.

The new cars of the wealthy and the ruling class glide through the traffic easily. Tuk-tuks offer me a clear view of the tourists: many are older men, between the ages of fifty and sixty, accompanied by girls between twelve and fourteen years old. The locals steal furtive glances at these tourists known as *dadas* or *papis*, foreign pedophiles who are used to being treated as white, rich men, the ones who have US dollars or euros, able to pay for all the luxuries they desire. Cambodia is classified as a source, transit, and destination country for sex tourism. This means that the selling, buying, and sexual exploitation of women and minors takes place within the country.

The reality on the streets clearly does not match the information handed out to tourists by military officers at the airport. Tourists are given a pamphlet with a local map and the behavior code: under the laws of the Kingdom of Cambodia, anyone who is caught using child sex tourism services may be penalized with a jail sentence. The effective presence of NGOs from many countries—including AFESIP Cambodia (Acting for Women in Distressing Situations), directed by the Cambodian trafficking survivor, Somaly Mam, and ECPAT (End Child Prostitution, Child Pornography and Trafficking of Children for Sexual Purposes), an international network of organizations— has succeeded in proving and quantifying the extent of sexual exploitation crimes. Thanks to the work of these NGOs, it is known that, each year in Cambodia, 2,000 girls and boys are victims of trafficking for sexual purposes; some are used as beggars and others as domestic slaves. As in Thailand, 70 percent of the consumers and accomplices of child sexual exploitation are men born in the region, whereas those who run and protect the trafficking networks are international mafia bosses.

After stopping at Western Union and having a double shot of espresso at a small restaurant—which will become my hideout during my free time—I make my way to Hagar—a Christian NGO that has worked for fifteen years in the region, specializing in the rescue and reintegration of girls who have been victims of trafficking for commercial exploitation. Pierre Tami, a Swiss Christian, founded Hagar in 1994. He was determined to implement programs to empower women and girls to give them a chance to be free and live in non-violent situations.

Sue Hanna, Hagar's representative, is Australian. She has short hair, a round face, red cheeks, and a sweet rhythmic voice. Her gaze is sincere, and her eyes dance between pain and kindness while she explains their approach to rescuing girls from traffickers. In the majority of cases, the local police officers accompany the rescuers. After chatting a while over a delicious salad, we take Sue's rusty white Jeep to go to the shelter.

The facilities are a stark contrast to the impoverished neighborhood around them. The western-style building surrounded by a high wall hints at foreign funding. A security guard greets us, takes my identity card, and hands me a badge. We leave our sandals at the entrance, and I am given a quick tour of the premises. I am able to see the girls' rooms, simple but impeccable, filled with colored objects made by the girls and their caretakers. Each room accommodates three girls and their mentor, who accompanies them on the emotional journey to reconstruct their lives based on new rules of respect and behavior.

Traffickers use the same techniques as kidnappers. They both provoke disagreements and rivalry among victims living in the same space in an attempt to prevent the victims from uniting and rebelling easily. They also use a system of unequal rewards and punishment. Victims can become "favorites" by adopting hypersexual, seductive, and submissive personalities and by accepting exploitation. The girls are so young that this emotional conditioning becomes part of their personalities. They do not pass moral judgments on each other for what they have lived through. Their whole lives have consisted in being slaves. Finding refuge in a shelter means being reborn, being able to reinvent one's self.

In the garden below, perched in a wooden tree house, a group of four adolescent girls speak in low voices. Some of them have lived in the shelter for more than two years. They cannot be returned to their families because they would probably be re-sold to traffickers. Almost 43 percent of these rescued girls stated that their own mothers had sold them. Some were brought from Vietnam, others from towns in southern Cambodia or the Philippines, and others were rescued from Thai brothels.

The girls observe us for a few minutes. I wave and they smile back politely and quickly get back to their conversation. Below us is a small plastic pool. Six girls between the ages of five and ten play and scream, splashing and pretending to be dolphins or fish. Some wear swimsuits, while others wear light clothing that allows them to move freely in the water. Sue tells me their stories. One of them was sold to a local trafficker who works for the mafia in Phnom Penh. Foreign tourists sexually exploited her. When Sue introduces me to the girls, I am moved at the sight of their big smiles, the smiles of girls who live freely.

This isn't the right moment to ask them anything. They've managed to extricate themselves from their pasts of systematic rape. I observe them: small, thin, some with copper-colored skin, others with skin the color of alabaster, all with long black hair. Some of the girls have large, almond-shaped eyes and others have narrower, more delicate ones. May, a nine-year-old, moves sensually, a telltale sign of abuse. Every so often, May stands up in the pool and flips her wet hair back, like a television model. She knows that we are watching her, and she is trying to hold our attention, just as she was trained to do.

The psychologist explains that, once the girls understand their captors' rules, they learn how to be seductive so the traffickers will mistreat them less. They are perfectly aware that they were trained to be prostitutes. They do not understand why, but at nine or ten years old, with their sweet, childish voices, they believe this is what they were born to do. At least this is what the traffickers told them. The psychologists work to deactivate this message, imposed on them at such a young age. It is a monumental task, for the development of a hypersexual personality and constant eroticization impedes them from developing protective barriers and keeps them from understanding the appropriate boundaries for relationships with other girls and adults. With much patience and respect, the therapists teach the girls to restructure their personalities and "de-eroticize" their daily behavior. The most difficult task is rebuilding their trust in adults without succumbing to feelings of guilt about their sexuality.

May smiles at me. I ask her if she likes to swim, how old she is, and what her favorite food is. She is exultant; she has won the attention of the unknown visitor. She touches my hair, points to a bicycle, and brags that she already knows how to ride it. She laughs at my interaction with the interpreter. I speak English and May speaks Khmer. She becomes distracted and begins to play again, yelling and making small waves with her hands clasped together like a cradle. Suddenly May yells in English: "That's it, baby girl . . . Good job." I show my surprise. The little girl's American accent is perfect. "Who knows who taught her that phrase," Sue says. Later on, we discover that this is the phrase that the traffickers used when May behaved well while she did *yum-yum* (performed oral sex) or when a client raped her. She had to smile and kiss him, so the rape would end sooner.

For May, and for thousands of exploited girls, this phrase, which would horrify almost anyone, is a tool of both domination and liberation. Their physical and emotional suffering is such that anything that mitigates the abuse seems miraculous. Their reasoning is much like that of a battered child who, after being beaten by his father from birth to the moment he was rescued, asked the psychologist: "And what do you hit with?" This question shows his certainty that at some point he will be beaten at the shelter. When the therapist responded that he would never be beaten at the shelter, the boy was disconcerted, bothered. His only way of interacting with people was through violence. He had to be taught other forms of interaction and helped to understand and value affection.

I walk through the playground in silence. I see a teacher in the distance reading a story to a group of young girls sitting in a circle on the ground. I take some photographs. One of my objectives on this trip is to learn about the victims' perspectives and to hear their deepest and most personal testimonies. I will not attempt to narrate their stories based on the caregivers' moral evaluations or on the authorities' moral panic and doublespeak. Seeing May, I am moved and I ask myself how I would have survived a similar tragedy at the age of nine. Immediately, I back-track: the circumstances in which these girls have grown up are unique. At their age, they have not yet formed a moral idea about sex or eroticism or about the differences between adults and children. Their mothers and fathers sold them when they were very young. In fact, our notions of motherly love have no place in their imagination or in their language. This is why they can laugh and have fun, while adults look at them, horrified that, as far as we are concerned, they have been robbed of their childhood. Other girls do not smile: those that are still subjugated to men; those who suffer abuse and clear threats; and those who are being used for child pornography have a difficult time smiling. Sexual exploitation varies; there are different types and levels of abuse, ranging from the extreme cruelty of the child-pornography cases that I documented in 2005, while exposing a child-pornography ring in Mexico. I think the challenge is to work out whether someday it will be possible to make the concepts of freedom, happiness, love, family care, and dignity universal.

As I look out at the garden, I ask myself if this socio-cultural normalization of child abuse, prevalent in many countries, can be reversed, without either imposing religious dogma or having a progressive philosophical debate on total freedom, which includes the belief that the limits and concepts of sexuality are outdated and should be reinvented beyond moral boundaries. Isaiah Berlin wrote: "Liberty is liberty, not equality or fairness

or justice or culture, or human happiness or a quiet conscience."
I breathe the warm air of Cambodia with a single question on
my lips: what is liberty for these girls, for women? Or perhaps
liberty is what allows men to foster a culture where slavery is
normalized?

I will leave the shelter after learning about the girls' process of
adaptation and education. Once they turn sixteen, the majority
of them will go to live in another community of young women.
Returning to their towns or family homes is not an option. The
families' contempt for these abused girls can become intolerable,
and, on many occasions, it drives girls to return to the traffickers. The girls become convinced that they belong to an undesir-
able caste and that their only way to survive economically and
emotionally is by returning to sexual slavery. The traffickers'
greatest triumph is the transformation of their victims into outcasts: nobody, except their captors, wants them.

Foreign families who want to give them a second chance
occasionally adopt some of the youngest girls legally, but it's
not an easy task. Overcoming the post-traumatic stress of girls
who were sexual slaves can take up to ten years, depending on
how badly they were exploited. Whoever adopts them needs
to understand that transforming the girls' views of themselves,
women, sexuality, and their relationships with men will be a
life-long mission. Otherwise the girls fail to adjust, they escape
from their new homes and return to the familiar world of prostitution, where the rules are clear: everyone lies; take what you
can get.

"Love and patience is not enough," says Claudia Fronjosa, a
Mexican psychologist and sexologist. Around the world, in the
United States, Europe, and Asia, the goal is to train thousands
of therapists as specialists who understand how to effectively,
ethically, and respectfully approach children and adolescents
subjected to sexual slavery. This approach cannot be the same
as for a child who has been enslaved as a manual laborer sewing

soccer balls in Indonesia. The development of highly specialized treatment for victims of various types of trafficking is just beginning.

Leaving the shelter, I wonder which mafia enslaved these girls. Within twenty-four hours I will have the answer, and, after seeing the captors' faces, I will have an even deeper respect for these girls' resilience.

Somaly Mam and Her Army

Somaly has the demeanor of a princess, the strength of a warrior, and the serenity of an old soul. This woman with copper-colored skin and a penetrating gaze goes through life like someone who knows the secret to world salvation and who fears that humankind will not react in time when faced with a moral catastrophe. She works day and night with one mission in mind: to abolish female sexual slavery. In her opinion, prostitution should be eradicated, but in a slow way, so as to avoid further abuse of those who are already trapped in the business. She believes that labeling prostitution as "sex work" creates a trap for women, as her story demonstrates.

This beautiful Cambodian woman is a worldwide symbol, renowned for her tenacity and for developing the best strategy for rescuing women and girls who are the victims of traffickers and sexual exploitation. When Somaly enters a room, she radiates warmth and light. Her voice is kind and deliberate, but full of passion. She looks, walks and moves like a typical Cambodian woman. The first time I met Somaly was in New York, when our mutual friend Mariane Pearl asked us to attend the launch of a book on universal human rights. Just like thousands of other people, I had read Somaly's story. She was sold in Cambodia and exploited in a brothel for several years. She escaped after witnessing the murder of her best friend, another girl prostitute, by a trafficker. She overcame this horrifying experience and made it her life's mission to save Asian girls from sexual exploitation and to eliminate trafficking in the world. She is a leading proponent of the abolition of prostitution.

When Somaly organized the first big operation to rescue eighty-three girl victims, the Cambodian police betrayed her. This left an indelible mark on her. Her team at AFESIP has adapted to the country's reality and developed strategies for security; they work with police officials, but they never fully trust them.

This time, when I visit Cambodia, Somaly is out of town, receiving an award for her work. A tuk-tuk takes me to the AFESIP offices, situated among wooden crafts shops, bicycle-repair shops, and small wooden and straw huts. Two kilometers of dirt road lead to this spot. Pavements do not exist here, and public utilities, such as water and electricity, have not yet arrived in this part of the world. I leave my sandals outside, and am greeted at the door by the organization manager and a British volunteer.

The offices are small and the desks are stacked up. There are hundreds of photographs of Somaly—with the queen of Sweden at a gala dinner, with the king and queen of Spain; at least twenty other world-famous figures, including Nobel Prize winners, appear in photos hugging this defender of the victims of sexual slavery. It is evident that these powerful people feel honored to be standing beside Somaly. It's no surprise, I think, especially after visiting Cambodia and taking a close look at the monumental challenge of eliminating trafficking in women and sex tourism, after observing the mafia's strength, and knowing how many times Somaly's team has confronted powerful officials who protect traffickers in the region. The founder of the AFESIP foundation is living proof that a person can survive slavery and heal her soul, body, and mind. Furthermore, she has proved that it is possible to work to save other victims without a trace of hate, bitterness, or anger rising up from the past. This is Somaly's magic, a quality that other trafficked survivors do not necessarily possess, as I will see when I travel to other, more economically powerful countries. Hatred is a poor advisor, even when a person strives to do good.

Sari, a thirty-year-old lawyer, explains to me that the young women are ready to be interviewed. We are going to the community health center, a kilometer away from the offices. We climb on to her Vespa, which Sari drives at top speed. My tuk-tuk driver follows us, smiling. Later he will tell me that he thinks that Sari drives really well and really fast. At the health center, three young women are waiting for me. Two of them are still working as prostitutes (they pay a percentage of what they earn to the owner of a squalid brothel), but have partial freedom that allows them to train for other types of work. The third managed to escape from sexual exploitation by a trafficking ring that operates in bars and massage parlors and she is now sheltered in one of Somaly's houses.

Taking time to speak with me means that the first two girls will be missing their work with clients. I make an agreement with them through the lawyer who is acting as an interpreter: I will pay them what the clients would pay for their time. I check my wallet, and find I have $120 in cash. I ask them how much it will be and if it is OK for me to pay them in US dollars. Three dollars an hour, this is what their clients pay.

Da is the saddest woman I have ever seen. She does not wear make-up. She is dressed in a rumpled red blouse with a black skirt. She was born in the province of Prey Veng. When she turned thirteen and her mother could no longer feed her, she was sent to Phnom Penh to support herself and to be with her sister. Her sister worked in a dance club for tourists, and Da began taking care of her sister's baby. Da's mother fell ill and needed money for her treatment. So Da took a job as a Thai masseuse. The owner gave her a loan of $400 to send to her mother. This is how she became indebted to the boss, who claimed that the debt would be impossible for her to pay unless she had sex with her massage clients. Da spent two years paying back the loan, and during that time she was denied the right to go anywhere alone. The tuk-tuks that form part of the trafficking network are responsible for ferrying clients to and from the hotels; they are also in charge of looking for the girls who have escaped and returning them to their captors so they can be punished. Da lived under the threat of death. The boss knew where her mother and sister lived.

Her cruelest client was a fifty-year-old Chinese man who owned a factory in Cambodia. He was a man who could not have an erection without being violent, so all the girls were afraid that he would pick them. He liked to insult the young girls, spit in their faces, urinate on them, and anally rape them, all for a big tip to the owner of the massage parlor. On one occasion, the Chinese man threw Da against a wall, fracturing a rib. By way of apology, he gave her $5.

The nicest client was a Frenchman who saved her life. When Da starts talking about Pierre, a forty-year-old boxer, she puts her right hand over her heart. Her eyes become even sadder, but she smiles as though she is savoring the secret of her freedom. Pierre was a client who came for massages and sex at the massage parlor. One day he paid the owner $1,500 to take Da to his hotel room for a month. One night Pierre told Da that he was leaving for Holland but that he had bought her freedom. For a year, Pierre sent Da monthly payments of $150. At some point, Da lost her bank card, and she did not go back to the bank. She never heard from the Frenchman again. She begged and looked for work for six months. A friend promised to get her work as a waitress and sold her to the Viva Nightclub for $200. The club owner was Vietnamese, and almost all of his clients were Thai laborers.

All of the bars, karaoke joints, massage parlors, and restaurants that offer "entertainment" have official licenses. They employ a large network of tuk-tuks and taxis whose drivers act as bodyguards for the young girls. Some of them carry a knife and are prepared to use it if the girls try to escape. "After all, the girls are the property of those who purchased them," state the AFESIP lawyers. Nobody who spends a few days immersed in this reality can say that these young women and girls lack the willpower to escape from this hell. They do resist, but weakly— their vital energy fails them because they have discovered as children that to be born a woman is a nightmare in itself. The only thing for them to do is to endure the nightmare, subjugated to those who own their lives, their economic survival, and their futures.

When Da turned eighteen, the owner of the nightclub sold her for $750 to Brothel 55, because she was too old and the clients wanted "fresh meat." "I'm lucky," she says with a half-hearted smile. "There are girls who start working when they are six years old; at least I was thirteen."

She became pregnant by a married man. She gave birth to a girl with black eyes and a sad expression, just like hers. Da says that she would never allow her daughter to become a prostitute. She is currently training to be a seamstress. She wants to work in a factory, save money, buy land and grow rice. Most of all, she wants to move her daughter far away from those who buy slaves. I ask her if the father of her child agrees with this. She looks at her short, grubby nails. The father of her child is a police officer who frequents prostitutes. He says that when his daughter has grown up he will find out himself whether she was born to be a prostitute. "What do you think of that?" I ask her. She simply shakes her head and gazes out the window. This is how we end the interview.

In the afternoon, I return to my hotel room. I lock the door, drop my bag on the chair, and collapse on to the bed. I look at the ceiling and feel warm, wet tears running down towards my neck. I think of the question that the young women asked me as we said goodbye: What does it feel like to do whatever you want, to travel, and write? With my freedom, I travel around the world to document their stories and to look for a possible explanation, a way out. Meanwhile, the victims, patient slaves, look in my eyes, wondering at the secret of my freedom. They observe how my writing covers my notebook, weaving together their words, the retelling of atrocities, the statistics, the names of those who buy them, and those who sell them. What they do not know and what they stopped looking for long ago are the names of those who don't care that they have been enslaved.

What suddenly comes to my mind is the curious, smiling face of one of the young girls I recently interviewed. "Someone is going to read our stories?" she asked me, with the nervousness of someone who has never read a book. "And what for?" she asked, smiling. Neither she nor I can explain the perversity of a form of slavery that allows the prisoner to speak and then, a few hours later, gives her back to her owners, returning her to hell. This would be impossible without the complicity of the government and society as a whole. I get up to take a shower. The search must continue; the truth must be revealed. All human tragedy is the result of an idea and a strategy. The accomplices must also be exposed.

Baby Girl Limo Services

I planned to meet with an American woman, a tourist at Naga World, Phnom Penh's only legal casino. It is a gambling Mecca, covering 25,000 square meters, complete with a Shanghai-style luxury hotel and a casino built to look like a boat.

I ask the concierge to get me a luxury taxi. He tells me that a limousine is safest for going out at night. A good tip gets me the concierge's English-speaking cousin as the driver. It turns out that the driver's French is better than his English, and we end up speaking in French. It seems absurd to rent a car to go to the casino, which is a mere 200 meters from my hotel at the intersection of Tonlé Basac, but this was an important part of my security plan.

I shower and put on a black dress, high heels, and some make-up. I check my evening bag and make sure that I have at least $400 (in $20 bills), plus 300 euros, some business cards with my false identity, and lipstick. Bags are checked meticulously at the entrance to the casino, and women who are not accompanied by men are always suspected of prostitution.

Naga World is owned by the Malaysian multimillionaire, Dr Tan Shri Chen Lip Keong. He is in his sixties, and, according to *Forbes* magazine, he is worth $195 million, earned from the gambling trade. The Monetary Authority of Singapore (MAS) recently decided to block the initial public offering (IPO) of shares in Naga Corp Ltd, which has its headquarters in the Cayman Islands. According to the report, Chen Lip was denied the IPO because his business is listed by the Singapore authorities as "out of bounds." Naga Corp's business transactions are not covered by the official regulations to prevent money laundering in casinos since they are beyond Singapore's territorial control.

Despite these problems, Chen Lip has achieved something seemingly impossible in Cambodia. He received an official, seventy-year, exclusive permit for his mega casino. The secret of his success is that Chen Lip is the economic advisor to the Cambodian Prime Minister, Hun Sen.

It is interesting to note that the Cambodian government actively enforces laws against the spread of gambling and betting throughout its territory, even though this is a daunting task, given the poverty and instability engendered by the Khmer Rouge years. However, in the case of Chen Lip, the government does not seem to care. Chen Lip is also the owner of the Cambodian National Lottery. The media and government officials frequently raise questions about the lottery because profits have been in the millions and nobody has ever won the first prize. National Congress members have demanded that Naga Corp Ltd provide accounting information for its legal and illegal activities, but Naga Corp's political influence has curtailed demands for financial transparency.

The investigation of casinos that are probably involved in human trafficking is extremely complex. From Las Vegas to Cambodia, high-level politicians protect the owners of these establishments. It does not matter if they are in Nevada, Hong Kong, Macao, London, the Caribbean, or if it is the Pai Wo Triad operating in Chinatown, New York; the strategies for paying off the police, including donations of undeclared money to the political campaigns of congressional or parliamentary representatives, senators, mayors, governors, judges, and police chiefs, have been fully documented by the authorities and by the media. According to Interpol, 100 million people gamble in casinos each year and business has increased with legalization in more countries. The gambling industry makes more money than sporting events, cinemas, the music business, theme parks and cruises, combined.

My local sources reported that some American and European human-rights activists naïvely believe that they can visit nightclubs in Cambodia or Thailand and take pictures of young girls being used as prostitutes in front of everyone. This is a dangerous belief, and nothing is further from the truth. The mafias controlling the trafficking of women and children know their business inside out. They keep an eye on human-rights organizations and they beat up or make death threats to journalists who poke around in their business. The casinos and the karaoke bars have security guards, who are intent on keeping activists and journalists from obtaining information about the sexual exploitation of minors on their premises. In contrast to most casinos, Naga World has an overwhelmingly male clientele. When I arrived with the American woman I was meeting, the only other women were the hostesses. I would have to be careful.

My sources also pointed out that the hotel gives special treatment to distinguished clients who like to gamble with large amounts of money and who seek sex with minors. My plan was to gamble, but, knowing that I am terrible at it, I had resigned myself to settling down at the slot machines and pretending to be hooked on them. Fortunately, it turned out that my new American friend was an expert at blackjack, and this put my plan back on track. We ordered a bottle of champagne, and the waiters immediately began treating us with more respect. Around 90 percent of the clientele consisted of men between the ages of forty and seventy. About 30 percent of them were Japanese, and they were gambling with large sums of money. The Japanese, together with two groups of Korean men who were on a special tour, were the loudest and most obviously inebriated patrons in the place. "Karaoke, karaoke," yelled one of the potbellied Koreans, as he fanned a handful of American dollars in the air. My friend and I looked at each other. The venues for the sexual exploitation of women and girls often operate behind the façade of karaoke bars in Thailand, Cambodia, the Philippines, Vietnam, and Japan. The front for a brothel is usually a karaoke bar perfectly set up for singing, but with rooms for private shows and for sex. This is also how the Korean and the Chinese mafias tend to operate in New York.

I walked to the elevator, which the first group of Koreans had entered, but a security guard in a black suit immediately blocked my way. In the elevator, a young girl, elegantly dressed in red silk and wearing only red lipstick, smiled at the men and said some phrases in Korean. Faced with the security guard's scrutiny, I asked for the women's lavatory. He answered in almost incomprehensible English, and insisted on searching my bag. He stuck his hand in my bag without looking at me. I thought he would take out the money, but instead he pulled out my fake business cards, which stated that I was a VIP tour operator. He looked at them, said something, and then took one. I tried to draw his attention to the money. He finally glanced at it. A second later, he signaled that I close the bag and then escorted me to the door of the lavatory. Once I returned, the security guard stayed within a meter of me from that moment on and his conversation with my friend always steered us back to the beauty of Cambodia. He was on to me, which meant that I would have to find another way to document sex tourism in Naga World. I was lucky; later I heard stories of activists and reporters who tried to uncover the syndicate and received death threats or were beaten up in "street assaults."

We left, and, as soon as the limousine pulled out to drive us to a bar, a black car began to follow us, staying close behind us all the way down the road. Later, it turned, and we never saw it again. We had a beer in a small bar belonging to a couple of English brothers who were volunteering in the offices of Somaly Mam. We played billiards and I managed to distract myself for a while. The next day I would meet a survivor who escaped from the Chinese mafia.

Escape from Death

I sleep very little. I get up early, do yoga, and go out for a walk when the sun is beginning to rise. On Phnom Penh's main avenue, entire families of beggars are still sleeping in chairs and hammocks on the street. Outside the Buddhist Cultural Ministry there is a young woman whom I saw the day before picking lice out of her daughter's hair. She had offered to sell me her daughter, without giving me a fixed price. I was supposed to make an offer, but it had to be in dollars and I had to promise to take good care of the girl. Poor and without work, this young mother has no way of providing for her daughter's future and well-being. When I asked her how I could take the girl back to my country, she surprised me by answering that she could get me "legal" documents for her daughter in three days. Or she could arrange for someone to hand her over to me in another country—whatever I preferred.

I take some photographs, and at 8 o'clock sharp, I am standing with a young man, Pao, and his seventeen-year-old sister, Qui, in the kitchen of a cafeteria, still closed to the public. He is a reporter for a local daily newspaper. She escaped from a gang of Chinese traffickers. I explain that I am doing research for this book, and Qui begins to talk. She is now in hiding and working for an NGO in Cambodia. She will soon be taken to another country where she will be safe and where she will train to do social work to help Cambodian girls rescued in other countries.

She was twelve years old when her uncle came from the capital to take her from her village. He promised her a house and schooling, instead of living in poverty like the rest of the family. Once they arrived in Phnom Penh, the uncle's attitude changed, and he was no longer her mother's adorable brother. He became cruel. On the second night in his house, he molested her, but he did not rape her. He told her that she would be better off with some of his friends. He took her to the house of a Filipino woman named Yi Mam. There was a group of girls there. They were all between the ages of seven and ten. She was the oldest. Before her disbelieving eyes, a man gave her uncle a handful of bills. Her uncle said, "It would be in your best interest to behave, because, if you don't, you're going to suffer a lot."

She never saw her uncle again. A group of men spoke in a foreign language, which she would later discover was Mandarin Chinese. Qui talks about her first days of training. She speaks in a very quiet voice, and her brother translates what she says into English. Every once in a while, she says a few phrases in English—she has a British accent—to help with the translation.

We were separated and taken to two different floors of the same building in downtown Phnom Penh. An older girl always accompanied the younger girls. Yi Mam pulled some plastic, skin-colored dildos out of a bag made of woven flowers. She called us and we gathered around the table. "This is a man; it is 'mister daddy,'" said Yi Mam, as though she were showing a child's toy. Some of the younger girls laughed when they touched the soft material. "Touch it," ordered Yi Mam. The girls who had seen a naked boy before understood that this was the part of the body called "pee-pee," but nothing more. I had never seen a penis.

Sitting on the floor, around the table, almost like a game, we touched the plastic medium-sized penises. "Now, *yum-yum*," said the woman watching a girl of around twelve, who instantly obeyed. Like a teacher, she took one of the dildos; with her fingers pressing on its base, she stuck it in her mouth. Yi Mam smiled, approvingly, with her eyes. She was the cruelest woman I have ever met, and she always smiled, even when she was beating you with a thin rod. Her three nephews, aged fourteen or fifteen, were with us whenever the clients came. If the police arrived, they would say that they were victims as well. They were as cruel as she was.

The gradual training made the girls understand that if they behaved well with the men, they would be treated well and given toys and food. A rapid English course taught them to say that one girl would cost $30 and two girls together would cost $60. They also knew how to say their ages, "Me, ten years old," and, "I am virgin, sir." The girls under ten would not have intercourse until the man paid for it. Those over ten were sold on various occasions as virgins for up to $300.

In comparison, women of twenty or thirty charge just $3 per session, which explains why traffickers look for younger and younger girls. The local clients pay little, but they help maintain economic stability to fund the purchase and reshuffling of the slaves, police protection, and advertising to attract "safe" sex tourism from Europe, Asia, Canada and the United States.

After the first rape, the girls understood that the only way to survive was to obey the bosses and the clients, most of whom were Korean and Japanese, with about 30 percent Europeans and white Americans.

One of the girls was considered special. She had long jet–black hair, light green eyes, and unusually light brown skin. She looked like a doll or the fairy in a children's book. She wanted to escape. Her father had sold her to a man in Vietnam, and she didn't speak a language that we could understand. One day, she escaped when Yi Mam left with a driver to go grocery shopping. She had hidden in the car somehow, we didn't know how, but the girl had always wanted to leave. She had always been angry and they often locked her in a room as punishment for spitting at the clients. The doctor came to see her twice. He checked her private parts because she bled a lot. They did not give her any clients for almost a month because of the bleeding, and this made her happy. She seemed to misbehave on purpose. We all knew that if you resisted, some clients would really hurt you. It was better to obey.

We knew that the doll had escaped because Yi Mam beat us all and locked us up in different rooms. That day, Yi Mam did not give us anything to eat, and she did not take us to any clients. The following day, she gave us only a bit of milk in the morning and at noon, she had us meet in the dining room. Yi Mam brought two men. One of them I had never seen before. They said he was Chinese, but I don't know. He spoke a language that we didn't understand, and Yi Mam said that what the doll had done was very bad.

Qui pauses. She takes a sip of water. She looks at her hands, which tremble slightly. I leave the notebook and pen on the table and take out a bottle of water from my bag. We both smile. Her brother gets up and ten minutes later appears with a teapot and three glasses. The three of us drink a bit of green tea in silence. I thank Qui again for her story and I tell her that I respect her pain. She sighs with weariness, but at the same time she says she is driven by great conviction and a sense of responsibility to document these crimes.

> She ordered us to eat. We were very hungry, and we devoured the chicken curry with rice. They stood there and watched us. When we finished eating, Yi Mam repeated what the men were saying: We had just eaten the girl doll's body and if any of us wanted to escape, they would chop us into pieces for the other girls to eat. We all got sick and vomited a lot that night, probably from fear. I didn't escape by myself. A Belgian client came three nights in a row, and he told me that he had fallen in love with me. He was good, very careful, and he didn't hurt me much. The third time, he took me to his hotel. He didn't tell me anything. A car came for us. He had his suitcase. They dropped me off at a house run by an organization that saves young prostitutes, and then the car took him to the airport. I don't know if he bought me, but during the first year, I wouldn't even go near a window. I'm still scared that they will kill me and cut me into pieces. I haven't eaten meat since.

I say goodbye to Qui and her brother. I promise them that I will continue to investigate why the Cambodian authorities insist on denying the mafias' participation in human trafficking.

When I interviewed some activists, mostly from Europe and North America, they give me a surprised look when I ask about mafia participation. "It definitely exists," states a British man. "But we don't have time for that; we want to rescue the girls and young women, not fight the mafia." A Christian priest responds, "It is the corruption of the authorities; the real mafia is the government that does nothing to stop clients." An American says, "Interpol states that there are no large mafias and that, in this region, trafficking is a cultural problem, a result of sexism and poverty." In Mexico, where I am from, the authorities said the same things, until I published my book, *The Demons of Eden: The Power that Protects Child Pornography* in 2005, which led to the broadcasting of recordings of an implicated magnate talking with governors, senators, and police officers about trafficking in girls and boys for pornography and sex tourism.

The Triads

> *I don't understand what the big deal is. People say, "They kill girls." The Chinese kill girls because they are only allowed to have one child. We don't kill them; we put them to work. They say, "Oh, they sell them; the Chinese are bad." But I say, "They get to have husbands and work; we help them get these things in other countries." And people say, "The Chinese are really bad." People are stupid.*
> —Trafficker arrested in Chongqing Province

"Who are you afraid of?" I ask the employee of the Welfare Ministry of the Kingdom of Cambodia. He looks at me without understanding the question. "Are you afraid of the Chinese Triads or of the corrupt police?" I insist. He widens his eyes as he leans closer to me and says, "Madam, please don't say that word out loud." He puts his hands together as if in prayer, takes a deep breath like a good Buddhist and refrains from looking me in the eye for the rest of the interview.

"The government of the Kingdom of Cambodia collaborates with the United States in the fight against trafficking in women, a problem of global dimensions," says the government official, who continues to talk as though he were reading from a script sent by the Minister of Tourism. After our brief meeting, he hands me a card without saying another word. The card has the contact details of a Cambodian police official.

"I do not know you, miss," he says as he bows goodbye. "Nor do I know you," I respond, bringing my hands to my face as I smile with gratitude at his trust. My friend at the IOM was a mutual contact; we trust each other, and I was the beneficiary of this professional friendship. In Cambodia, as in all other counties, there are public servants willing to collaborate in the battle against corruption, and they know how to fight the monster because they live within its guts. For this reason they avoid speaking in the government offices, where the walls listen and the mafia allies could be secretaries, waiters, assistants, or bosses.

People are scared to say the word "Triad" out loud. The word originates from the triangle emblem of the Sanhehui mafia, the Society of Three Harmonies, to represent the unity of heaven, earth, and humanity. According to the Hong Kong police, the Triads date back to the seventeenth century, when Manchurian invaders destroyed the Ming Dynasty, and the Qing Dynasty, also known as the Manchu, took political power. A resistance force loyal to the Ming Dynasty, called Tian Di Hui (the Society of Earth and Heaven), incited an uprising of workers and citizens willing to defend their tribal ideas. In order to get weapons and supplies, they started to commit more and more crimes. During the nineteenth century, Queen Victoria, who may be considered the first woman to head a government-run drug-trafficking cartel, stimulated the economy through the opium trade. The British colonized Hong Kong as its commercial port while millions of Chinese became addicted to opium and the drug was exported via different maritime routes under the royal seal.

While Western nations supported the corrupt government of

the Manchu Dynasty, the British named the resistance groups the "Triads." After the 1911 revolution, Sun Yat-sen took power. The various groups split, and the Triads became more powerful than ever before.

No longer involved in politics but retaining its influence over government affairs, the Sanhehui mafia created a monopoly in gambling, betting, prostitution, and trafficking in women, girls, and opium. The Triads gained great political power and criminal influence imbued with mysticism. To this day, Triad members must undertake a series of thirty-six oaths, including loyalty until death. Like the Yakuza, the members of the Chinese Triads have hierarchical ranks, which are numbered: 489 for "Mountain Master," 438 for "Deputy Mountain Master," 415 for "White Paper Fan," and 432 for "Straw Sandal." Like the Yakuza, the Triads punish treason or informing the police with brutal executions. Their weapons of choice are meat cleavers and the type of machete traditionally used for harvesting rice. They are renowned for using knives rather than high-caliber weapons. However, they also use military-grade arms, especially AK-47s, the easiest weapons to get, to protect their commercial interests involving the buying and selling of people and gambling-related extortion.

In contrast to the monolithic structure that the Triads maintained at the beginning of the twentieth century, they are now organized in a similar way to the powerful Mexican cartels. The sex trade, with its inherent overlap between legal and illegal activities, is more powerful than any other. It does not yet make as much money as drug or arms trafficking, but it has infiltrated the global market in a remarkable way. This may be because of the large number of mafiosi who have succeeded in moving from the provinces to central governments, strengthening what Misha Glenny, author of *McMafia*, calls the "political-criminal nexus." This is a profoundly corrupt relationship between tycoons and party leaders, whether it is Chen Kai in Fujian Province, China; Kamel Nacif in Quintana Roo, Mexico; or Michael Galardi in Nevada in the United States. The tycoons, whose "shady" activities have made them rich, launder their money through political campaigns, buying candidates with gifts of pleasure and women. In this way, they get laws passed in their favor and thus gain impunity. In developing countries, the mafias' social impact on their communities is more evident. They are the cartels that build schools, pave roads, and erect hospitals and churches. It is difficult to find a high-level mafioso who has not entered the global marketplace, diversifying his operations and his criminal and political connections. His two favorite places are the casino and the brothel. His favorite things are pleasure, power, and money.

The Mafioso's Wife

The policewoman arrives for our meeting on time, accompanied by another woman who is dressed in Western-style clothes— jeans, a white T-shirt under a purple cotton blouse. Her fake Dolce & Gabbana sunglasses cover half of her small face. With her palms together, she closes her eyes and lowers her head, "Ms Cacho," she says softly. "Thank you for coming." I return the Buddhist greeting. We walk in the public gardens of Wat Phnom, the mountain pagoda, among small monkeys who eat gherkins, and we climb the narrow paths, talking about the weather and the beauty of this place. We reach the top, and walk around the temple. I take a seat on a side step, and they do the same. I photograph an elephant whose trainer makes it do tricks for the tourists. The policewoman explains to me that the Chinese mafia's extensive reach is deeply rooted in Cambodian culture. The other woman, the ex-wife of a drug trafficker, is here to help me with this book. She will be leaving in a few days for a shelter in Europe, where she hopes her ex-husband will be unable to find her:

They have a lot of money and power. This country's economy would collapse if they decided to move their money; Cambodia would be devastated. They work together. King, my ex-husband, belongs to the Malaysian-Chinese mafia. They started with girls and young women, all under the age of eighteen, and with time, they saw that they could exchange them with their partners in the region. They rotate the circuit of girls every two years. After exploiting them sexually with tourists, they send them to the factories they own. They specialize in virgins, which allows them to sell the same young ones to different groups. They have their sons working in the police departments: they enter the police academy; they train them to be the best; and from the inside they work for the brotherhood. King said that it was better to make a long-term investment in the police force rather than buy a dumb cop. They have investments in the mines, in the factories, in construction, and in tourism. There are three methamphetamine factories; one of them is here in Phnom Penh. They send the unprocessed chemicals, ketamine and amphetamine, from Beijing. [In China, there are at least 110,000 chemical factories; the majority of them are unregulated.]

King's partners send pirated merchandise—DVDs and music—in shipments of raw materials for the factories. No one looks through the ships' containers entering the Gulf of Thailand or the charter planes that leave and enter Phnom Penh, at least not the ones that are protected by King. People think this is all new, but it's always been here. Despite political changes and the Khmer Rouge genocide [which annihilated a third of the population], the commercial networks were kept intact. Now the mafia has taken them over again, but this time the mafia has returned with more force and better marketing.

With regards to international connections, Ms King recalls:

> I was twenty years old when he took me to London. We
> went to a famous casino, and there he met with his partners.
> We have been to Mexico four times since 2000, twice to
> the capital and twice to Sinaloa, where he set up contracts to
> send workers. He went to Cuba several times, but he didn't
> take me with him. He returned with boxes of cigars that
> the general had given him as a gift. They entered into an
> agreement to bring two Chinese workers to Cuba and from
> there to Miami and then to Mexico. They were negotiating
> a contract to open a factory to make medicines for the poor,
> which was really a lab to make synthetic drugs. [She does
> not know whether the business was ever opened or if it is
> still in the works.] In Mexico City, we visited the home of a
> Lebanese businessman, in a very elegant mansion. In Sinaloa,
> we were with a man who, from what I saw in the newspapers,
> was murdered a few years ago in the drugs war.

I ask for the names. She seems to doubt herself, and tells me
that she cannot remember. She lowers her gaze and tells me that
she is very tired and must go. A small women's group rescued
Ms King when she was fleeing from her husband's abuse. They
decided to talk to the head of the Cambodian police, who told
them not to get involved. Later they went to the US embassy
and told the story. At the time of publication, it is unknown
whether an investigation has been opened on this case.

This thirty-year-old woman, like thousands of criminals'
wives, knows the inner workings of the mafia, which she lived
with for many years. She tells me that they have been in Cambodia for a long time, since the nineteenth century, when the
Cantonese merchants, Chinese-Khmer, controlled the tourist
and petroleum markets. The historian William Willmott states
that the French colonists allowed the Chinese to control 92

percent of commerce in Cambodia in 1900. Some were barefoot doctors (traditional Chinese medicine healers), but there were also great landowners who created the worldwide market for Kampot pepper. Others, the most powerful, were moneylenders or usurers. Many of them created their own codes of conduct for business.

Chinese businessmen control the tourism industry in Cambodia, which earns about $1.8 billion, more than twice what the government recovers in taxes. The Cambodian government favors investment from Chinese companies, even though there is evidence that some of them are involved in organized crime. "They prefer them because, unlike the Europeans, Chinese businessmen do not believe in human rights. They don't care if children work twelve-hour days in a factory, and they care even less when it comes to making pirated products," says the policewoman. "And we shouldn't even mention transparency; it's not an issue that they discuss," interrupts Ms King. "My husband and his partners traffic in girls, pirated products, and synthetic precursor drugs. He doesn't smoke or drink because he says that stuff is poison," she adds.

The policewoman interjects, "It's not that they buy police officers; it is that the bosses and military officials are the ones who sit in international conferences to speak about laws and campaigns against trafficking and sex tourism, and they are the ones running the operation from the inside; they also consume commercial sex. It's perverse . . . very perverse. Don't forget what happened in Chai Hour II."

In 2005, Somaly Mam and her husband Pierre Legros gave information to the police to rescue 250 girls trapped in a prostitution ring in the Chai Hour II hotel. The girls were exhibited in small glass cages like animals in a pet shop, marked with numbers. They were bought by Asian and European tourists and by some powerful local men who raped them. The police entered the hotel and took eighty-three girls to the

AFESIP shelter directed by Somaly. However, the next day, police officers, soldiers, and civilians entered the shelter by force and took the girls back to the brothel. In an attempt to show its power, the mafia took some of the girls to demonstrate outside the US Embassy against "Yankee interventionism in Cambodian businesses." Furthermore, in an attempt to undermine the AFESIP, the mafia boss brought a lawsuit on the victims' behalf against Somaly Mam for $1.7 million (a fourth of the shelter's annual budget), arguing that the girls were massage therapists and dancers. Since that time, AFESIP employees have received death threats, and they have even faced hired gunmen. This is one of the main reasons why the international organizations that work in Asia to rescue trafficking victims of all ages concentrate on prevention and raising awareness. They feel overwhelmed by the government's corruption and the strength of the political-criminal nexus.

The Cambodians in London and the Chinese in Nicaragua

The Triads expanded their operations from the British colony of Hong Kong to London. Next, they extended their reach into Malaysia, Singapore, Cambodia, Kyrgyzstan (where they have fought over territory with the Russian mafia), and all of French Indochina. They have formed Chinese branches for trafficking in pirated merchandise, Chinese workers, and women and children for sex tourism. All of these businesses are run by diverse groups of Triads in the United Kingdom, South Africa, New Zealand, Australia, Canada, the United States, Guatemala, Nicaragua, and Mexico. I slowly discovered that in all the cities of the world where there are Chinese factories, trafficking in men, women and children exists.

According to the Mexican Attorney General's Report (PGR 2007), written in collaboration with the National Institute of Mexican Immigration, there is evidence in Mexico, in the provinces of Yucatán, Campeche, and Quintana Roo, that a network of illegal Chinese immigrants uses Nicaraguan and Mexican airports to transport illegal aliens to the United States. An investigation was opened in 2006 after a complaint was filed in Managua claiming that a Chinese network of slave traffickers existed.

The Chinese mafia, according to the authorities, specializes in the buying and selling of young Asian girls. These girls have been found working in factories under substandard conditions, in brothels, and in Asian massage parlors (serving as fronts for prostitution), along the trafficking route that begins in Cancún, continues to Los Cabos, and ends in Los Angeles, California.

In Yucatán in Mexico, the exploitation of a young Chinese woman and two Filipinos in a factory in Guanajuato led to the discovery of the human-trafficking route. They had been brought into the country via the Caribbean with the help of corrupt Mexican immigration officials.

The network, overseen by the Chinese mafia, involved about 300 factories in Mexico. The factories were investigated because of Li Ye, a Chinese woman aged thirty-four, from Fuzhou, the capital of Fujian province. She was found after she escaped from her captors, who had held her against her will in a house in Cancún. Ultimately, none of the factories in Mexico was closed because they had used official and legal means to get temporary work permits for their employees.

With the help of an interpreter, Li Ye testified that she had traveled from China to an airport in Central America, where traffickers imprisoned and abused her in the hold of a boat. Boats from Nicaragua arrive in Puerto Progreso, Yucatán, and Seybaplaya, Campeche. From there, the victims were taken by car to Cancún and Playa del Carmen in Quintana Roo. The Triads have become experts at creating international networks providing child and adolescent sex tourism to clients. They have clearly defined their clients' preferences: there are the gamblers who like prostitution and then there are the businessmen who need cheap labor from people who do not speak the businessmen's language and are unable to fight for their rights. The victims are taken to countries for forced labor, primarily in factories and brothels. Between 2000 and 2008 alone, there was a 300 percent increase in the legal opening of new Asian massage parlors in Mexico, a business that was practically non-existent in this country.

In an interview with José Luis Santiago Vasconcelos, the Mexican anti-drugs prosecutor, I asked him why the Mexican authorities did not act if they had clear evidence that the Chinese mafias were operating trafficking routes from Fujian in China, to Mexico and the Caribbean. The answer was clear: "We need the Chinese government's cooperation, and the victims must give us sufficient proof." "But shouldn't you be the ones to investigate?" I insisted. "Yes, we should, but when it comes to trafficking, we depend on the victims because there are not sufficient resources to carry out transnational investigations of this scope."

It is globalization's Achilles' heel: the inequality of cultures, economies, and legal systems, as well as the disparity in intervention capabilities among countries and regions, make it practically impossible to follow cases such as those presented here, no matter how well documented they are. Political will or its absence is a key factor in understanding why human slavery has remained a horrific issue; focusing on isolated cases makes it seem like a criminal phenomenon, a complex conundrum of disparate, individual stories, exaggerated by the fevered imaginations of NGOs. Beyond opinions and sociological hypothesis are the facts: these women and girls show us the route like sailors in the middle of the night who point to land and warn of the obstacles that must be faced in order to arrive there alive and on time. Their stories, with concrete details, such as addresses, names, telephone numbers, travel routes, false passports, photographs, and even telephone recordings, are dismissed, just as the voices of the first domestic-violence victims who fled their homes were ignored as they sought better lives free from subjugation and humiliation.

5

Burma: The War Against Women

Charm Tong was six years old when her parents crossed the Burmese border to take her to Thailand. They left her in an orphanage, the only safe place for a girl of Shan ethnicity. The Shan belong to a minority group that is persecuted and attacked by the Burmese military dictatorship.

Many of the young girls who were Charm Tong's friends in Thailand would become victims of the sex trade. She considers herself very lucky to be alive and to have avoided being sold into forced prostitution. She went on to become an activist for girls' rights. At sixteen, while other teenagers across the globe were busy finding love and planning their futures, Charm wrote:

> The military has damaged our hearts, our beliefs, our souls, and our rights . . . It is difficult for people to forget the military's violations. Every day there are more human-rights violations in the rural areas and borders of Burma. The best we can do is fight with our minds and our hearts and not let fear take over.

In 2005, Charm won the Reebok Human Rights Youth in Action Award. Undoubtedly, her greatest contribution has been the report entitled *License to Rape* (2002), in which, with the help of organizations such as the Shan Women's Action Network (SWAN) and Shan Human Rights Foundation (SHRF), she documented the rape and killing of more than 600 women and girls, some as young as four years old, by the Burmese military. Charm also established a crisis center for victims of sexual violence. She demonstrated that in the twenty-first century her country's military uses rape as a weapon of war. She showed that ethnic minority women and girls were enslaved, forced to work in the fields during the day and raped at night to satisfy the soldiers, just as the Japanese military had done with the "comfort women" during World War II.

A quick note regarding names: after the coup of 1988, Burma was re-named the Union of Myanmar. Opponents of the military dictatorship have refused to accept the new name and they continue to call the country Burma, whereas the United Nations and the European Union have recognized the new name. In this text, I will use the name Burma in order to avoid confusion.

Burma shares a border with China in the north; the Andaman Sea in the south; Laos and Thailand in the east; and India, Bangladesh, and the Gulf of Bengal in the west. It has a tumultuous history of conflict and turmoil.

In 1962, Burma became a one-party socialist state. In 1988, students and monks led an anti-government uprising known as the "8888 Nationwide Popular Pro-Democracy Protest." General Saw Maung grabbed power through a coup and established a military dictatorship. Saw Maung also sent troops to suppress the protests, killing thousands. In 1990, Aung San Suu Kyi, a democratic leader opposed to the regime, was arrested after winning democratic elections, which the dictatorship declared invalid. Despite being awarded the Nobel Peace Prize in 1991, Aung San remained under house arrest until her release in November 2010. In 2007, there were mass demonstrations in Burma. The media seized on the dramatic images of the military violence against Buddhist monks during the protests and broadcast them around the globe. In 2009, Aung San was sentenced to another eighteen months of house arrest to keep her locked up during the 2010 elections. For many years, she has called for an international boycott of tourism in Burma. Her stance has created controversy among her supporters, since poverty has been exacerbated by the economic downturn. The absence of mass tourism like that in Thailand and Vietnam, has also made journalists, investigators, and activists more conspicuous and their work more difficult.

Staying in Burma as a journalist is not a good idea. I decided to keep a low profile while conducting my interviews, in the light of the military dictatorship's reputation for arresting and torturing those who try to publicize human-rights violations. I planned my trip to Burma while I was still in Thailand. The easiest way to enter would be to go to Myawaddy, across the Moei river from the Thai border town of Mae Sot. I needed to stay in Burma for at least two days to complete the interviews I had scheduled. This posed a potentially serious problem because crossing the bridge from Mae Sot requires a special visa whose conditions stipulate that tourists must return to Thailand that very same day and through the same border crossing by which they entered. In fact, the only way to visit locations throughout the country is to enter and exit by air.

The soldiers who serve as border patrol agents at the small outpost retain each visitor's passport in exchange for a receipt. I wanted to find a way to stay more days without the authorities finding out. I would need two things to happen in order to pull this off: the Thai authorities stationed at the bridge would have to agree not to stamp my passport when I exited Thailand; and, the Burmese soldiers would have to do the same when I re-entered Thailand. A Thai activist commented that this would allow me to put the borders to the test and thus discover what it's like for those who cross illegally from one country to the other.

The idea was to return to Thailand a few days later with my passport and evidence of the border patrol agents' corruption in my hands. For security reasons, I was traveling on a tourist visa throughout Asia. As a precaution, I decided to give my local contacts and friends at the IOM copies of my itinerary.

How hard would it be to cross the border of a country whose military dictator is connected to organized-crime groups involved in human trafficking? I needed to find someone who would be able to accompany me to Mae Sot and, from there, cross the so-called Friendship Bridge. Fortunately, I was able to find a travel companion; colleagues had recommended him. The price for this feat would be $250: I would give him $50 for his services, $100 to bribe the soldiers at the Thai border crossing, and $100 for the soldiers at the Burmese border crossing. This included permission to enter Burma without a visa and not having my passport stamped on either side. I would also be charged the same price for my contact's cousin to accompany me on my safe return to Thailand. The plan was simple: I would silently enter Burma with a group of seven local tourists accompanied by Tomy, the "tour guide" to whom I had paid $250.

Mae Sot's market is noisy and filled with men and women dressed in traditional clothing. The tourists blend in with the human-rights activists who live near the border so that they can monitor the situation in Burma without placing themselves in grave danger. However, soldiers occasionally confront and arrest those trying to gather information about the country. This is black-market central for the Burmese, Chinese, Thais, and Karens, a Burmese ethnic group. Here, they exchange as many illegal items as legal ones. Among the picturesque restaurants and the handicraft stalls, vendors offer almost anything, including fake passports, women, girls, and boys for adoption. There are also Chinese products arriving from Mae Ramat, Ban Tha Song Yang, Phop Phra, and Um Phang. The Friendship Bridge unites Mae Sot with Myawaddy on the Burmese border. From there, the highway takes us west to the Burmese cities of Mawlamyine and Rangoon. Even before crossing the bridge, I started acting like a tourist, buying a small Buddha while strolling through the market, overwhelmed by the vendors.

The border crossing on the Thai side is much more modern and organized than its Burmese counterpart. There, Tomy was able to make arrangements and get us through in less than ten minutes, as though it were business as usual. We walked the 420 meters of the Friendship Bridge. Then I had to exchange another $200 into Burmese kyat; the Burmese government requires that all tourists exchange this amount. There is no other option.

In February, the weather is hot but bearable. It was 36°C that morning. We lined up when Tomy approached a soldier. I believed that having a Mexican passport would make me less conspicuous than having one from some Western country that has an inflexible stance against the military state and its criminal activities. Two impeccably dressed armed soldiers carefully examined our passports. The money was folded into the pages of each passport. In another line, soldiers were studying the passports of some older Europeans dressed like Indiana Jones. A soldier suddenly became very interested in the professional video camera held by a German man, and severely scolded the group's tour guide: "No journalists, no journalists!" he insisted. The tour guide tried to calm the soldier down by reassuring him that they were visiting Burma to see its natural wonders. They were ultimately given one-day visas, and their passports were retained.

I felt nervous, uncomfortable. I glanced over at the desk of the soldier holding my passport, and I suddenly froze. He had a computer: all he had to do was enter my name into Google to discover that I was a journalist. Staring at the ground, I began to take deep breaths in an effort to calm down. I jumped when I felt the tour guide's hand on my arm: "Let's go; let's go," he said in English, as he gently pushed me forward. Later I laughed when I learned that the soldiers didn't have Internet access.

An hour later, I was walking through the streets of Myawaddy.

The cars on the roads were from the 1950s, some run-down and others lovingly well-maintained. They reminded me of Cuba. So, too, did subsequent interviews when speakers suddenly became stiff as they tried to hide their fear of offending the government while reassuring me, with fake smiles, that there was total freedom in their country.

The hot, humid air struck my face as I noticed toxic black water flowing from exposed drainage pipes. Outside a temple, I saw an old man sleeping beside some children who were watching over a basket that contained a cobra. A group of fair-haired tourists approached and the children immediately started the snake-charming show. From the corner, a soldier watched the spectacle attentively from a safe distance: group meetings are prohibited in Burma to avoid the organization of political protests and rallies.

In Burma, trafficking and the sexual exploitation of women can clearly be identified as a business run by the state and, more precisely, by the military. Taking extraordinary precautions, my contact and I went to a monastery to meet the activists who have documented hundreds of cases of Burmese women and girls who have been raped and killed by the military; they have also managed to photograph and document the conditions of slavery in which these women and girls live. The Buddhist monks' activism and solidarity, like that in Sri Lanka, gave me hope. They stand in stark contrast to monks in Cambodia and Thailand, who avoid any interaction with women: if a woman needs to give something to a monk, she must do it through a go-between. What the Buddhist monks of Sri Lanka and Burma have in common with their Tibetan counterparts is a sense of compassion for the suffering of their people and a rejection of sexist traditions.

The emotions I sensed in the streets seemed similar to those of people living in war zones and under oppressive regimes, such as Iraq, the occupied Palestinian territories, and

Afghanistan. Those who defend human rights in Burma work clandestinely in an effort to protect the victims. "There are more than 700 prisoners of conscience. We don't need any more people dead, injured, or silenced," said a Spaniard who has secretly made a documentary about social movements in the Burmese countryside. The people I interview speak about the demoralizing effect of the military's sexual violence, waged against peasant women and girls. Outside the monasteries, most Burmese social movements tend to be led by women; men also participate, but, in general, the women are the ones willing to risk their lives for the community. The military knows that by raping and intimidating these women, it sends a warning to the communities that they are being watched.

Nan is thirty years old, even though she looks fifty. She is uncomfortable with her appearance and lowers her head from time to time because she feels embarrassed at the enormous scar left by the bayonet that gouged out her left eye. Miraculously, she survived. I tell her that she should be proud of her bravery and strength. She speaks almost like a child, responding that she doesn't like to frighten people by the way she looks. She slowly begins to tell me about how she was sold to a brothel in Thailand and then punished in Burma after being deported by the Thai government.

In 1992, Nan was fifteen and lived with her family in a village in northern Burma. One night her father introduced her to a soldier who claimed he was looking for young, healthy virgins for government employment. The soldier had stressed to Nan's parents the importance of virginity. They did not want dishonorable girls who would get into trouble, he said. Her parents received the equivalent of $60 and the promise that their daughter would return in a year, ready to work. Just a teenager, Nan had heard rumors about soldiers who raped and killed girls, but at the time she didn't really comprehend what it meant. "At home, my parents never spoke about sex," she said. "They are uneducated, conservative peasants . . . After walking for a long time, I was put in an old vehicle with soldiers. When one of them touched my leg, I wet my pants. They laughed at me and called me names."

After a brutal gang rape, Nan was sold to a brothel on the Thai border. She was sexually exploited for two years before a Christian organization intervened and asked the authorities to raid the brothel. The traffickers were never apprehended and Nan, along with twelve other young girls, was sent home. While still in Thailand, a Bangkok daily newspaper interviewed her. In the interview, she revealed that a Burmese soldier had sold her to a brothel. When the Thai authorities turned her over to her country, Nan was arrested. They kept her blindfolded for days. A soldier then accused her of treason and attacked her with his weapon, leaving her for dead. Despite Burma being ranked number 190 out of 191 countries in terms of healthcare, Nan lost her eye but not her life. This was due, in part, to the work of a good doctor from the Red Cross who attended to her in the cockroach-infested hospital where she spent two months recuperating from an infection and post-traumatic stress.

Nan has managed to survive and become an interpreter for clandestine human-rights groups working in Burma. I believe that she is driven by an extraordinary combination of compassion and willpower. There is no anger or rage, not even a hint of revenge, in the almost mystical sweetness of this brave woman. She doesn't know how to write, but her prodigious memory retains detailed statistics and rapists' names.

The ethnic cleansing carried out by the military has resulted in massacres of women from several ethnic groups: Karen, Mon, Shan, and Rohingya (a Muslim ethnic minority). Members of the military have created camps for sexual slaves, and they have kidnapped hundreds of girls of Shan or Mon descent.

In 2006, Colonel Myo Win ordered fifteen villages of the

Ye district to hand over two young women from each village. They had to be single, more than 1.6 meters in height, and be between the ages of seventeen and twenty-five. A small unit of soldiers was responsible for picking up the candidates for their participation in what the generals called the "catwalk" on Independence Day. The chosen ones, all peasants from the Burmese state of Mon, were taken to military quarters and obliged to parade for the soldiers during the three days of rapes. When they returned to their communities, no one dared ask them anything. (This account can also be found in the report *License to Rape*, at www.shanwomen.org.)

According to the women's organizations, in Rangoon alone there are between 5,000 and 10,000 women forced into prostitution as a means of subsistence, and Burmese citizens often seek protection abroad from oppression and ethnic violence. In Thailand, there are 74,000 Burmese women living in refugee camps. There is heightened political tension between Burma and Thailand, due in part to the refugee situation and to an ongoing land dispute. Despite the tension, Thailand continues to enter into trade agreements with Burma's dictatorship.

Between 800,000 and 1.5 million people flee Burma for other countries, where they are often exploited or treated as slaves. The Coalition Against Trafficking in Women (CATW) reports that 200,000 Burmese women and girls have been trafficked to Karachi, in Pakistan, to be sold as sex slaves and used as beggars. The Asian Development Bank has reported that 25 percent of adolescent girls forced into prostitution in Burma carry the HIV virus and many of them already have AIDS. Without healthcare services, they will die very quickly.

The stories collected by Burmese organizations operating in exile in Thailand describe rapes by the military; cases of women, even seven-months pregnant, being subjected to sexual abuse by groups of up to fifty soldiers; and summary executions of victims who resist and of those who are no longer of interest.

The interviews have been filed under the first name or the initials of the women and girls who have been victimized. The files also include a number and a photograph of each victim's half-hidden face. It is almost impossible to read them without crying.

Burma is effectively a concentration camp for women. If the country manages to liberate itself from the military junta and develops into a democracy, the world will be horrified by these facts when the media uncovers them. What is happening in Burma is similar to what occurred at the Nazi concentration camps, different in scale but no less dramatic or unforgivable.

The Mafia and the Restoration of Law and Order

Traveling around the world, crossing borders by air, land, and sea, has given me a deeper understanding of the effects of corruption and how it makes it easier for organized criminal networks to traffic in drugs and human beings. In 1997, the Burmese military junta, formerly known as the State Law and Order Restoration Council (SLORC), rechristened itself the State Peace and Development Council (SPDC). Its members included officers who created various sex-slave camps. They have ties with organized-crime groups that facilitate or participate in trafficking in humans, gems, animals in danger of extinction, hardwoods, and other contraband that travels along the Southeast-Asian trade routes.

In recent years, Interpol, the United Nations Office on Drugs and Crime, and the US Congress have reported an increase in organized crime in Burma, which has enjoyed legal impunity under the military junta. The reports are cautious, with no specific details of government officials being connected to organized-crime groups. According to reports from Transparency International, Somalia and Burma are the two most corrupt nations in the world.

The economic sanctions imposed by the United States

under President George W. Bush, along with serious human-rights concerns, combined to isolate Burma and increased the government's drive to obtain, by any means, resources and more power in an effort to legitimize itself. One method has been to charge "taxes" for protection services provided by military commandos to transnational organized-crime groups. These groups seek protection for the transportation of drugs, persons, and arms along the Asia-Pacific trade route. International sanctions on tourism and commercial activities will not debilitate Burma. The isolation that results from such sanctions not only worsens the general population's poverty, but also strengthens and enriches a military junta that acts outside of any international control.

In Burma, there are "entertainment" businesses dedicated to promoting "fashion shows." These businesses are fronts, similar to karaoke bars in other Asian countries; they cover up trafficking in women for the purpose of forced prostitution. Some of the cases that have come to light reveal that members of the military junta own these types of establishment. In addition, it is widely known that the military regime has invited mafia members to invest dirty money in Burma, particularly in infrastructure and transportation. The government-controlled banks manage some accounts that facilitate the laundering of money from Bangkok and Singapore cartels.

The Burmese military regime receives huge amounts of revenue from the following contraband, in descending order: opium, methamphetamines, hardwoods, exotic animal species, and humans. Its largest markets comprise China and Thailand, which are also transit countries. Other destinations include India, Laos, Bangladesh, Vietnam, Indonesia, Malaysia, Brunei, South Korea, and, of course, Cambodia. According to the US Drug Enforcement Administration (DEA), the mafias have succeeded in importing large amounts of methamphetamine pills manufactured in Burma into the United States.

Burma is one of the poorest countries in the region: according to the Asian Development Bank, 27 percent of its population lives in extreme poverty. As in other countries, such as Mexico, poverty has driven rural communities to engage in drug cultivation, the hunting of endangered animals, and illegal harvesting of hardwoods. More and more peasant farmers are becoming the weakest link in the chain of organized crime. They are willing to plant opium and enslave women and girls to harvest it. Intelligence reports also show an increase in the number of people willing to kidnap children to be sold as soldiers to the military junta and women to be used in brothels.

The Golden Triangle

The statistics on opium production are shocking. According to the DEA, Burma produces 80 percent of the heroin in Asia. After Afghanistan, it ranks second in the cultivation of opium poppies that are converted into illegal drugs. Most recently, methamphetamine production and the cultivation of opium for heroin have increased considerably: the annual exportation of drugs generates $1–2 billion. According to the United Nations Office on Drugs and Crime, in 2007 alone, the re-sale price of opium crops from Burma amounted to $220 million.* Once refined into heroin and sold on the market, the profits exceed $1.8 billion.

Burmese drug traffickers freely drive their old trucks through the "golden triangle," a mountainous area between Burma, Laos, and Thailand that covers approximately 350,000 square kilometers, almost three times the size of England. While other Asian countries were making commitments to fight opium production, Burma, which was not party to such agreements, became the chief exporter of heroin and methamphetamines,

---

* United Nations Office on Drugs and Crime, *Opium Poppy Cultivation in South East Asia*, October 2007

so much so that by 2010 the "golden triangle" had been re-christened the "ice triangle."

In November 2003, the Financial Action Task Force on Money Laundering (FATF), an inter-governmental organization, classified Burma's Mayflower Bank and Asia Wealth Bank as establishments specializing in laundering money for drug cartels. After significant pressure was applied, the military junta revoked these banking institutions' permits, while simultaneously authorizing the creation of *hundis* or *hawalas*, which are banks that handle small transactions, as also happened in Cambodia and Thailand. Most immigrants use these organizations to send small amounts of money, but local traffickers also use them to pay and charge on a daily basis without being detected. As described in the chapter on Cambodia, I tried sending money through a *hundi*. Without a passport and under a false name, I was able to send $600 without leaving any trace of the money's origin or its destination.

An Interpol agent who is currently investigating a case of Spanish money laundering in Bangkok and Singapore sheds light on the flow of dirty money:

> A door closes and a new window opens for the laundering of money. In developing countries there are more small banks opening, like *hundis* or *hawalas*. Dirty money can even be moved through Western Union. The capital that flows through micro banks—which are also local retail stores or pawnshops—is impressive once you do the math. This is what allows the links on the chain of organized crime to survive and receive their share.
>
> We have a case involving a child slave trafficker in the "golden triangle" region. One farmer moves between $1,700 and $2,000 per week by dividing this amount into three installments. Most people would say that a peasant farmer is insignificant to organized-crime networks, but after fifty

weeks—supposing that he takes two weeks off for vacation—he will have moved $85,000 without anyone imagining that he is part of a scheme to launder dirty money produced by the purchase and sale of child slaves. Making modest assumptions, if in Burma there were 1,000 intermediate traffickers moving $85,000 annually, we are talking about a flow of $85 million, not an insignificant amount for the mafia and its collaborators.

One farmer sells five girls under the age of eleven for $5 dollars each. A broker re-sells the girls for $30 dollars to a soldier. The soldier then re-sells the girls to opium traffickers, who have already bought fifty girls from local recruiters. The soldier facilitates transporting the girls to work as bookbinders in the factories that print underpriced books in Thailand. Publishers all over the world will most likely buy these books. Each girl is required to carry a small bag of opium paste ready to be turned into heroin. When they arrive in Thailand, the traffickers receive the drugs with one hand and the slaves with the other. It couldn't be a better business.

Two days later I return to Thailand with my guide's cousin. My notebooks, my small voice recorder, and my small camera will never be able to convey the profound human suffering seen in the passionate expressions of those who believe in freedom and are willing to give their lives for it.

I walk through Mae Sot. Some girls run toward me when they see me take off my backpack and rummage through it for a bottle of water; they think I'm looking for coins to give them in exchange for some of the trinkets they are selling. They are barely six years old. They are small and malnourished from the look of their pale skin and thin hair. I bend down and buy small plastic and wooden elephants. One of them holds my gaze. It is as if we are suddenly alone. I, a Mexican woman, am on a dirt road on the border of Thailand and Burma. Meanwhile, in my country, hundreds of girls are being trafficked as slaves.

The girl smiles, as though she knows a secret, while selling trinkets in the streets without suffering the unfortunate fate of thousands of girls like her, locked up in brothels to satisfy men from all over the world. I pat her cheek with the back of my hand and she does the same to me, and we are both surprised by this connection. A smiling, thin young man, probably around twenty years old, approaches me. "Guadapochion," he says. I look at him and indicate that I don't understand what he is saying. Then he slowly repeats the words with the attitude of a powerful man, and I realize that in broken English he is asking me, "Want adoption?" I stand up without responding.

I take a deep breath and walk toward the market's immigration stand. An agent looks at me in a friendly way and offers me a one-day visa to cross the bridge. I shake my head and ask him if he knows anything about the atrocities, such as forced prostitution and massacres, perpetrated by the Burmese military against women and girls. "Yes, terrible, terrible. Here, it is a crime," he replies. I smile a little and I sigh to expel my fear while the man continues to speak: "But you know, many of them like it . . . Those girls are very much prostitutes . . . They like it." His voice sounds involuntarily cynical, like that of millions of men in the world who repeat over and over the argument that slaves cause their enslavement and they, the potential or actual clients, are doing no more than giving in to the slaves' desires.

I turn around and silently walk to the spot where I will meet my driver. At this moment, under the Asian sun, I am not a journalist or a human-rights activist; I am simply a woman who is walking along the world's routes of evil, looking for someone who knows the secret, maybe utopian, of saving humanity from its own cruelty.

6

Argentina–Mexico: Arms, Drugs, and Women

Raúl Martins: The Untouchable

The unique color of the Caribbean Sea and its clear blue sky welcome tourists seeking an earthly paradise. Large five-star hotels attract families planning to swim with the dolphins at Xcaret. These hotels also provide a private space for single men who are looking to have sex with young women and girls. Some of these men have heard that Mexico is now the "Thailand of Latin America." Here, laws to punish clients of forced prostitution and sexually exploited minors are not enforced, making Cancún and Playa del Carmen the ideal destination for American and Canadian sex tourists.

In the heart of the hotel district, Raúl Martins Coggiola—an ex-agent of Argentina's Secretariat of State Intelligence (SIDE), accused of being connected to groups that carried out genocide during the last dictatorship in Argentina—runs the brothels and lap-dancing bars known as The One and Maxim. In these bars, young women, no older than twenty-three, from Argentina, Colombia, Cuba, and Brazil, dance and sell sexual services under the close surveillance of a tough security force. Under municipal law, prostitution is illegal in this district; however, Martins' friendships and protection networks override even the power of the current governor of the state, Félix González Canto. Martin receives protection from federal judges who prohibit local authorities from shutting down these bars.

It was October 2005, and hurricane Wilma had just destroyed the Caribbean coast of Mexico. Cancún was left temporarily paralyzed. A few weeks later, only a few restaurants and bars had re-opened. The hotels were rapidly rebuilt, but all the tourists had fled from the disaster. One afternoon, I met with a group of friends (all men) for lunch. I asked them if we could go to The One. I had already been to Maxim on Playa del Carmen—owned by the same business—where I had seen girls aged seventeen and eighteen working as dancers. Now I needed to speak with the girls in Cancún, but it was almost impossible for me to enter The One alone.

My friends gladly accepted the assignment. As soon as we arrived, I discovered that a 75-year-old architect in our group was a frequent guest of The One. We climbed some metal stairs toward a dark door. The architect greeted some of the employees, and they immediately treated him as a distinguished client. We did not have to wait to enter, and the bouncers barely glanced at me as I crossed the threshold, something I was silently grateful for. As soon as we entered it was obvious that The One was also paying the price of hurricane Wilma's devastation: there was only one client with a young woman near the dance floor.

When the men in my group ordered a $300 bottle of alcohol, three women approached them. They rapidly turned their attention to the most attractive man in our group, who was tall and athletic; he made up a story that we were celebrating our anniversary. I stood up and began to speak with these young women. I gave them a false name, as false as their own. Next, they invited me to join them on the dance floor. I realized that this was my chance to gain their trust, so I accepted their invitation.

The place was beyond sordid. The pimps, normally agitated and suspicious, were outside smoking, except for one of them who was drinking at the bar with a couple of women who appeared to be employees. My friends asked to have the music turned up, and the architect, as though he owned the place, took the microphone to introduce us. As a joke, he invented a name and nationality for me and announced that I would be dancing next. I was dressed in jeans, high heels, and a purple blouse. I was uncomfortable, but with these young women cheering me on, I managed to dance beside them. I grabbed the pole and twirled around it, lifting myself off the ground, which was no easy feat.

The initial tension dispelled, I asked the dancers to teach me some moves. My years of doing classical ballet and Hawaiian hula dance helped me to avoid making a fool of myself. An hour later, we left the dance floor and began to talk alongside my group of male friends, who continued to drink the most expensive whiskey in the house. They also paid for a bottle of champagne that I ordered and shared with the women. I told them that I write stories about women, love, and sex, something that is true. It did not take long for them to start speaking as though we had been friends forever. "You're not going to get in trouble for talking with me?" I asked them. They answered that they had done their job as long as the clients were drinking, and we were with the clients. They did not sit down at any point, and I carried on standing up with them. Every now and then, I would dance with the young women near the sofas where my caring and somewhat drunk accomplices were seated and doing their best to assist me with my journalistic mission.

As on countless other occasions, I confirmed my suspicion that most of these young women feel much more comfortable with other women than with men, even in an erotic sense. The four women with whom I spoke for almost three hours were very young. A Colombian woman, a friend of the manager, always knew that she would be a dancer and prostitute. A Brazilian woman, aged twenty-two, had been brought to Mexico when she was seventeen years old under the false promise that she

would become a model. She was brought to The One by the
bar owners who control the prostitution circuit that begins
at the border city of Tijuana. A nineteen-year-old girl with a
baby face, the daughter of a Colombian man and an Argentine
woman, came to Cancún on vacation, ran out of money, and
stayed. Her aunt then recommended that she contact a family
acquaintance who could get her a job and fix her papers.
This acquaintance turned out to be the wife of Raúl Martins.
Another twenty-year-old from Cuba, who had left two small
children behind with her parents, was convinced that she would
be sending lots of money home to her family as soon as she
managed to pay off her debt to Martins.

I managed to see them two more times outside the bar. On
the days following my initial meeting, the bar closed early
because there were no tourists and the locals were busy rebuilding their homes and businesses. The security team at The
One lowered its guard and the young women could meet with
me while returning to the apartment where they lived under
weak surveillance. Martins had confiscated all of their papers
as collateral until they paid their debts to him. They did not
seem interested in backing out of their agreement, even if it
was unfair. This life was better than being back on the streets,
poor and without options, they reasoned. None of these young
women had finished high school, and they came from troubled
homes where domestic violence prevailed. Raúl Martins' team
of lawyers fixed their papers, including their passports and visas.
The young women did not know whether the papers were fake
or official, but it wasn't something that worried them too much.
They said that the only nice man they had met while getting
their papers in order was a man named Claudio.

I found that three of the four women I interviewed had
young children from unwanted pregnancies. They told me that
they had learned to love these children. Two of them became
pregnant when they were still teenagers. The four of them

confirmed that they disliked their work, except for dancing and occasionally meeting an interesting person. Getting paid to have sex was something they refused to analyze since it was just a temporary job and the best way to quickly pay off the debt owed to Martins. Smira, the young Cuban woman, said that the men who frequented The One were disgusting. The others agreed: "The clients are insecure drunks who believe whatever we tell them. Some of them are very vulgar, and they believe we are going to fall in love with them." They described their work as a performance and their clients as powerful fools who paid for someone to pretend that she could stand their presence.

The young women's stories, along with the details provided by some of the waiters, clearly show that Martins, like other traffickers, understands the importance of mixing professional prostitutes and the victims of slavery in the same group. The former have paid their debts, have chosen to stay in the sex trade, and enjoy freedom of movement, whereas the latter are forced to submit under threats of assault. These victims are stranded, with no immigration papers, and vulnerable to deportation at any point.

As we said our goodbyes, Nina, the Brazilian woman, asked me: "You're not going to give our names, right? They say that Martins killed his son-in-law. He's a very cruel man." According to the director of the federal judicial police, Nina was telling the truth. In 2004, the Norwegian Peterson Kenneth Turbjorn (aka Mike Arturo Wilson Garcia), Lorena Martins' boyfriend, was found murdered in Cancún's hotel district. The official police report stated that the primary suspect was Lorena's father, but the case was never solved and Lorena found refuge in Spain. My local police sources confirmed that forensic evidence showed that Kenneth Turbjorn had been tortured before he was murdered. When asked the question directly, the director of the federal judicial police told me that Martins was one of the suspects but that the Argentine was untouchable. I asked him what he meant by "untouchable." He answered, "Don't even bother with it. He's the mafia."

"And you should watch out; when you write this, Martins will not leave you alive," the Cuban dancer said to me as she hugged me goodbye. I never saw these women again. A short time afterward, I came to understand just how serious they were, when Claudio Lifschitz, Raúl Martins' former attorney, publicly denounced Martins. According to Lifschitz—allegedly Martins' accomplice in the trafficking of women from South America and Central America to Mexico—Martins had already controlled these trafficking routes when he was an intelligence agent working for Argentina's SIDE. This required a political network extending from Buenos Aires to Cancún, and all the way to Tijuana.

On January 11, 2007, the prestigious Mexican newspaper, *Reforma*, ran a front-page headline that got the authorities' attention: "Ex-spy owns VIP brothel." Alejandro Pairone, an Argentine journalist, signed the article, which exposed the globalization of trafficking syndicates and the syndicates' access to judicial and political power:

> Buenos Aires. "An ex-spy for the Argentine dictatorship dominates VIP prostitution scene in Cancún and Playa del Carmen, thanks to a network of official protection," said Claudio Lifschitz. Raúl Luis Martins Coggiola, a former intelligence agent, lives in Mexico, even though his residency visa has expired.
>
> According to Lifschitz, this Argentine citizen runs The One in Cancún and Maxim in Playa del Carmen, two bars where around 150 women provide prostitution services in circumstances that are comparable to semi-slavery.
>
> The attorney confirms to *Reforma* that Martins' best clients are drug traffickers, businessmen, and Quintana Roo politicians, who frequent these bars or have young prostitutes

sent to their private parties in mansions or on yachts and cruises.

"Martins brags that on his cell phone he has the private numbers of Cancún's attorney general [Pedro Ramirez] and that he is protected by the powerful businessman Isaac Hamui, whom he told me was a partner of the ex-governor Joaquín Hendricks," the attorney remarked.

Lifschitz also confirmed that the current governor, Félix González Canto, continues to protect him, just as the former governor, Joaquín Hendricks, provided protection to The One, maintaining its position as the only brothel in the hotel district.

"There has always been speculation that the owners of The One had state and municipal protection. Supposedly, under the new governor, they don't enjoy such protection. However, no one has touched them," stated Raúl Poveda, manager of Plaza 21 [the red-light district of Cancún] . . . *Reforma* checked and confirmed with anonymous sources that local authorities provided protection to the Argentine's businesses.

Raúl Martins was a SIDE agent from 1974 to 1987. During the military dictatorship, it was his job to decide who would be tortured at army headquarters and made to "disappear." According to Lifschitz, Martins' work included following and photographing dissidents who would be kidnapped and would then disappear.

After Martins retired from the intelligence service in Argentina, he focused on running a high-class prostitution business. He managed eleven establishments and became the boss of the sex trade in Buenos Aires. However, the judicial, political and police network that protected him suddenly collapsed, and Martins had to leave town. In 2002, he arrived in Mexico by way of Tijuana, a city that would allow him to thwart Argentine justice, which was lapping at his heels.

Claudio Lifschitz is still the defense attorney for some of the officials who carried out the oppression during the Argentine dictatorship, and he was also Martins' attorney for seven years in Buenos Aires and Mexico until they had a disagreement and Lifschitz returned to Argentina, out of fear of reprisal. To protect himself, Lifschitz revealed his ex-client's operations and stated that he was prepared to testify against Martins if he was granted certain guarantees. Martins and Lifschitz began to part ways when Martins began to pressure Lifschitz to "change his testimony in an investigation that involved high-ranking officials in ex-president Carlos Menem's government." Martins wanted Lifschitz to retract his testimony in the case involving an attempted attack on the Argentine Israelite Mutual Association (AMIA). It was Lifschitz who had discovered and denounced the cover-up in which the guilty parties were being protected against murder charges.

In his testimony to the judge, Sandro Ossipof, Martins' former partner, revealed all the places where Martins had set up hidden cameras to record clients as they had sex with prostitutes. Also, in Buenos Aires, a former administrative employee brought a lawsuit against Martins accusing him of threatening bodily harm and assault. The case was sent to magistrate's court number twenty-eight, in Buenos Aires. Another case against Martins, named Megacase 103933/97, was still pending in Argentina while the Mexican authorities were giving him permits for his businesses involving the internment of the young dancers. The Megacase included charges of police corruption and bribery to give Martins' protection, and of running a prostitution ring in Buenos Aires.

Martins decided to move to Cancún and Playa del Carmen after being charged with fraud in Tijuana. In southeastern Mexico he reconstituted and strengthened his VIP prostitution ring, which he had managed for more than a decade in Argentina. He gradually pieced together a web of protection for the traffickers, a web that extended from the Southern Cone—Argentina, Chile and Uruguay—to Mexico.

Until I read Lifschitz's allegations in a Mexican newspaper, I did not realize that the young women at The One and Maxim were referring to Martins' attorney when they told me about the nice man, named Claudio, who had helped them get their immigration papers in order. I searched for him, so I could hear his side of the story first-hand, but I never found him.

Useless Scandal: Martins Reloaded

The newspaper article detailing Martins' activities revealed a web of complicity that had not been investigated by Mexican federal or state authorities. For a month after its publication, different government officials tried to place the blame for this lapse on third parties. González Canto, Quintana Roo's governor, blamed the judges who had issued six court orders that prevented him from having Martins' nightclubs raided and shut down and from having Martins arrested. Martins accused his ex-attorney of violating attorney-client confidentiality. The National Institute of Migration blamed the federal police, and the federal police blamed the municipal authorities that had granted Martins permits for the sale of alcohol. The scandal's aftermath unfolded in Mexico just as it had in Argentina.

Martins then disappeared from the scene. His brothels closed, and some of the women who worked for him were detained by the authorities, photographed, and deported to their native countries without any questions asked. A federal agent told me that Martins had fled. However, according to the director of the National Institute of Migration, Cecilia Romero, the immigration authorities had received an order for Martins' deportation, which was "a priority" and they were following him "very closely because of the prostitution cases that were a matter of common knowledge." However, Romero also stated that they could not carry out these orders because some federal judges were protecting Martins. If the judges continued to protect Martins, they were never going to be able to arrest him. The reason is simple: some levels of the judiciary are part of the web of corruption, and some judges are clients of prostitutes. On the one hand, they are afraid of having been taped in such situations; and, on the other, they consider prostitution a "normal" business and do not see any moral reason to punish the crimes related to it. As such, they become "de-facto accomplices" or "moral accomplices" of the men controlling prostitution.

"Why hasn't anybody taken any action against Martins for trafficking in persons, falsifying official documents, fraud, or suspected homicide?" I asked all the relevant Mexican authorities. "Nobody, not one judge wants to touch him," they responded.

The explanation for the authorities' surprising paralysis and silence about this case was given to me by one of the young Argentinean women who was taken to Playa del Carmen under false pretenses and then put to work as a prostitute: "Here and in Buenos Aires, Raúl Martins' thugs recorded everything, including our visits to five-star hotel rooms in Playa del Carmen and Cancún. They taped drug cartel bosses, politicians, and businessmen; that's his life insurance."

It was obvious that I probably appear in one of these videos, making a fool of myself dancing in my jeans, twirling around the pole, or drinking with the young dancers who trusted me enough to help me with uncovering this story. I kept thinking that if I were a man, I would have been able to enter those bars without any problem, have a drink, and pay for a few hours of female company while gaining the trust of the dancers. To be a woman in this investigative field means having to become part of the "merchandise," and bait for the mafias, whereas a male journalist can pretend to be one of the "consumers."

On September 9, 2007, eight months after the Lifschitz's re-marks caused a scandal, after the authorities had assured me that Martins had fled Mexico and that nobody knew his whereabouts, a new brothel bar called Sex & Girls opened its doors. Among the honorable guests on the VIP list was a bald man, dressed in black, sporting a bright Rolex Oyster on his right wrist: it was no other than Raúl Martins, the prostitution czar. He was intro-duced as the manager of the new bar in Cancún's "red light" district outside the city. This bit of news went almost unnoticed.

In December 2009, Raúl Martins was seen dining at Rolandi's, one of the most prestigious restaurants in Cancún's hotel district, with a few women who looked like models or dancers. Without any apparent legal problems, he became partners with some businessmen in Mexico City and opened VIP lounges, where women from South America and Eastern Europe dance, strip, and are forced to sell sex to pay off their debts.

When I asked the women who worked in Martins' brothels if they considered themselves slaves, the majority of them smiled or asked disingenuously what I was talking about. However, if I asked them whether they would take the opportunity to stay in Mexico to work freely as salespeople, teachers, waitresses or as anything they could imagine, they all answered: "Yes, definitely."

Denounced by His Daughter

On January 9, 2012, the Argentine newspaper *Página/12* reported that Martins' daughter, thirty-five-year old Lorena Martins (whose boyfriend was allegedly killed by her father), presented Argentina's Justice Department with documents and other evidence of her father's criminal activities and his involvement in a prostitution ring in both Argentina and Mexico. Lorena stated that in Buenos Aires her father owned "seven businesses, and he also owns Cancún nightife." According to Lorena, he pays a total of approximately 85,000 pesos a month (approximately

$8,000 dollars) in bribes to the Argentine Federal Police.

Lorena, who had been estranged from Martins since 2010, when he broke off all relations with her and the rest of the family, feigned a reconciliation with Martins in order to infiltrate his inner circle and find the evidence necessary to denounce his illegal activities. She gained access to his personal bank accounts and emails, which allowed her to uncover valuable information on how he operated his businesses, the names under which he registered his nightclubs, and, more importantly, the practice he referred to as "breaking girls." Lorena explains how he "rescues" girls:

> [They] have gone through hell with domestic violence, or have been raped, and he becomes a sort of father figure; he gives them a place to live and a job and they feel grateful. They are promised work as a receptionist or as a model. They are told that they can earn lots of money. [My father's organization] pays for their airfare, lodging, and promises to get them papers to work and reside in Mexico legally. With the excuse that they need their passports in order to process their immigration permits and to ensure that they will settle their debts, they retain the girls' passports.

Once they are settled in their new lives, they gradually begin to lose the "help" they were promised, such as lodging. Their immigration turns problematic and they are placed in a situation of distress. My father calls this process "girl breaking" and this results in the girls agreeing to offer their "services." Martins keeps half of what every girl charges.

On April 10, 2012, I traveled to Buenos Aires in order to launch the Spanish edition of this book. Upon my arrival I met with a secret service agent. He informed me that Nilda Garré, the head of Argentina's Homeland Security, had assigned six bodyguards to accompany me at all times during my visit to Argentina. In the hotel lobby I was briefed by the head of the security team; they knew about Raúl Martins' death threats, and as this is a high profile case and he is an ex-spy who belonged to Videla's dictatorship, his threats are taken seriously by the Argentine government.

That afternoon I met Lorena Martins, who attended the press conference amongst forty journalists. Our eyes connected and at the end she approached me, hugged me and said, "Thank you for coming; together we will make sure my father pays for his crimes of enslaving women." Later, at the hotel bar, I talked to Lorena, her mother, and Lucas Shaerer, a well-respected human-rights activist.

Lorena's mother, a woman in her sixties, looked at me with her eyes full of tears, and apologized that when I first wrote a newspaper article about her husband Raúl Martins, she had called me a liar. I smiled and told her not to worry: being a journalist is not a popularity contest, and telling the truth earns you more enemies than friends. She said her husband had always kept her away from the business; she did not know he was a sex trafficker, nor did she know he was also married to another woman, the madam who controls the young women in Martins' lap-dancing clubs in Cancún and Playa del Carmen. She explained that she is bringing a case against him for bigamy.

Lorena is a strong, slender woman with beautiful brown eyes and blonde hair. She opened a briefcase and handed me a file on her father. It includes original photos of all kinds of politicians, including the current governor of Buenos Aires, Mauricio Macri, posing with Martins in his brothels. Lorena has evidence she has given to the police of Martins paying $10,000 dollars for Macri's campaign when he ran for office last year.

I have a copy of that file, which includes the documents showing that Martins belonged to SIDE in 1974 during Videla's dictatorship. His name appears next to some of the agents currently sentenced for crimes against humanity, crimes such as torture and forced disappearances. "He was a part of it, Lydia. I know it, that is why he wants to get me killed, because I know and I am willing to help the authorities go after him," said Lorena.

Lucas Shaerer, who works for La Alameda, an Argentinian NGO that helps to fight human slavery, explains how the organization has investigated more than 8,000 brothels in Argentina, and has rescued hundreds of slaves, mainly men, from illegal clothing factories. Most of them come from Bolivia and Paraguay. Lucas emphasizes how worried they are about the prevalence of labor and sex trafficking in Argentina, and about the South American trafficking route of Bolivia, Paraguay and Brazil. His organization has brought three cases to the Argentine courts and believes traffickers will be properly sentenced now that they have a good anti-slavery law.

While in Argentina I met an amazing woman known as "Mother Courage." Susana Trimarco lost her twelve-year-old daughter, Marita Verón, in 2002, when the girl got on a minibus and never came back. Susana, convinced that her daughter was kidnapped by traffickers, began searching for her in every brothel in Buenos Aires. Since then, even though she has not found Marita, she has rescued more than twenty minors from brothels all over Argentina. The good members of the police force admire her; the corrupt ones fear her ability to investigate and to pressurize the authorities into saving the underage girls. After the Spanish edition of this book came out and Lorena Martins testified against her father, Susana Trimarco followed the trail of Martins' brothels in the province of Mendoza. She told us that Darío Biglione, alias "Ivan," Martins' cousin, owns the Red Club brothel in that province. "I have been hearing Martins' name for a while," Susana says. "He has taken minors to Mendoza to prostitute them. I also remember one policeman who was paid a set fee to protect drug traffickers and helped them protect the brothels." She mentions the video Lorena turned in to the media in January 2012, filmed in Martins' Cancún club The One, showing exactly how he operates.*

Susana and Lorena know Martins cannot go back to Argentina for fear of being arrested. That is why José Alejandro González, known as "Rocky" or "El Cachorro," and Guillermo Martín Soto, are the ones sending the girls to Mendoza, under the supervision of Virginia Inés Solís, Martins' mother-in-law, who appears in the nightclub videos. Susana and Lorena both live under protection, having been threatened by the trafficking mafias. They insist that the police have everything they need to ask the Mexican authorities to arrest Raúl Martins in Cancún and extradite him to Argentina. But the Mexican attorney general does not seem to have any interest in the case. Martins is still living in his oceanfront condo in the Mexican resort, and as this book goes to press, he is still operating his brothels there.

Before I left Argentina, Arodi Orea, an immigration officer in Mexico, declared: "At this time, [Martins] is being protected by the judiciary . . . He has very important connections within the government and they are the ones delaying the situation." He explains: "Martins is a powerful man in the state of Quintana Roo. On a national level he wasn't well-known until this situation was uncovered a few years ago by a Mexican journalist."**

Arely: Rescued from Death

Arely, aged nineteen, is a Venezuelan with platinum-blonde hair. She is hugging a soft toy, a rabbit, sitting on a chair in the

---

* http://www.youtube.com/watch?v=m56IwgSdU1A
** Arodi Orea, "Martins se encuentra amparado por la Justicia en México," February 10, 2012, www.radiolared.multimediosamerica.com.ar/mananasyl vestre/noticia/7276.

Center for Integral Support of Women (CIAM), a shelter for battered women and children. At times she talks seductively and at other times like a scared girl. Her neck shows the marks of the man's hands that tried to strangle her; on the left they stand out like purple stains, the size and shape of the aggressor's fingers. She speaks non-stop, gesturing, holding back her tears:

> I wanted to study, to be an important businesswoman, an intelligent one who makes money and has a car. When my mother died, back in Maracaibo, my grandmother said that I would have to go out with her and sell empanadas on the street. When cars passed by, I smiled. Men said, "What a pretty blonde girl." I thought, "What is the advantage of being pretty if I can't study or play outside like the other girls?" One day on the street, I met Mariel, a beautiful, elegant woman who told me: "If you wanted, you could be a model and make loads of money, study, and take your grandmother off the streets. In Mexico there is lots of work for Venezuelans like you." And I thought: I'm tired of dragging myself through the streets all day. I wanted to study and not end up like my grandma: a *cabeza de chola*, a dumb loser, forever. And Mexico . . . I thought, How cool, there you can live life to the max. I watch Mexican soap operas. Everything is so exciting, so gorgeous there!
>
> I went to an Internet café with Mariel. I didn't know how to use the Internet, but she showed me how to find a website called Divas.com. She said, "Look, it is such an important business; if not, it wouldn't be on the Internet!" Wow, I thought . . . It's Mexico, and the business looked very professional with its cool advertising and its logo "Prestige," and there was a school for models and singers.
>
> I registered my information on the website. I sent my photograph, which Mariel had paid for me to get. And not more than a week later Mariel got in touch with me at home.

She already had my plane ticket for Mexico! She took me with my documents to get my passport and put everything in order. Everything was legal. How was I supposed to know that I would end up like this, a whore? Models are not whores; they're beautiful and they appear in magazines; and men adore them.

"Once you get there, you'll pay them back with your work," she said. I never imagined that upon my arrival in Monterrey they were going to take my papers and tell me that I owed them $5,000 for the plane ticket. And, there I was, alone. I couldn't think about returning to the poverty of my home, so the only thing I could do was obey; and before I knew it, I was training six hours a day to dance. Later, I met the boss. They called him "the Devil." He's a very rich businessman from Monterrey. He owns bars and restaurants. He told me that I was his favorite, but that I needed to get some tits. They took me to a doctor and got me these. [Arely lifts up her augmented breasts as though they were balls.] I felt beautiful and super sexy, but never like a whore.

The lawyer is called Luis, and he made me sign all the papers regarding the debt. He kept my passport. One night, before going out to dance, Mr Luis sent a message that he wanted me to go to his office, and the chauffeur took me there. As soon as I entered, I froze. There were two immigration officials, and I thought, God, what did I do? Why are they taking me away? But Mr Luis told me to relax. He said that the agents were there to help with the process. On the desk were the papers of seven other girls. The youngest ones were from Brazil and the others were my age, from Colombia. They made me sign papers, and they fingerprinted me. Later, the agents showed up at the bar wearing plain clothes to watch us dance. They were handsome and loving.

One day, I saw that I already owed them more than $10,000 for the plane ticket, housing, food, the doctor, the pretty clothes they had bought me, and my immigration papers. This is why the first time they asked me to go to the hotel with that wealthy businessman from Nuevo León, I accepted. I didn't want to mess with the hornet's nest, so I obeyed. Later, I couldn't stop. They were politicians, and they all told me the same thing: that I have the face of a child, of an angel; that they liked my soft voice; and that I was obedient. At night, I would figure out how much I still owed. Héctor, the chauffeur who took care of us, bought me a little book, and I wrote things down in it. One day I asked Héctor if he would help me find another job once I had made enough money. He told me that I should never say anything like that and that if Mr Luis found out he would punish me. Here, nobody goes anywhere alone. It was Héctor who told me that Luis was the governor's brother and that this was why he was able to run these fine escort agencies. In the club, Luis videotaped everything. The clients had no idea, but they are all on the tapes. If any of them does anything, then the whole world can see what they've done. When Carmen, the most experienced dancer, explained to me how to work the booths, I felt uncomfortable. It's a small, dark space, with a sofa that fits three people. I dance for them and I'm allowed to touch them, but they are not allowed to touch me. She told me not to worry because everything is videotaped. If a client went too far, it would be videotaped and I could ask for help; that was what the security guards were there for.

One day I was sick of it and I started crying because a client had been very rough with me . . . I told the boss: "If they want my tits, then I'm going to return them." I grabbed a knife and I said to him, "I'll cut them out, you bastard!" They laughed at me, slapped me a few times, and I was punished. No food for two days. No chance of seeing anyone. Then I behaved. They were right: what did I have to return to in

Venezuela? To fucking poverty on the street, without money
for my studies . . . If a person has no opportunities, she does
what others tell her to do.

I asked Arely about living in the mansion, a large house in San
Pedro Garza García, the richest city in Mexico, located in the
state of Nueva Leon:

It was nice, very well kept and protected, with a police
officer at the entrance. We had a big TV room. They would
keep the TV tuned to the Playboy channel all day. Marta,
the housekeeper, a woman around fifty years old, would say
to us, "Look, girls, you should take care of yourselves and
make yourselves classy women so you can be like those
girls." You know, the ones from the Playboy mansion; those
girls have a good life. Hugh Hefner treats them well; he
respects them . . . and he gives them everything they want.
He never makes them dance in front of drunks with stinky
mouths.

Arely's story is strikingly similar to the stories I have heard from
young women and girls in other countries. In the houses where
they live, pornography and erotic movies are used to create a
culture of acceptance and to normalize their exploitation. The
traffickers convince these women that they should dream of
becoming porn stars and that these dreams can come true. In
this way they make them believe that the exploitation will be
only temporary and that they will soon become famous and free
women in the sex trade, which is their only option. They assure
them that they are being trained to be the best and that once
they reach a powerful position they will be able to make their
own choices.

The induction techniques are similar throughout the world,
especially in the high-class businesses, providing escort services,

masseuses, and dancers for businessmen and the powerful. This type of man does not want to be with a woman who looks like a prostitute or who makes him feel like he has to pay for sex. Instead, he wants to be with a young, beautiful, obedient woman who pretends that she is in love with him or that he is her "special date." For this reason, Arely learned early on to call her clients "my love," "my life," "darling," "big daddy," or "my king," names that are supposedly affectionate and help to make the exploitation seem like an honest business transaction among equals.

The National Routes

Arely tells the story of how she met Juan Carlos at the bar. He was twenty-three and apparently had a lot of money. In the beginning he paid to be with her and have sex. Later, he began to fall in love with her and he would bring her gifts. It was romantic. He gave her expensive costume jewelry and stuffed toys. One day he gave her a movie which he said was his favorite: *Pretty Woman*, starring Julia Roberts. When the Venezuelan girl saw the film, she was delighted. Juan Carlos would be her Richard Gere and he would definitely ask her to marry him. Why not?

One morning, the group of girls who had been in Monterrey for a year were sent to see the Devil, the owner of the bars. He told them, "You are professionals now, which makes it boring, so I have a surprise for you: you're going to Cancún; there you'll work in a nice place by the ocean." Some were going to a nightclub called Black Jack; others were going to Caribbean Escort Services; and others would end up at The One. Arely was upset by the news. When she told Juan Carlos, he said that it was a fantastic idea because this way he could visit her in Cancún. Later they would run away together, he added. She could not believe her good luck; she was finally on her way to freedom.

Later, Arely spoke to a Brazilian girl and she discovered that Juan Carlos had made the same promises to other girls. It turned out that he was working for Luis, helping to keep the girls hopeful and allowing them feel somewhat free. She was devastated. She cried all night and prayed to her mother. How could he have deceived her in this way? In the darkness, Arely decided to find a way to escape in Cancún. She felt as if she was a slave, as if all these men had the power to mess with her head, to put her in chains, not physically, but in her head—to make her lose her mind, she said.

> Yes, I felt like a crazy person. They told me, "Look at yourself; you are ungrateful and miserable." They had pulled me out of poverty in Venezuela and this was how I repaid them, with tantrums. And I thought: Am I crazy? I don't like to be forced to have sex. Sometimes they [the men] are disgusting. I'm tired. They smell bad. I don't like drunkards. "This is a job like any other," the mansion housekeeper said to me. All I wanted to do was dance. I don't know if I'm crazy because I don't like to obey.

Arely was in the municipal jail in Cancún when the CIAM team rescued her. The day before, she had tried to board a plane without her passport—the traffickers had confiscated it—but the airline employees had told her that she could not fly without it and the FM3 visa form. Arely then spotted the immigration agents she had met before. At that moment, she decided to run. After running an extraordinary distance, she jumped into a taxi. She could not pay the fare because the police at the airport had taken her money. The Cancún taxi driver got angry so he took her to the local police station. The police officers took one look at her and immediately knew what she was: with platinum-blonde hair, large (obviously fake) breasts, big lips, sculpted legs and wearing shorts and high heels, she must be a prostitute. The authorities' criteria are clear: according to Cancún's chief of police, prostitution is a blot on society, and, like the municipal president, Gregorio Sánchez Martínez, he considers these women the trash of the town. They arrested Arely and in jail four officers raped her. While she was crying, the police officer in charge asked her, "Why are you crying? You are a whore, and this is what whores do."

A few days later, when I interviewed the prison governor, he told me with a smile on his face, "You don't understand. These girls make a living from this. They provoke the boys and later they regret it. She most likely offered sex as a way to get out of jail, but here we comply with the law. Also, my officers tell me that it isn't true that they raped her; she had already been raped before she arrived . . . She was no virgin."

The CIAM rescue team entered the Cancún prison, along with two Red Cross paramedics: the prison doctor had injected Arely with drugs "to calm her down, because she was screaming that they had kidnapped her and raped her." The paramedics found her drugged and tied to a bed in the infirmary. They filed a report and noted what medications had been used: an overdose of benzodiazepine, which had caused psychotic shock. The prison governor assured the paramedics that the young woman was insane, and discredited the story that Arely had tried to tell the officers. What she had told them was this: she had escaped from a trafficking ring and that they had threatened to kill her because she knew the names of everyone involved. However, the police officers decided to focus on the fact that she was a prostitute, giving no value to her words or what she had to say.

After the nurse and social worker—who care for victims twenty-four hours a day in the CIAM shelter—helped Arely take a bath and go to bed in a room at the shelter, the psychologist stated that Arely would be fine, now that nobody could harm her. Arely, however, could not believe it: why would a group of strangers help and protect her? The men who had bought her had convinced her that her life was worthless to anyone other than them. The authorities, the clients, and the airline employees had clearly demonstrated this. Earning Arely's trust was the hardest task for the rescue team, who had to find a way to make her believe that she had rights and that her life was important just because she was a woman.

The shelter's psychologists explained their observations of Arely:

> We knew that Arely was not insane. She, like thousands of other victims of violence and trafficking for sexual exploitation, showed signs of desperation when confronted with a desperate situation. The owners of the nightclubs in Monterrey sent her to work in Cancún. She was determined to escape from this form of slavery. She knew that any attempt to escape could cost her life, but she did it anyway. Arely vomited everything she ate for two days, and we were almost certain that they had addicted her to some drug, although she denied it. She had all the symptoms of withdrawal. Later we realized that the symptoms she had were due not to an addiction, but to the overwhelming realization of the victimization she had suffered, exacerbated by post-traumatic stress and an overdose of narcotics injected irresponsibly by the prison doctor.

The plump lips and voluptuous body were only a shell in which a young woman was hiding, still drugged. She continued to cry like a little girl, incessantly asking for her mother. The nurse spent the first night by Arely's side until she fell asleep, hugging the toy rabbit that had been placed in her arms.

While she was coming out of the drug-induced stupor, Arely, still half asleep, asked if she was back at the mansion. It took her two days to comprehend that she was really free and that nobody was going to use her for any purpose. A few weeks later, after undergoing some therapy, taking walks in the garden, and doing yoga in the shelter, Arely sat down to tell me about the journey that had led her to enslavement. Together, we could clearly plot on the map how the syndicate had taken her from Venezuela to Monterrey, and finally to Cancún.

Just like many other victims of trafficking, she could recall with astounding clarity the names and physical traits of the buyers, sellers, and the public servants who make it possible for an international syndicate to peddle women as if they are objects.

Face-to-Face with the Accomplices

When the CIAM social worker offered Arely the opportunity to seek help from the immigration offices, Arely turned pale. She knew who they were, at least she knew the bosses who had met the girls arriving from Monterrey. The girls had been sent in a private jet to Cancún, and it had landed in the area designated for the plane belonging to the governor of the state of Quintana Roo.

In a minivan with tinted windows, the CIAM chief of security, a psychologist, and I took Arely to the National Institute of Migration. Wearing dark glasses and a hat to cover her hair, Arely got out of the minivan with the psychologist, and we entered the building to ask to speak with the office director. One by one as they appeared, Arely was able to identify the men by their first names. It was an astonishing experience: all of them, including the top bosses, were involved, some as clients and others as facilitators for the arrivals and departures at the airport.

When I met Fernando Sada, who had recently been appointed director of the National Institute of Migration, I told him Arely's story. He stared at his hands as I spoke. As I got deeper into the story, beads of sweat covered his forehead. The air conditioning in the office was set at 18°C: it wasn't the heat that was making this bureaucrat from Monterrey nervous.

"She should come in and make a statement. We will gladly help her," Sada said. I explained to him that Arely was certain that they would kill her because of what she knew. As though he were not joking, he asked, "Who would want to kill a dancer?"

"She says 'the Devil' would, the owner of the bars, a powerful businessman from Monterrey. Do you know him? She is also certain that the lawyer who coordinates the foreign girls' entry into Mexico and their movement on the prostitution route between Monterrey, Cancún and Puebla is the governor's brother. Could you send a report to the Secretary of the Interior in order to protect this young woman's life until she can be repatriated?" I asked.

Sada nervously got up, opened a small glass jar full of candy, and offered me one. I accepted it. Obviously lost in thought, he unwrapped one and put it in his mouth. He silently paced around his small office. I sat still, just listening to the sound the candy made as he chewed it. It seemed like he was stalling for time, searching for the right words. Finally, he looked at me and said, "Look, Lydia, I know nothing about this. It's better to stay on the sidelines. It's not in my hands. Don't put yourselves in harm's way. This conversation never happened."

"Are you telling me that this trafficking ring is above the law?" I protested. He looked at me uncomfortably, sheepishly, almost pleadingly. He straightened his glasses. I looked at his neck, where the white skin was turning red and I could see signs of controlled anger.

"I didn't say that; I didn't say anything." He did not return to his seat, but he continued to speak: "It's better for you to do what you know how to do: help the young woman recuperate."

"You don't think it's better to arrest the people who sell women instead of having to rescue girls indefinitely?" I asked him as I rose from my seat to get my bag and notebook. He merely said, "Yes, definitely," and added that he would have to evaluate the situation with the "competent authority." Every time a government official gives me this answer, I ask myself whether he defines himself as an "incompetent authority."

The CIAM coordinator sent Santiago Creel, Secretary of the Interior at that time, a letter, with a list of the names of the immigration agents involved, various photographs, and Arely's story. Three weeks later, the newspapers published the news that Fernando Sada had resigned from his post to become dean of a private university.

The social worker assigned to Arely's case explained to me that the Venezuelan ambassador refused to help Arely. They recommended sending her to the immigration center in Cancún. The immigration center at that time was more like an overcrowded, smelly prison for juveniles. The agents guarded the trafficking victims as though they were delinquents. In 2009, things changed for the better and an adequate building replaced the old immigration center.

I decided to call Emma Toledo, Venezuela's consul general in Mexico City. The ambassador had refused to take my call for an interview. Toledo was friendly but succinct: "Look, Lydia, I understand that the people at the shelter do commendable work. It's not that the consular office refuses to help a Venezuelan citizen; it's simply that we do not have the budget or the staff to undertake the necessary steps. Every year, thousands of Venezuelan girls fall into these traffickers' hands, and there is no budget to cover their repatriation with protection as the social worker proposes. We will do what we can with what we have." Her consternation was clear from her voice, and her frustration seemed genuine.

Going Home

The shelter's team was able to contact Arely's family by Internet and by telephone, and her relatives immediately sent copies of Arely's papers. The Venezuelan embassy in Mexico was able to issue her a new passport based on these copies. (The Monterrey traffickers had the original papers locked up in a safe, and it was clear that no government official wanted to retrieve them.) Six weeks later, in complete secrecy, thanks to the help of an official at the National Institute of Migration—a sensitive individual, not the government—Arely was driven to Mexico City, where she stayed for five days in the immigration center with special status. Finally, she returned on a flight to Venezuela, where her older brother met her. With great excitement, the family called and sent messages to thank the shelter for returning Arely, whom they never expected to hear from again.

Most cases do not have such a successful resolution. Sixty percent of women lured into forced prostitution are not welcomed back into their homes. This may be due to the family's prejudices or because, in many cases, a member of the family was involved in the sale of the young woman or girl in the first place. Equally, some of the victims have grown accustomed to another type of life and in their homes they feel judged or oppressed. Unfortunately, they have been conditioned to sell their bodies, and they believe that prostitution is the only way for them to make a living.

Many women who have suffered sexual exploitation become outcasts once they return to their countries. In Asia and Europe, they are often forced by circumstances to go back to working for local prostitution rings. They have told me that at least in this environment, they don't feel judged and they are with the other outcasts of the world, the slaves who have been taught not to trust anyone and to consider themselves objects for sale. They belong in a different social category, which the feminist anthropologist Rita Laura Segato calls, "the others, the women for sale."

In October 2008, I received a last message from Arely. She told me that she was studying to be a social worker at a shelter like the one that rescued her in Mexico. Later, she closed her e-mail account. I hope she did so in order to remake her life and forget about her past completely.

Sitting in front of my computer screen, I stare at a photo of Arely taken right after she was rescued. There are marks of violence on her neck. She is lying in a chair, exhausted. I feel desolation invading my office and spilling on to my keyboard. I hope that this book finds its way into the hands of people who really care about the lives of these women and girls; of men who stop to look at themselves and are able to see in these women their very own daughters, sisters, nieces or granddaughters. I hope readers realize that all of the girls whose stories I tell deserved safe, dignified, and happy lives, lives that none of them got to have because there are not enough people in the world who worry about and work to prevent sexual slavery.

Killing the Messenger

One morning I opened the Mexican newspaper *La Jornada*, and found an article about the dismantling of a trafficking ring that was using the Internet to contact women in various countries and transport them to Mexico for sexual exploitation and forced prostitution. According to the tabloid, the website that the traffickers used was called Divas.com—the same one that Arely had used.

The article went on to say that the Office of the Attorney General in Mexico was investigating Federal Preventive Police officials and National Institute of Migration officials for their alleged participation in providing protection to the organization Divas.com. They were also suspected of allowing Divas.com to establish links with criminal groups that operate in Eastern Europe and South America, making it one of the most active pimping and people-trafficking organizations. The Deputy Attorney General's Office for Special Investigations into Organized Crime (SIEDO) came to the same conclusions in its investigation.

In October 2001, Antonio Santoyo Cervantes, known as Sony, and José Antonio Martínez Villeda, known as Tony, created their website. The market research was impeccable, and they managed to identify and contact women in various countries and offer them contracts in Argentina, Chile, and Mexico. In five years, Sony and Tony, along with Diana Patricia Quintana, Mercedes Luján, and Susana Arzamendia, consolidated a prostitution network through the Internet and established connections with international organizations dealing in prostitution and human trafficking.

Between February and June 2007, Divas.com was apparently shut down after the arrest of two people; however, the website was immediately reactivated under the name Zonadivas.com. This website was eventually used by trafficking rings in Argentina, Chile, Colombia, Brazil, and Spain to facilitate the exchange of "merchandise." This was the word some high-level SIEDO officials used when explaining their investigation's findings to me.

The testimony of the women involved, who gave the investigators the "legal contracts" drawn up by the company that moved them from country to country, provided important leads. Human trafficking has been integrated into the "escort service" branch of the prostitution business. As you read this book, you can go to the website Zonadivas.com and hire a woman from one of these countries. How does a client know whether the woman is working voluntarily or is the slave of a trafficking ring that controls her through debts she can never repay, threats, and isolation? He cannot know this, because the owners of the business, once some of the key players were arrested, understood that they needed to mix the slaves into the group of "voluntary" prostitutes in order to keep rotating the women on the sex-trade circuit.

I made it my goal to find out who was the owner of this business. The attorney general was investigating links to organized crime and to one of the most powerful drug-trafficking cartels in Mexico, which buys and sells women as gifts and trophies, as incentives to close deals, and as a "thank you" to powerful men for favors. One of the lines of investigation related to the traffickers' strategies to cover up their activities, such as mixing adult women with teenagers and girls in groups of voluntary and forced prostitutes.

Many of the facts coincided with my investigation in 2005 into Succar Kuri's child pornography ring in Cancún, published in my book *The Demons of Eden*, for which I was tortured and wrongly imprisoned. I decided to talk to the public prosecutor for violent crimes against women and human trafficking in Mexico: Dr Alicia Elena Perez Duarte. When we met, she could not give me more information than what had been published in the newspapers, but she helped me piece together the puzzle. We both agreed that these organizations are connected to each other and that there are invisible links that protect them. I guessed that it was the same network of government officials that protected the child pornographers and the sex traffickers, but it still needed to be proved.

In April 2007, Nemesio Lugo Félix, the general coordinator of information at the National Center for Planning and Analysis to Combat Organized Crime, phoned my office. He asked to meet with me. I had previously interviewed him for my investigation on child pornography, and some names had coincided with other investigations he had been working on. A year before, Lugo had visited Cancún, accompanied by US agents, including agents from the US Immigration and Customs Enforcement (ICE). They were involved in an operation focused on finding American criminals.

On this occasion, Lugo asked me if we could meet in a public place, so I gave him the address of a small café in the city center, owned by friends of mine, where we could have some privacy. During the conversation, he asked me twice how I stayed calm when confronted with death threats. I told him that attending therapy sessions helped, along with a strong social network. He said very little; the truth is I never even knew whether he was married or in a relationship. We talked about how the Divas network had recruited Arely. He then asked me whether I had proof that government officials of Nuevo León and Baja California, particularly Tijuana, took part in the human-trafficking syndicate. I responded that the only evidence I had were the victims' stories and the fact that government protection was provided in the victims' work places, which were untouched by the police. He was worried that a deputy of Joaquín "el Chapo" Guzmán, the Mexican drug traffickers' most powerful leader, might be implicated.

Lugo told me that if he managed to get recorded conversations between the trafficker they had arrested and the governor's brother accused by the victims, he would turn them over to his bosses and give me a copy for publication, "in case something goes wrong," which I understood to mean in case of political corruption and the all-too-common disappearance of evidence handled by Mexican officials.

When we said goodbye, he asked me where my bodyguards were. I pointed them out by glancing at them: they were inside a bulletproof vehicle, taking a nap. "You're not scared that you'll be killed?" he inquired. I answered, "Are you?" He answered, "That they kill me, not really. That they make me suffer—the truth is, yes." We smiled, and said goodbye with a squeeze of the hand. That was the last time I saw him alive.

On May 14, 2007, at 7:05, Nemesio Lugo Félix was murdered, shot eight times, a few feet from his office. I heard the news at 8 o'clock. It was a Tuesday, and I was listening to the radio. At that moment, a wave of paralyzing heat ran through my body, and the bitter taste of bile rose in my throat. I called the ICE agent with whom Lugo had traveled to Mexico; he was now in Texas. "Nemesio was killed. Do you know anything?" I asked nervously. "No, Lydia, but you should leave town for a few days; this thing's very hot right now," he answered. I contacted my sources at the attorney general's office, because I wanted to find out if they had found the USB that Lugo always carried with him; it contained all the information related to his cases. Two days later, one of the criminologists told me that they had only found Lugo's wallet and a pen. As this book goes to press, his murder remains unsolved.

Before Lugo's death, I had decided to continue with the investigation and I traveled to Monterrey, where I interviewed some local sources. A journalist colleague from the *Milenio* newspaper asked me if I knew anything about the rumors of a trafficking syndicate being run by some members of the governor's family. I told him that I was investigating it but that I did not have any proof, just victims' stories.

I subsequently spoke with Gamaliel López Candanosa, a young, very active reporter, fired up with adrenaline, at TV Azteca. An expert on police activities, he knew every corner of the state of Nuevo León. He knew the names of the policemen responsible for protecting the traffickers of women and minors. He had tried to contact me the year before, after I won my case against the mafia and the millionaire Kamel Nacif. López had a video of an attempted kidnapping carried out by the same policemen sent by the governor and Nacif to arrest me. Some colleagues had warned me not to trust López because he liked money too much, but, in the end, there is almost no way to minimize the risks we take when investigating the underworld of organized crime and corruption.

López was offering to help me. He had some information that could prove useful; he would not publish it in Monterrey. He gave me some photographs of nightclubs that exploited minors: there were girls aged twelve and thirteen; most of them were Mexican, but some were Brazilian. They had been making child pornography with a company in Rio de Janeiro called Rua das meninas (Girls' Street). We decided that we would each keep investigating and then talk on the phone. Like many Mexican journalists, he had already received some death threats, so we agreed that he would contact me using a public telephone.

On May 4, 2007, I received an e-mail from López saying that he would send me some important information related to the case. On May 10th, Gamaliel López and his cameraman, Gerardo Paredes Perez, of TV Azteca Northeast, were kidnapped by a group of people in several cars. Immediately, Reporters without Borders, the French NGO that defends freedom of the press, made an urgent announcement. At that moment, I believed that the reporters would be found alive, but it didn't turn out that way.

Novices in La Merced

With help from various NGOs, some human-rights activists and I dressed up in white coifs and black habits like novices, or nuns-in-training, and we walked through the neighborhood of La Merced, in the Venustiano Carranza and Cuauhtémoc districts of Mexico City. The purpose of this visit was to verify evidence that I had received. Just in this area of the Mexican capital, there are 1,528 trafficked women who are kept in mafia-protected brothels, 947 of whom are girls under the age of seventeen. A third of them come from Brazil, El Salvador, Guatemala, and the Dominican Republic. In Mexico City's Chinatown, seven sexually exploited girls were found; the girls came from northern China and were eight to ten years old.

Walking through the neighborhood in a disguise was a tremendous experience. Some pimps greeted me with a slight nod of their heads. The older prostitutes said to me, "Pray for me, sister." The owner of a motel even told my colleagues that he had just donated a large sum to the basilica of Guadalupe. It was clear from people's eyes that they feared and respected the nuns. Undoubtedly, there are only two ways that a woman can walk through these mafia-controlled neighborhoods: either as a nun or as a prostitute.

It was very difficult for me to take in what I heard and observed in those places. I grew up in Mexico City, in a lower-middle-class neighborhood. Ever since I was a young girl, I have seen how the dispossessed live in my country, and I knew that poverty was never too far away. However, maybe because a month earlier I had interviewed various women in a union trying to validate prostitution, unconsciously I expected to see something less dramatic than what I witnessed. I had interviewed and listened attentively to scholars, political experts, activists, and sociologists in favor of the regulation of prostitution. They all assured me that confusing slavery victims with voluntary prostitutes was a result of the moral panic and sick obsession of activists and journalists who wanted to exaggerate stories of sexual exploitation. I secretly hoped to find something different in these neighborhoods to what I found in Bangkok and Cambodia, but it was just the same. Streets lined with brothels have their own language: pimps lounge in the doorways of a house, a small building, or an hourly-rate motel; teenagers, almost always in pairs, stand in the streets wearing clothes that look like costumes. They wear fuchsia-pink lipstick and blue, green or black eye shadow. Their eyes are outlined in black, and they wear fake eyelashes. Their attitude seems to indicate exhaustion. They simply observe cars and wait for men.

I know that to investigate sexual slavery it is necessary to shield your emotions behind armor of steel. Nobody can deny the emotional impact of observing mafia-controlled areas and forced prostitution; it's even worse when girls and boys are involved. My visit to La Merced shocked me to the core.

We continue on our pilgrimage. A girl of about seventeen, dressed in fishnet stockings and very high heels, stares at me. My eyes are transfixed by her gaze. I remember that I am dressed as a nun, and I smile slightly. She looks down out of guilt, and I do the same. We continue walking. On the corner, a patrol car is parked. Inside, two police officers look around, showing no particular interest in their surroundings. On the other sidewalk, in front of a wall painted green, three women in their forties, their wrinkled, haggard faces plastered with make-up, talk among themselves without taking their eyes off the passers-by. Two young men go up to them and negotiate a price. The woman with big breasts goes with the man who is probably no older than twenty-three. They walk past a hardware store and enter a hotel.

Seated on the sofa of an hourly-rate motel, I see five girls, no older than twelve, sitting in plastic chairs, having some soup. One of them slurps her soup while her eyes follow a couple that has entered. She swings her legs back and forth, not reacting, indifferent, just observing reality. In this building, various girls, her co-workers, have gone upstairs with clients. "Soon it will be her turn," says one of the real nuns, who knows very well that the authorities will not intervene. She guides me through the lobby. If the police rescued all the young girls and teenagers, there would be no safe place to send them. The few shelters for trafficking victims that exist are crammed full. These nuns have slowly gained the trust of this community, and with great courage they are able to rescue victims from time to time. The traffickers have more respect for them than for the police. At times, the nuns are able to negotiate the release of some girls, but the nuns themselves have also received death threats.

What would happen if I approached one of these little girls and asked her if she would like to have a different life? Maybe I would start crying if she told me that her mother is there; that this is the way life is; and that it's all right. Or if she told me that her father, seated about thirty feet away, told her that he will love her more if she brings home money . . . And she, like everyone else, wants her parents to love her. This is what some of the girls said, dressed in pink polyester and wearing a necklace with a gold medallion engraved with the protective image of the Virgin Mary.

7

Clients: A Man's Secret

Between trips, I found myself home in Cancún, Mexico, enjoying the view of the Nichupte lagoon and having a beer in the Puerto Madero restaurant. Once my two friends arrived, we ordered tequilas to celebrate my return. After the meal, a waiter came over to us with a bottle of champagne, followed by a young waiter holding three crystal champagne glasses. "Señora Lydia, this was sent over by the man at the table over there," said the waiter, glancing discreetly at a man, whom I had already noticed had been observing us for a while. He was tall and well built; he ate a steak and drank wine in the company of two young platinum blondes, wearing revealing dresses and transparent acrylic platform heels. They were no older than twenty-five. The man persistently looked at my table. Accustomed to living with death threats, I tend to be alert, especially in crowded places.

"Tell him, thank you, but I don't accept drinks from strangers," I responded. The waiter became very nervous and in an even quieter voice insisted, "Señora, the man said that he won't take no for an answer." I stared at the waiter, and my friends quietly suggested that I accept the bottle and keep my mouth shut. "Tell him that I appreciate it, but no thank you." With the bottle still in his hands, the waiter returned to the man's table. Given his appearance, we suspected that he was a mafioso working for drug dealers, a suspicion that was later confirmed. The man discreetly gave me what looked like a military salute—he touched his forehead and curled his fingers downward. I simply lowered my head a little and assumed that the episode was over.

Drug dealing is a thriving industry in my country. The cartels continue to grow, recruiting more and more men from various walks of life into their ranks and operational networks. The Zetas, for example, are recruited from the national army's pool of soldiers; and, in the last few years, they have expanded their business by selling "protection" to the upper echelons of Mexican society against the violence surrounding the "war against drugs," which was initiated by President Felipe Calderón in 2006. The violence generated by wars and dictators ultimately works in favor of those involved in organized crime, who are always looking for ways to enter the legal economy and to expand during times of crisis.

A few minutes after the champagne incident, I excused myself to go to the lavatory. When I returned, the man was leaning against a pillar, waiting for me. In the distance, my friends were watching me.

"Look, Ms Cacho, you are the bravest woman in this country, and I want you to know that we have more in common than you may think. We are both fighting against the same perverts, because there are some things that are allowed and others that break God's and man's laws."

I looked him straight in the eyes. He was tall, with a military demeanor, wearing Armani sunglasses and a luxury watch, denim trousers, Italian shoes, and a gold medal depicting the Virgin of Guadalupe on a chain around his neck. The man seemed confident, although he was obviously making an effort to speak good Spanish. He spoke as though we were discussing the weather.

"If you allow me, I'll eliminate the precious governor and Nacif. We have to clean up this country by getting rid of the rats that touch our children."

I felt my blood freeze, my stomach contract, and I could only reply that I appreciated his offer but that I didn't believe in violence.

"It doesn't have anything to do with believing in it or not. Violence is just out there and there is nothing anybody can do about it," he said with conviction, looking at me intensely. He said that he understood my wariness but that he was a man of his word. A waiter walked past, glancing at me anxiously. He did not know what to do, so he kept walking.

"Look, you go back to your table, and before I leave, if you drop your napkin, then I'll know that together we are going to save our children from those bastards. You can count on me," he insisted.

"I believe you. Good afternoon," I said politely, faking composure, and making my way back to the table.

My friends and some acquaintances at two other tables were visibly worried and didn't take their eyes off me. I took my seat and immediately asked them to make sure, no matter what, that none of our three napkins fell to the floor. In fact, we placed all three napkins in the center of the table as a symbol of our rejection of violence. My hands were sweating and my mouth was dry; I sipped a little tequila and told them what had happened. We understood that this hit man for the drug dealers was offering to assassinate Mario Marín, the governor of the state of Puebla, and his associate, Kamel Nacif, who had incarcerated and tortured me in 2005 to persuade me to retract the contents of my book, *The Demons of Eden*, an investigation of an international child pornography ring run by their accomplice Jean Succar Kuri. I became famous, not only because I survived but also because soon afterwards voice recordings that proved their involvement were publicly released. These recordings showed the entire country that these men had bought and sold girls, as young as four years old, for sex tourism and pornography. I brought charges against them, and the case went to the Mexican Supreme Court, where corruption won the day and the defendants remained free, despite the outrage of most Mexican citizens.

What this man was offering me was the core of the mafia's business: the use of violence for protection. It was a prime example of the mafia's "criminal ethics." If I had felt daring enough, I would have asked him whether the same offer would stand if the trafficking had involved not young girls and boys but young women, like the ones at his table. I know very well that the trafficking rings in Cancún, Playa del Carmen, and the state of Yucután survive thanks to the protection of the Zetas and other hangers-on of the drug cartels, who offer kidnapping and protection services.

Thanks to the journalist Misha Glenny, I discovered that Diego Gambetta, a professor of sociology at Oxford University, wrote a book that should be read by anyone wanting to understand how organized crime operates: *The Sicilian Mafia: The Business of Private Protection.* The author explains that the mafia uses violence as a means and not an end, contrary to what the police have had us believe for years. The general view is that the mafia deals in violence. Gambetta refutes this perception and argues that "protection" is in fact what the mafia is selling on different levels. Violence, to a greater or lesser degree, is a tool that allows the effective delivery of protection—whether for a local trafficker who wants to ensure the safe transfer of his slaves from the airport to his bar; for a Colombian or Ecuadorian drug dealer who doesn't want to get involved in the machinations of local cartels while his cargo is in transit through Mexico or the Caribbean; for a Russian producer of child pornography who is tired of the effectiveness of the cyber-police in England; or for the owner of new prostitution hotels in the Caribbean, such as Dr Nights, Charlie's Angels, and others resorts operating in the Dominican Republic, which has become a safe haven for European and North American tourists trying to avoid the laws against prostitution and sex with minors.

The mafia does not necessarily manage the sex industry directly (with the exception of the Yakuza bars in Japan), but it provides protection and looks for new ways to protect the industry beyond the reach of the law. On my travels over the years, I have found that there does exist a "new breed" of mafia, which specializes in human slavery.

The great problem for NGOs providing aid to the victims of trafficking is that the mafia profits from their intervention. When these organizations rescue exploited women, the businessman who has lost his slaves taps into his network for finding "fresh meat." Within seventy-two hours, his brokers have usually found replacements. The businessman also needs the mafia to provide him with protection in case his victims testify and, in the unlikely event that an investigation is initiated, to ensure that corrupt police officers intervene. The mafia definitely charges extra for its involvement in a trial. Some mafias, such as the Yakuza, count on attorneys who specialize in financing shady businesses such as casinos and brothels. To understand how human slavery works, we need to accept that the mafia runs businesses, that prostitution is an industry, and that women, girls, and boys are the commodities being sold.

The Mafia's Business Tactics

On the trail of the Yakuza in Japan, I board the subway at Ginza station in Tokyo, two blocks from my hotel. I will have to change to get to Kabukicho, Shinjuku's "red light" district, where child-pornography videos are sold. There I will meet up with my contacts and get in touch with the girls I am going to interview.

My eyes wander to a poster, part of a Japanese social-awareness campaign. It prohibits the use of cell phones on the subway: "Avoid disturbing others," the poster urges. Next to the poster, a man in his fifties is reading a book. His upright posture and the delicate way he turns the pages draw my attention. I notice something unusual about his hand—a closer look reveals that his little finger is severed, a mere stub remains. "Yakuza!" I think. He looks at me, covers his hand, and slightly purses his lips in disapproval. I look around: I am the only person shocked by this man's presence on the train.

Three women trafficked to Japan helped me better understand how the networks of traffickers have modernized and transformed their slavery strategies. Sarah, the singer, Carmen and Marcela—forced into prostitution in Tokyo—have something in common: the three managed to escape with their lives and with sufficient proof to implicate the Yakuza and their gangs in the women's countries of origin: the United States, Mexico, and Colombia.

Unfortunately, nothing was done in these cases, beyond the survivors being put through legal hell for many years, suffering multiple interrogations and institutional mistreatment. The mafia structure remains intact, possibly because the mafia has influence over some of these governments' officials. The inaction may also be the result of cultural changes that have not embraced laws against human trafficking. The feminist boomerang effect of the twenty-first century has encouraged impunity for those who traffic in women and girls: sexism is back, stronger than ever, with new marketing strategies. In reality, sexism never went away in most countries; in others it is simply disguised by politically correct arguments.

Criminal Techniques in a New Marketplace

In 2000, I interviewed a young woman from Belarus who had been trafficked to Mexico three years earlier. I could see that her captors had got her addicted to morphine. The women were given small doses, injected with pediatric syringes commonly used for the treatment of diabetes, with the promise that thanks to this "little medicine," they would not suffer. The parts of the body used for the injections are unimaginable; the traffickers had to make certain that their "models" did not show signs of addiction. The good clients of VIP brothels frequent this type of establishment to ensure that they are getting "healthy" women.

Around this time, books were beginning to be published, television programs were appearing, and reports were being written about the enslavement of women and the methods used to transport them. The journalist Victor Malarek wrote *The Natashas: Inside the New Global Sex Trade*, which described how traffickers take women from Russia to bordering countries and then on to the United States. At this point, traffickers around the world, who function through a network of protection, changed their techniques. They knew that it was imperative to modernize their business. To defend slavery, traffickers and pimps in various countries started repeating the arguments of academics and feminists. They argued that the sex trade represented the true liberation of feminine sexuality in a capitalist society. The traffickers changed their methods: prostitutes no longer had to be drugged, hit, or terrorized; now a trafficker focused on reinforcing sexist cultural norms by lavishing sophisticated make-up and luxury goods on potential prostitutes to make it seem like they were acting by choice, as liberated women.

According to a Filipino trafficker who spoke with me in Cambodia, it is still necessary to teach the women and girls through a reward-and-punishment system; and to reprogram them by normalizing sexual exploitation through systematic exposure to pornography. They have to be convinced that they were the ones who chose to do this, and they must constantly be reminded that their lives are worth nothing; if they break the rules of the game, they will die.

"Difficult choices are still choices," said the trafficker who made the girls call her "godmother" in the brothel she controlled. This is one of the central premises in the global debate on prostitution: there are women over the age of eighteen who "freely" choose to live by means of prostitution. The mafias exploit and capitalize on the debate about "free choice" among intellectuals and activists. The philosophical argument about the definitions of free choice and coercion in a society has become part of the traffickers' discourse. I heard it from their own mouths.

The counter-argument of those who seek to abolish prostitution rightly focuses on the philosophical concept of freedom and on the ability of women to make decisions in a cultural context of submission and profound inequality. Almost 60 percent of the people engaged in prostitution start between the ages of fifteen and twenty-one under misleading circumstances, including threats and coercion. It is important to make clear that those who control the illegal sex trade have taken advantage of this philosophical, intellectual, economic, and even religious debate. The fact is, the organized-crime syndicates buying and selling sex slaves do not consist of isolated, underground groups who operate covertly. I repeat: they are active members of an industry, and they should be investigated with this in mind. You don't have to go very far; attorneys, bar owners, massage parlors, food stands, and restaurants are a starting point, and then there are the producers of adult pornography, casino operators, factory owners, and hotels. They all pay taxes; the sex industry yields very high returns for governments through tax revenue, the cost of permits and official licenses, and attracting tourists. It is also the sector in which most money is laundered for drug traffickers and arms dealers.

As in other industries, slavery has been bolstered by the liberalization of global markets. Sexual slavery is the extreme form of sexual exploitation, and it follows the capitalist model which seeks to increase profits and lower costs. If women or girls work for free for two years, profits are increased and any associated costs are quickly recovered, especially since the costs for maintaining a slave are so low.

Welcome to the New Century

Until the beginning of 1990, traffickers ran their networks in isolation, albeit with help from the government (corrupt police and public servants) and the local mafia. When global markets opened up, and George W. Bush spread moral panic about trafficking, local and international mafiosi developed the market for protection and global connections. The protection that the mafia could provide was perfect for high-profile clients like the Interpol agents filmed with prostitutes at a party in Cancún, or the governors, senators, and magnates who are regular clients of brothels, karaoke bars, and escort services.

Just as the tourism industry has created its own culture, the sex-slave industry exploits the most popular female stereotypes, as confirmed by clients around the world. On hundreds of websites, we can find advertisements offering sex with "silent Japanese geishas; submissive Thai masseuses; wild, uninhibited Colombians; insatiable Cuban nymphomaniacs; Russians who like dirty sex; gentle and loving Dominicans; North American playgirls, lovers of rough sex," etc.

The organized-crime networks move like leopards, and, in contrast, the international groups fighting crime move like lumbering old elephants. One of the fundamental differences between the trafficking networks and the international crime-fighting institutions is that the former lack bureaucracy and scruples. They are immoral. If someone in the mafia breaks the rules or commits an act of betrayal, he is simply eliminated, whereas at Interpol, if an employee is suspected of taking bribes, he will be investigated within strict legal guidelines, a process that usually takes one to two years. If the suspect is found guilty, he is sentenced for his crime. Mobsters assassinate traitors, and they don't have any trouble finding a replacement within a few hours. What a pimp told me in Guatemala is key: "We are not afraid of the cops. Not at all. We fear the bosses; they kill without mercy, and they know where our families live. Cops can be bought; the bosses are not for sale." As long as corruption exists, international agreements to fight trafficking from country to country represent no more than good intentions.

If I have learned anything on this journey around the world, it is the opposite of what experts have claimed: the mafias of traffickers—large and small—have clear operating rules and procedures and "codes of ethics;" in many cases, they are elementary, absurd, and inconsistent, but ultimately, they are still codes. In researching this book I found that the police forces of at least forty-six countries lack minimum operational standards for data capture, professionalism, and transparency.

Market Distribution

Walking at midnight through the neighborhood of Shibuya in Tokyo, we find a happy, smiling black man in the middle of the street. I look at my two Japanese colleagues, a journalist and a women's rights activist. We chat with the man and, in English, he offers us what "we need to be happy," in other words, liquor and methamphetamine pills. I joke with him and ask him where he is from. He is Nigerian and his thing is "making women happy." According to his story, he had been in Tokyo for five years; he was a businessman and a "man of the night." He tells me I can get what a woman needs, including pleasure, in a karaoke bar where young people know how "to make women happy." We finish our chat, he laughs a little and makes more sexual innuendos. As we are saying goodbye, he asks me where I come from. I tell him to guess. He answers, "Colombian, definitely. The most beautiful brunettes are Colombian." This is an overused line that I repeatedly hear in Japan. "What would you recommend to a Colombian so she can have a good time in Tokyo?" I ask him, fishing for information about the drug and sex trade in the city. With a pious expression, he responds: "Beware of Iranians; they are the bad guys around here." He is referring to the Iranian mafia, responsible for the heroin market in Tokyo. This man and other Nigerians handle synthetic drugs provided by the Chinese mafia, while the Yakuza are the kings of trafficking in women and of the prostitution scene. My friends and I walk toward a store where one can find sex toys and child pornography in comics, along with Hello Kitty dolls, bears, and other toys for children.

On the corner, before entering a bar to speak with some young people who work as prostitutes, I stop dead: I see a brightly lit police cabin with four police officers inside. On the opposite corner, there are four young Colombians "working the street" under the silent watch of their keeper, a trafficker. This scene occurred just six hours after the Japanese police chief had assured me that trafficking in women was practically non-existent in his country.

The following day, a journalist colleague showed me a report on the ceremony held to mark the succession of a new mafia godfather. The Yamaguchi-gumi—the largest Yakuza syndicate—had officially selected a new boss: Kenichi Shinoda, aged seventy-three. The ceremony took place in Kobe, clan turf in western Tokyo. Hundreds of bosses of the Yamaguchi-gumi and affiliated groups from all over Japan were there, offering their congratulations with toasts of sake, as required by Japanese mafia tradition. According to the report, which was later published in the national newspaper, various police officers dressed in civilian clothing patrolled the perimeter of the party during the ceremony.

Numbers on the Skin

Time and time again, the prostitutes I have interviewed tell stories about having to hand over a certain amount of money each night to their "godmother" or "godfather," while another percentage would go to the mafia and police officers protecting the streets and motels where they have sex. They can recall the precise figures, because they are written on their bodies and in their memories.

The Colombian, Mexican, and Russian prostitutes whom I interviewed in Japan were enslaved through debt bondage: they owed millions to the Yakuza. They have four clients on a bad night; six clients on a normal night; and up to fourteen on their best. A Colombian woman, aged twenty-one, pulled a small Hello Kitty notebook out of her purse. She had noted down how many clients she had had in Tokyo in the last eleven months. She was eager to pay her debt of $15,000 to her trafficker, who had bought her from an international network and had her brought from Medellín in Colombia. Only after paying off the debt would she be able to get the money to return home. In the time she had worked as a forced prostitute, she had had sex with 1,320 men. The girls who had been rescued from Pattaya in Thailand told me that they had six or seven clients for *yum-yum* (oral sex) every day, year-round. The sixteen-year-old who had fled her traffickers in Ciudad Juarez, northern Mexico, had up to twenty clients per day; two-thirds of them were Mexican and the others were from the United States. She had been forced to have sex 6,750 times, and only 10 percent were regular clients.

Where are these men? Do they understand the part they play in this global tragedy? The answer is simple. They are in their houses with their wives, with their girlfriends, or with their same-sex partners. They are in their respectable companies and in churches, giving or helping out with mass. They are making policy, in congress, parliament, and local councils. They appear before judges in court cases, and they investigate stories for the most prestigious newspapers. The clients of prostitution, who fuel the growing supply of sex slaves, work in schools, universities, as website programmers and football players; they are everywhere. During the day they brag about their sexual prowess to their friends in hundreds of electronic messages in more than twenty languages.

Thailand, Cambodia, and Japan are three of the Asian countries where the sex trade has the highest number of consumers: approximately 70 percent of men pay for sex. Thailand, despite its laws against trafficking and forced prostitution, receives 5.1 million sex tourists annually, and, according to ECPAT, between 450,000 and 500,000 local men pay for sex with adults and minors. In Europe, Spain tops the list of countries for the amount of prostitution consumed.

In the tourist centers of Mexico, such as Cancún, Playa del Carmen, and Acapulco, there is an increase in the number of US citizens and Canadians looking for sex with young, docile, obedient women, as I confirmed during my investigations into several nightclubs in Cancún. As two young dancers were laughing with me, a forty-year-old American watched us nervously, hoping that we would turn toward him. We immediately approached him and asked: "Why are you so lonely?" One of the girls started to work on him as we walked away. I couldn't resist turning back and asking him what he liked most about Mexico.

"Its beautiful girls; they are hot and sweet. I'm sick of American women; they are demanding and always looking for an argument. But Latin women are, I don't know . . ."

"Obedient?" I ask him gently.

"Yes, that's it! Latin women still believe in the sanctity of marriage and in showing a man respect. You are real women."

I smiled as politely as I possibly could and moved to the opposite corner of the bar.

In his investigative report, *The Johns: Sex for Sale and the Men Who Buy It*, Victor Malarek dares to unravel the secrets of prostitution's clients. He reveals the real face of those who generate the slave market. Some of the passages in his book remind me of comments made by tourists and traffickers I have met: a young Spaniard smoking a cigarette at midnight said to me, without turning a hair, that instead of making an effort to treat a girl his age as an equal, and to talk to her rather than just fucking her as though she were an inflatable doll, he preferred to simply pay to have sex with someone who would obey and keep her mouth shut. On that occasion, I was in Madrid's Casa de Campo, a neighborhood where Latin and African prostitutes work selling sex under the intimidating gaze of their traffickers and the soft hands of the authorities' protection.

8

The Military and Prostitution

*In spite of my most diligent efforts, there would un-
questionably be some raping in the war.*
                              —General George S. Patton, Jr.,
                                       War as I Knew It (1947)

John is young and tall, with a sculpted body. He is twenty-six
years old. He was trained by the US army to join the elite special
forces for combat in Iraq. At eighteen, he was selected for his
passion and knowledge of cybernetic communication systems.
Now, in October 2009, he is in Texas, undergoing therapy for
severe post-traumatic stress disorder, and one of the questions
he asks himself, in an effort to understand his nightmares, is why
his fellow soldiers raped Iraqi women and girls when they were
there to restore peace.

In a coffee shop in New York City, I sit in front of Jim, aged
sixty, from New Jersey. He understands why. While he pours
cream and sugar in his coffee, I study his fair complexion, his
forehead and cheeks wrinkled from unforgiving weather and
age.

Jim is married. He has three granddaughters and one grandson.
He now works for a NGO. When he was a soldier in Vietnam
he thought of himself as a true patriot. Age has made him wiser
and he now asks himself how he could have done the things he
did without questioning any of it:

Being a soldier means obeying. Being a patriot means not questioning your superiors and not allowing your subordinates to do so. They train you to do something absolutely unnatural: hate a whole village that you don't know anything about; hate the village's inhabitants so much that you are unable to recognize them as human. You have to see children as potential enemies, and women as objects or hostages; it is the only way you can keep from going crazy in a war. Despising, hating others. All the training has to do with releasing your inner rage, getting in touch with that anger and with the darkest side of yourself.

The army dehumanizes you until you drop, and that process follows the rest of your activities as a man. After all of these years of working on myself, doing yoga and becoming a peace activist, I don't recognize myself in that young man, but he is still a part of me. When they took us to Thailand for the first time, the general showed us a slide show of the brothels that were US army approved. The brothel doors had stickers with a green beret. This meant that the Thai government had recruited their prostitutes with funds provided by the US government to ensure that the girls were virgins upon arrival and that they were healthy. Every time we went to the brothels, we saw very young girls. No soldier questioned anything; we simply used them, and that was it. But we were not the only ones doing this; all armies have used prostitution as a sort of relaxation therapy for their soldiers. It didn't matter whether the girls wanted it or not, or if they had been kidnapped or not; the important thing was that we were enjoying our days of R&R. The fantasy was that they were in love with us and we would tell them whatever was necessary for them to act as our slaves, not only in a sexual sense, since they also gave us massages and made us feel like the most manly of men.

In 1957, at the start of the Vietnam War, it is estimated that there were between 18,000 and 20,000 prostitutes in Thailand. After opening seven military bases, the US army invested $16,000,000 in the Thai economy annually. In 1964, the population of women available for sexual exploitation had grown to 400,000. The Pentagon was responsible for creating what Senator James William Fulbright called "an American brothel" in Asia.

The presence of "comfort women" in war zones became well-known when groups of women in Korea and Japan reported the existence of prostitution camps or military brothels created by the Japanese military during World War II. Between 150,000 and 200,000 women and teenagers were sexually enslaved in these camps and brothels. Most of the victims originated from the Philippines, China, and Korea. Others were trafficked from Thailand, Vietnam, Malaysia, Taiwan, and Indonesia. According to the historian Yoshiaki Yoshimi, the Japanese Imperial Army leadership feared that its soldiers would rebel under the exhausting demands of the war, and, for this reason, it created sex-slave camps to "pacify the soldiers and entertain them with women."

To begin with, the Japanese army hired local prostitutes and took them to locations under their control. But very soon, more women were needed because many fell ill or became exhausted from attending to so many soldiers, so the army used brokers to advertise jobs for nurses and maids. After being recruited, the women were forced to become sex slaves. Historians and human-rights groups have documented the testimony of thousands of victims. The majority of women interviewed do not speak of sex but of a deeper form of violence filled "with some type of hatred expressed by penetration with a penis or with objects, but also with words and abuse," according to a seventeen-year-old from Mozambique. The doctors who attended to women in Mozambique and Rwanda describe unspeakable destruction of women's bodies. Human Rights

Watch is one of the organizations that has documented such cases.

On April 17, 2007, Yoshimi and Hirofumi Hayashi discovered documents from the Tokyo Trials, a military tribunal established to adjudicate cases against Japan's alleged war criminals after World War II. These documents show that seven officials from the Tokeitai military police units admitted to trafficking women to brothels in China, Indochina, and Indonesia. The women were meant to provide sexual services to Japanese soldiers. In May of the same year the historians discovered documents from 1944 that unveiled the military strategy of creating military camps for massive sex exploitation.

Until then, people were not aware of how the movie industry had exploited the image of geishas and "comfort women" as young and beautiful, crazily in love with soldiers from North America, Europe, and Asia. These women were usually portrayed as being fascinated and willing to serve as prostitutes for brave soldiers. It turned out that many of these young women and girls had witnessed the killing of their parents and siblings or they had been raped and deceived by soldiers. Hollywood and Asian films have played an important part in idealizing forced prostitution in times of war. Many great authors of classic and contemporary literature have also played a role in idealizing forced prostitution as an expression of sexual liberation. Films and books dealing with this issue are rife, with scenes of soldiers in the company of beautiful, young Asian women, at parties, dances, on romantic strolls on moonlit beaches.

However, survivors tell a very different story, a story of slavery, rapes, sometimes perpetrated by as many as twenty soldiers per day, unwanted pregnancies, sexually transmitted diseases that left them isolated and punished, bearing the blame for the soldiers' refusal to use condoms (when there were any). Thousands of these sex slaves died in the camps where no one was able to claim their bodies. In reality, Shanghai was the most important sexual exploitation camp of the Japanese army, and Thailand and the Philippines were the playgrounds of the North Americans and Europeans.

During the Tokyo Trials, conducted by the International Military Tribunal for the Far East from April 1946 to November 1948, it was proven that when World War II ended, the Japanese government received North American funds for the creation of new forced-prostitution camps, but this time the camps were set up for the occupation forces. In 1945, the Recreation and Amusement Association (RAA) was created; the RAA was really just a euphemism for the military sex camps. The Japanese and Americans, despite having been enemies, were able to negotiate the establishment of brothels that met North American standards and in order to "protect Japanese women from the sexual demands of soldiers and to preserve the genetic purity of the Japanese race by avoiding unwanted pregnancies from rape," according to post-war reports included in Herbert Bix's book *Hiroshito and the Making of Modern Japan*, published in 2001.

In 1946, the US First Lady, Eleanor Roosevelt, fought for the prohibition of the military's use of "comfort women." The reports reveal that in reality General Douglas MacArthur led this reform because 50 percent of soldiers had contracted sexually transmitted diseases and their poor health affected military operations. In the brothels, pimps and traffickers charged 15 yen up-front (the equivalent of $1 in 1945 or $9 in 2010) for one sexual service. In the Philippines, Cambodia, and Thailand, the families who made their fortunes from forced prostitution during this time still maintain their monopolies on the industry; they have never been held accountable by their governments.

Despite the proof and the testimony of thousands of women who were subjected to sexual slavery for the military in Burma, China, Japan, the Philippines, the Balkans, and in other European and Latin American countries, few people, besides the experts, understand the role that sexual violence plays as part of military training, and its consequences for women and girls in war zones around the globe. Today, despite the proof provided by Linda Chavez's investigation carried out as Special Rapporteur for the United Nations (published in 1998 as a UN expert report, *Contemporary Forms of Slavery*, by her successor Gay J. McDougall), there are people who insist that teenagers and adults subjected to military sexual exploitation "like being there," "they do it for the money," or "they were looking for a soldier husband."

In 2007, the governments of the United States, Canada, the United Kingdom, and the European Union publicly criticized Japan, asking it to apologize publicly to the world for creating the military sex camps. But these same countries avoided any mention of their own participation over the centuries in similar forms of enslavement and sexual exploitation during invasions and conquests of other countries. Of course, these governments and the media have not disclosed evidence of their militaries' role in sexual slavery and the promotion of human trafficking. On the one hand, 175 countries have declared their willingness to abolish trafficking and sexual exploitation. On the other, they themselves have been the principal actors in creating this evil practice on a massive scale.

Sweeping Reality under the Carpet

Armies and police forces around the world have chosen to conceal the philosophy that underlies the well-documented cases of trafficking of women for occupying troops. Denying the facts will not make them go away. Sexual violence has always been a weapon of war, and in the twenty-first century new forms of extreme cruelty and unusual sexist practices have been adopted. It is not coincidental that many human-rights experts ask themselves how soldiers can be responsible for fighting human trafficking when they themselves are the perpetrators and clients; there are even documented cases of UN peacekeeping forces being involved in rapes in foreign countries.

During the armed conflicts between India and Pakistan, women were raped and sold as sex slaves. Two years later, 75 percent of victims were still on the sex-slave market. Many of them were branded just like African slaves: they were given tattoos and other marks with a hot branding iron, as documented by the Indian author and publisher Urvashi Butalia in 1997. Many of these women were unable to return to their families or communities because they were considered "tainted" by the enemies' virility. After being forced into prostitution, many of them became outcasts or pariahs for the rest of their lives, only accepted by their equals, other raped women, sexual slaves, and the untouchables. After a certain age, some of them choose to move up in the prostitution business and thus victims become victimizers. The tortured become the torturers.

One of the most shocking issues that Hindu and Sikh men had to face was the possibility that their women and daughters were raped by the enemy, became pregnant from these rapes, and thereby created a race that was genetically and religiously impure. Whereas the Japanese negotiated and constructed brothels for enemy soldiers to prevent any genetic mixing with their women, many rural Sikhs chose to kill their women rather than allowing them to be "sullied" by the enemy.

Sexual violence is employed to show who is in control and who has the power, but it is also used as a form of revenge against the "other," where women are seen as objects that belong to the enemy. In a culture that considers a woman to be the property of a man, the soldiers burn houses, kill livestock, and rape women to show their power. In this context, prostitution cannot be seen as an act of eroticism or sexuality, although some would like to believe it to be so; instead it is sexualized violence and a violation of the human rights of women and girls. Since 1994, the International Criminal Court has considered rape a war crime when used as an instrument of war and colonization, yet numerous cases continue to be revealed in diverse corners of the world:

- Rape as a tactic of war in Bosnia has been documented by a special United Nations commission and human-rights organizations: from 1991 to 1995 the Serbian paramilitary groups promoted the rape of Bosnian Muslim women as a strategy to expel Muslims from their homes and villages.
- In Africa, Hutu troops raped thousands of Tutsi women during the genocidal war led by the Rwandan Hutus in 1994.
- In Chiapas, Mexico, during the Zapatista uprising of 1994, Mexican soldiers raped indigenous women in the mountainous resistance zones as a way of releasing tension and overpowering them. As many as 700 rapes have been documented, but the Mexican government refused to recognize them as war crimes.
- In 1997, dozens of Algerian women accused the rebels who fought desperately for the Islamic Revolution of kidnapping them and making them their sex slaves.
- In the Democratic Republic of the Congo more than 500,000 women have been raped and hundreds of men have also suffered sexual violence since 1998 in the on-going conflict. As the journalist Caddy Adzuba put it: "Violence against women has become a weapon of mass destruction."
- In 2006, five American troops raped an Iraqi girl, Abeer Hamza al-Janabi, not yet fourteen years old. Afterwards they killed her in front of her relatives, including a six-year-old girl. According to the official reports, all those implicated in this crime, which occurred in Mahmudiya, near Baghdad,

were under the influence of an "uncontrollable orgy of blood and alcohol." This type of description is used all around the world to minimize the crime of rape.

On September 27, 2009, it came to light that at least ten soldiers of the 4th Infantry Division's 4th Brigade Combat Team from Fort Carson, Colorado, had been arrested for crimes ranging from murder, attempted murder, and manslaughter. All of them had suffered severe psychological damage and an "uncontrolled propensity to violence" since their return from Iraq. Once the media released the reports, the military publicly admitted their veracity. One of the soldiers, Kenneth Eastridge, who is serving ten years for being an accessory to murder, told an American newspaper: "The army puts it into your head until it's instinct: kill all; kill all. You obey. Later they believe that you can just return home and stop." This also occurs in the case of sexual violence; combat situations normalize the fact that when a soldier wants to have sex, he looks for a young woman or girl and makes her his own by buying or raping her. Eastridge's statements exemplify the military's doublespeak around the world. In many countries, the military gives each soldier a pamphlet on human rights. However, war represents the antithesis of these rights—the imposition of power through violence. Death and sexual violence are intrinsically linked as part of the military's accepted rituals to reinforce masculinity. These rituals are used in almost all cultures to celebrate victory over the defeated.

In *Prostitution in Thailand and Southeast Asia* (1994), Justin Hall reported that a study of the sex trade involving students, soldiers, and laborers in Thailand showed that soldiers are more frequent clients: 81 percent admitted to having visited a brothel in the past six months. The students admitted to having visited a brothel twice on average, and the soldiers six times during a six-month period. A poll of soldiers in northern Thailand revealed that 73 percent of the soldiers lost their virginity in brothels and that 97 percent regularly visited brothels.

The reports on the sex trade and trafficking in women and girls show that, in general, the police and military are the ones who protect the traffickers, as well as frequenting the brothels along with tourists. How can they fight something that seems normal to them and is also profitable?

Once again we discover that laws and international agreements on the sex trade are not enforceable if they have not been integrated into a country's domestic laws. The global reach of certain laws is in fact a fantasy of the United Nations. This explains how a US president can go to the United Nations, take the microphone, and deliver a diatribe against the sexual violence committed in 1943, while his own military's current war strategy includes mass rapes of women who are seen as their enemy's property.

Most countries that have approved laws against the trafficking of women and girls provide training on the subject to their police forces and state security agents (who are often military or former military officers), but they fail to raise the awareness of sexual violence and masculinity with those same police officers, immigration agents, and military officials who are consumers of prostitution and who assume that prostitution and sexual violence are something normal.

Dirty Work in Iraq

The reason the Japanese government was able to deny the existence of the sex-slave camps for so long is the same reason why the United States has been able to deny its role in the sex trade in Thailand, the Philippines, Panama, and in Iraq: the special brothels for soldiers were independent businesses run by contractors who, like vultures, lived around military bases to take on all the dirty work.

John Perkins, author of *Confessions of an Economic Hit Man* and the *Secret History of the American Empire*, clearly explains how the military allies itself with companies that do the dirty work during wars, including the capture and purchase of women and girls for military brothels. In 2006, George W. Bush made much of the law to abolish worldwide human trafficking, and since then the military has had to manage its soldiers' R&R (rest and recuperation) with more subtlety.

In a 2005 series called "Pipeline to Peril," the *Chicago Tribune's* Cam Simpson published information about the channels used for trafficking in human beings for the purposes of sexual exploitation and illegal labor. The journalist David Phinney reported that US-funded Kuwaiti contractors illegally hired laborers brought in from India and the Philippines to build a new US embassy in the Green Zone of Baghdad—the area where the Americans live. He also discovered that women were being trafficked to work there as prostitutes. And, according to Debra McNutt's report, "Military Prostitution and the Iraq Occupation" for *CounterPunch*, these prostitutes were being put to work in brothels disguised as beauty salons, Chinese restaurants, and even a women's hostel.

The military authorities insisted that they had prohibited soldiers from paying for sex. US Secretary of State Condoleeza Rice presented herself as the world's moral leader working for the abolition of slavery, at the same time as these contractors— responsible for security in the Green Zone and surrounding areas—advertized on the Internet and bragged about their diverse offerings: Belarusian, Chinese, and Iranian women. According to McNutt, in 2005, when soldier Patrick Lackatt returned from Iraq, he said that in Baghdad, "For $1 you can get a prostitute for one hour." Still, for a soldier it was better to go to the United Arab Emirates (UAE), because laws concerning prostitution and trafficking in women from Asia are very lax there. Undoubtedly, American R&R now takes place in the large hotels of Dubai. Some of the young women I interviewed in Uzbekistan in 2009, who had been trafficked for sexual exploitation in the UAE, told me how they had attended to young soldiers under orders from their traffickers.

Although the US government has implemented various programs and policies to eliminate trafficking in women, they are not enforced, according to Sarah E. Mendelson, in a 2005 report called "Barracks and Brothels," cited by McNutt. Without enforcement, these programs become a mere exercise in public relations. Military authorities frequently look the other way when it comes to the sexual exploitation of women by soldiers and contractors, because they want to raise their troops' morale.

Sexual Violence as Punishment and Fate

"What underlies sexual violence? Why do women seem obsessed with this subject? Is it really so serious?" a Mexican journalist asked me when I spoke with him about this investigation. His questions made me look deeper at how attitudes to sexuality are built into the construction of masculinity. Why do so few men in the world, despite being sensitive and compassionate, understand the implications of sexual violence?

The conquests of Africa, Asia, and Latin America included the colonization of land, women, and, ultimately, the indigenous populations. Innumerable women were abducted. In fact, many mixed-race people were born as a result of the conquerors' sexual violence against women. Carolina González, a Chilean historian and feminist, explains why there has been a normalization of sexual violence:

> To understand the cultural consistencies that legitimize vio-
> lence against women, it is paramount to think about the idea
> of the power sustaining it. In this sense, it is important to
> reflect on sexuality. Even though we know that sexuality is

a product of culture, understood and lived in different ways throughout history, it continues to be understood as something established solely by nature—or by "God"—and, thus, as something normal, universal, timeless, unchanging.

The primary victims of sexual violence have been women. Their victimization by men is one of the most brutal paradoxes of male domination: on one hand, historically, in the Judeo-Christian tradition the female ideal has been defined by women's duty of submission and chastity; on the other, men must exercise their masculinity through women: men's sexual feats must be evident to the whole male community to reaffirm its virility, one of the basic tenets of being a real man.

In many cases the sexual abuse of women is explained through the paradigm of virility. We have been taught that men are naturally programmed to give in to their sexual impulses and that they are unable to restrain them. Even though this lack of control is denied publicly, in practice, the difference between sexual violence and "consensual" relations is strategically blurred—especially when the aggression has occurred within the home or by known men. Therefore, violence against women, in particular sexual violence, in general ends up being tolerated in private spaces.

In a broader sense, although rape is condemned *a priori*, it continues to be seen as something perfectly plausible.

González expounds on how girls and women around the world are taught to dress a certain way and not to venture out into the world without a man by their side to protect them. Here, we are reminded of how feminists in Iraq and Iran have come up with a similar analysis of why women have to cover their provocative bodies from head to toe:

The bodies we have are suspected of provoking the violence of men. Such constructs feed fear and blame and are reflected in the reserved feminine gestures and other "womanly" habits that females are taught from infancy.

Women's fear of being raped is not a product of the imagination, but something learned empirically. Would the incidence of rape drop if prostitution were legalized? The mere fact that police officers, sociologists, psychiatrists, and journalists have spent thousands of hours trying to answer that question shows that some believe that rapists use prostitutes instead of abusing women who are not recognized as such. González concludes:

> Sexual violence then becomes a right for men, or some men, a tribute that women are at risk of paying in a patriarchal society. Sexual violence, like torture, has historically been ignored, despite leaving marks on the most intimate parts of the body of victims and society. Thus, in heterosexual societies, where the norm is for sexual desire between a man and a woman, and in societies where women are not valued because they are women, sexuality must be understood as a system of power, a system that expresses itself in sexual violence.

Power and Masculinity

There are clear parallels in the sex trade. Clients use sexuality as an affirmation of power in the world and as a way of obtaining the recognition of other "real men." Many of them resist the cultural changes advocated by feminists. For many men from diverse countries, women's right to choose—when, how, and whether they want sex with men—represents an affront, leading them to the false conclusion that the only thing women want is to gain power over them. In response to this "challenge," these men resort to more violent acts against women and girls in the sex trade as a way to reassert their virility. In *Machismo in Motion*, a study of the values and attitudes of a group of Peruvian truck drivers, the anthropologist Ralph Bolton showed that machismo is based on power, envy, self-glorification, and sexuality.

Machismo exists almost everywhere on the planet, not just in developing countries. One of things I have discovered on my trips around the world and in my interviews with men from all backgrounds, is that the majority of them are slaves to a masculine culture that has not been questioned, either by them or by those who are in a position to promote cultural transformation, such as religious leaders and editors of print and electronic media. Directors, scriptwriters, and producers of films and television programs perpetuate the values of machismo and sexual violence, which may be depicted subtly or overtly. In general, even academia has not been able to change its patriarchal ways through a reappraisal of roles and genders.

The intellectual and political elites speak with each other, imposing a single way of thinking. As a result, diverse cultures adopt the values of the most powerful countries and incorporate them into their traditional value system. This is the only way I can explain the fact that, in the Philippines, a whole generation of girls between the ages of twelve and eighteen assume that women are born to be raped and sold: they have been raised in a hostile environment and educated by women who thirty years ago were forced into prostitution during a process of colonization. Or the fact that the teenage girls I interviewed in Vietnam—twenty-three of the 200,000 existing sex slaves—do not see any way to support family members who are addicted to gambling other than earning a few dollars from the Dutchman who controls a group of child prostitutes. They return home to sleep every night, and every morning they are sent to see the Dutchman, in the hope that they will return with more money. Their trafficker knows that they have no options; he doesn't even need to provide them with food or a bed, or to lock them up. His allies are poverty and the culture that normalizes prostitution and sexual violence against women and girls, which began in the war and has continued long after the foreign soldiers left Vietnam.

In the military, soldiers are trained not to be sentimental or cowardly; in other words, they are trained not to show their emotions. They are constantly expected to demonstrate that they are men, not women. As more women are recruited into the military in different countries—a trend criticized by the more conservative elements of society—they are finding that they, too, have to be more masculine to be perceived as good soldiers. They must also endure unwanted sexual advances and attacks, as is demonstrated by the dozens of complaints filed by women pilots, marines, and lieutenants who were raped by their military colleagues in the US military. Even though they are soldiers, these women continue to be seen as sexual objects, as inferiors in an environment that promotes a traditional, sexist, violent, insensitive masculinity. These characteristics are not seen in all the armies of the world, but the most powerful ones support and promote these violent, misogynistic, and patriarchal values. Military training often involves breaking down empathy and purging sympathy for the pain of others, and prostitution provides the perfect arena in which to learn this. It requires avoidance of all types of connection, except between genitals.

For desensitized soldiers, these sexual encounters—whether rape or paying a prostitute—are viewed as the only place where they can express their emotions. According to anecdotes from veteran soldiers, they convince themselves that the Cambodian, Filipino, Peruvian, or Salvadorian girls aged fifteen or sixteen whom "they touched" are there willingly and that "they fell in love with them," because "they like soldiers," or that they were definitely "born to be sluts."

The military plays an important role in the formation of its soldiers, strengthening their sexist values, and the objectification of people. But there is another factor that is almost always ignored: sexual violence as an aspect of an individual's personality. The statistics on soldiers who buy sex throughout the world speak for themselves. After a war, away from the battlefield, soldiers continue to choose women in vulnerable situations, where they can control them and demand obedience and submission.

Kathryn Farr, professor emeritus of sociology at the University of Portland and author of various reports, including *Sex Trafficking: The Global Market in Women and Children*, writes that "Military rape and sexual enslavement are backed, at least indirectly, by patriarchal systems across cultures that legitimize male control over and sexual access to women. Among them are the major world religions, which have had an enormous impact on social thought throughout history and are often referred to for norms on gender relations."

9

Money Laundering

The bad guys no longer rob banks, now they buy them.

—Jeffrey Robinson, *The Laundrymen* (1996)

The term "offshore" has always fascinated me. It is such a lovely word for what lies beyond the coast, beyond local laws—perhaps a Caribbean island or a country whose banking system has strict rules on confidentiality. A perfect example is the Cayman Islands, a British territory situated south of Cuba and northeast of Jamaica. It is a place where treasures are hidden at the bottom of the sea and on land. For those who launder money, it is a haven that allows them to conceal profits from the sale of drugs, weapons, and people. Like other offshore paradises, the Cayman Islands not only has radiant sunshine and luxurious yachts and hotels but also is home to unpaid taxes, fortunes based on real-estate speculation, and interest-bearing bank accounts filled with money made illegally by politicians.

I have often wondered how the authorities calculate the amount of money large mafias make and move. The first time a DEA agent told me in an interview in Mexico that the drug traffickers make many billions of dollars a year, I naïvely asked him why they had not frozen their accounts; why they had not investigated the Swiss, Bahaman, and Cayman banks, as well as their shares on Wall Street. He explained to me that even though the international banking system follows clear rules, money-laundering investigations depend largely on bankers' willingness to cooperate. In most parts of the world, the average amount one can deposit, without disclosing its origin, is $10,000. Bankers, car salesmen, stock-market investors, casino and real-estate owners must report to the authorities any "suspicious client" who tries to pay in cash, but this type of activity is rarely reported. The power of money is stronger than ethics, according to the anti-drug agent. Undoubtedly, there are businesses, such as casinos, that are set up for the sole purpose of laundering money.

The DEA agent's answer sparked my obsession with understanding how money laundering really works and why the authorities of the most powerful countries do not scrutinize banks that move dirty money. The US Iran-Contra case of the 1980s demonstrated that the CIA diverted and laundered money in shady banks for the Pentagon's dirty-war activities. "The world's policeman," as the United States is sometimes called, committed its own international money-laundering crimes under the convenient smokescreen of "national security." Yet the US government has the highest standards when it comes to investigating the mafia and other nations.

How do money-laundering scams work? Let's imagine the case of an Argentinean who owns brothels and bars in Argentina, Mexico, and Florida in the USA. In Argentina and Mexico, he runs businesses exploiting women through debt bondage, and in Florida he owns two restaurants in his wife's name, where only cash is accepted, no credit cards. This businessman needs to launder money from his illegal businesses, so he speaks with his attorney, who contacts a Swiss bank.

Seated in an elegant office, both dressed in dark suits, white shirts, Hugo Boss or Armani ties, the trafficker's attorney and a banker discuss the importance of having distinguished clients in their portfolio. They smile. The banker gives the attorney an official bank document that states the following:

> Swiss bankers are obligated to keep any information about you and your account strictly confidential.
>
> This banking confidentiality is one of the strictest in the world and originates in historical tradition. It is enshrined in Swiss law. Any banker who reveals information about you without your permission risks spending several months in prison.
>
> The only exceptions to this rule are those related to serious crimes, such as trafficking in arms or drugs.
>
> The bank's confidentiality is also not affected by tax evasion. This is due to the fact that, in Switzerland, failure to report some income or financial transactions is not a crime. Thus, neither the Swiss government nor any other government can obtain information about your bank account. First, they would have to convince a Swiss judge that a serious crime punishable under the Swiss penal code had been committed.
>
> Private matters, such as inheritance or divorce, do not affect the banking confidentiality agreement. The plaintiffs have the burden of proving that a bank account exists if they want a judge to hear their complaint. In this respect, the numbered bank accounts offer the maximum degree of confidentiality.

The attorney does not lie when he tells the banker that there is no possibility that his client could be held responsible for the sale of drugs or arms or for financing terrorism, because his client only buys, exploits, and sells girls between the ages of seventeen and twenty-five for the sex trade.

A "numbered" bank account is not listed under the client's name. Everything is managed through codes. A numbered account needs a minimum balance of 250,000 Swiss francs, or approximately $237,000 USD. The banker explains to the attorney that, in accordance with EU and UN regulations against money laundering, the client must identify himself, even though the account will only be numbered. The attorney knows that his client gets authentic and fake passports not only for the prostitutes in his brothels but also for himself. The client has four passports: from Mexico, Argentina, Venezuela, and Italy. They all have official stamps and the same photograph, even though each one was issued under a different name. As a back-up, the trafficker also has a valid Florida driver's license, which was issued based on the information taken from a fake passport.

John Christensen, an ex-banker, held secret offshore accounts for politicians and the mafia. One day he dared to reveal the doublespeak used for laundering dirty money and why banks are so successful at it. Thanks to him, I was able to look in the right places when following the trail of money generated from selling people into sexual slavery.

Other experts have shed light on this matter. I often carry a bible under my arm, but not the Christian one. Mine is *The Laundrymen* by Jeffrey Robinson, which analyses the ins and outs of money laundering. It helped me understand that money laundering cannot be explained without looking at its origins. After foreign-currency exchange and the oil industry, money laundering is the third most successful business in the world. It is calculated that in 2009, almost $1 trillion was laundered worldwide, the equivalent of 6 percent of US gross domestic product.

Those who paved the way were very powerful indeed. For example in the nineteenth century Queen Victoria became an important trafficker of Chinese opium in order to strengthen her country economically as it dealt with a spectacular fall in the slave trade. In 1972, US President Richard Nixon and his team devised an elaborate strategy for laundering money through offshore accounts to finance his re-election campaign. The US attorney general, John N. Mitchell, and Maurice Stans, the financial director of the Campaign to Re-elect the President (CRP), orchestrated an impeccable money-laundering scheme, which still serves as a model for hundreds of politicians, business-men, and criminals. Of course, the large and small human traf-ficking groups have also learned from its intricacies:

> When Mitchell and Stans squeezed American Airlines for $100,000, George Spater, then chairman and chief executive of the airline, was faced with the dilemma of how to divert cor-porate funds that were otherwise accountable. He arranged to have a Lebanese company called Amarco submit a fraudulent invoice as commission on parts sold to Middle East Airlines. American Airlines paid the invoice and Amarco deposited the money in Switzerland, then wired it to their account in New York. There, Amarco's agent withdrew $100,000 in cash and handed it to Spater, who turned it over to Mitchell and Stans.

This is Robinson's description, in *The Laundrymen*, of how the CRP found new ways to escape the eye of the law and receive illegal campaign contributions from US companies. These businessmen were contributing to electoral democracy in the United States. Robinson quotes Nixon's famous line: "When the president does it, that means it is not illegal." Undoubtedly, governments' double standards have encouraged new and innovative ways of laundering money.

According to *The Laundrymen*, four elements are common to money-laundering schemes:

- The ownership and source of the money must be con-cealed. There's no sense in laundering money if, at the end of the process, everyone knows its origin and to whom it belonged.
- The money cannot be transferred as cash. Contrary to popular belief, you cannot stuff $1 million into a briefcase.

A stack of $100 bills would stand five feet high and weigh around 10 kilos.

- The process must not leave a paper trail. The whole purpose of money laundering is defeated if someone can follow the money from beginning to end.
- The process must be tightly controlled. After all, if the money is stolen, there's little the owner can legally do about it.

Everyone who takes part in the process of money laundering—bankers, lawyers, accountants, and administrators—knows or suspects when there is dirty money involved in a transaction. For this reason, the businessmen, minor criminals, or politicians who launder funds need protection. And the mafia defends them against anyone who tries to deceive or rob them or break the rules of the game.

At home, you know that to keep your clothes looking like new, you have to pre-wash, wash, dry, and iron them. The money-laundering experts must take similar steps to consolidate their cash.

Let's look at an example: a producer of child pornography whom I investigated in Mexico needed to launder $1 million that he had earned in cash from video production and sex tourism. He charged $2,000 for every time he arranged for a politician, visiting businessman or tourist to have sex with a thirteen-year-old. This man owned a restaurant in the airport, a jewelry store in a five-star hotel, and a beachfront hotel. To consolidate his cash (which he could not carry in a briefcase), he converted part of it into American Express traveler's checks, some made out in his name and some in the names of his wife and his three children. His manager converted another sum into Visa traveler's checks at various banks. His driver, claiming to be a tourist guide, bought 500 euros every third day at local bureaux de change. The man sent small sums of money through financial institutions such as Western Union and Banco Azteca to Los Angeles, Arizona, and Miami, where his partners retrieved the money. Another portion was recycled through his hotel through phantom guests. According to his neighbors, the rooms on the beach remained vacant for long periods of time, even though the reservations book was always full of guests' names, such as John Jefferson or Jane Jackson, who, coincidentally, paid in cash. In thirty days, twenty-five phantom guests paying $400 per day allowed him to recycle $300,000.

This criminal transported young women and girls for the purpose of sexual exploitation from Arizona, Miami, El Salvador, and Venezuela to Cancún. All plane tickets were first-class and purchased from a travel agency owned by the trafficker's partner. They also paid the travel agency for suites at a hotel, which was owned by the child pornographer.

The cash, which was a product of illegal businesses, was deposited in bank accounts in Los Angeles as clean money. Through these various ruses, within four months, the million dollars profit was transferred and made to appear legal.

As if that wasn't enough, another business partner, the owner of a casino and a textile factory, made two loans of $1.5 million to the trafficker for renovations on his hotel. The loans were guaranteed by a bank in Hong Kong, and the trafficker repaid them little by little from his profits from the hotel.

Another Mexican trafficker—who is associated with a powerful politician who served as a congressional member and as an advisor to three presidents on espionage—laundered more than $50 million through property ownership. He bought a mega-yacht that sank off the coast of Belize and was written off. Two years later, when the insurance company paid compensation for the yacht, the owner had clean money in his bank account. In Mexico, the Deputy Attorney General's Office for Special

Investigations into Organized Crime (SIEDO) cited this case but argued that it could not clearly prove where the original money came from, and thus the trafficker remained a free man. His children and wife own a large number of properties in the Riviera Maya in Mexico, but the source of the funds used to buy them is unknown.

People Who Live in Glass Houses Should Not Throw Stones

At the beginning of 2009, the US government's Internal Revenue Service (IRS) demanded that various Swiss banks reveal the names of several clients who had been accused of tax evasion by the FBI. This was a serious blow for the Swiss banks: their clients would feel very vulnerable if they began cooperating with the IRS. After long diplomatic negotiations, the names of some bank account owners were revealed.

At the time, Washington made a great fuss over the Swiss banks' lack of moral judgment. But what they didn't say to the international community was that the US banks' system for international money transfers was contributing to world economic instability, as James Petras, a sociology professor at Binghamton University in New York, pointed out when I interviewed him. The transfer system allows money to be consolidated into small "offshore" banks, which means that money laundering is carried out by central banks on both sides of the Atlantic with government complicity. All this suggests that the growth of the developed nations is intimately linked to a form of capitalism built on the basis of pillage, criminality, and corruption.

Europeans are not undermining American honesty; rather, they are competitors when it comes to handling dirty money. On the one hand, the large US companies moralize and criticize corruption; on the other hand, they are sustained by the juicy profits of dirty money. The Citibank scandal proved to be a watershed event. In 1999, investigations by the US Congress revealed that Citibank helped launder nearly $400 million on behalf of at least four corrupt politicians: between $80 and $100 million for Raúl Salinas, brother of the former Mexican president Carlos Salinas; $40 million for Asif Ali Zardari, husband of the former prime minister of Pakistan; $130 million for Hadj Omar Bongo, dictator of Gabon; and $110 million for the sons of General Sani Abacha, the ex-dictator of Nigeria.

Close the Doors and Open the Windows

In February 2010 leading Mexican and US newspapers published an article by Jonathan Stempel: Western Union had agreed to pay $94 million to stop a decades-long investigation into its role in money laundering in Mexico. The federal investigators believed that between $18 billion and $39 billion was illegally transferred each year to Mexico from the United States.

Terry Goddard, the attorney general of Arizona, the state that led the investigation, told the press: "This is a major step in our ability to crack down on drug cartels and organized border crime . . . Attacking the flow of illicit funds from the United States to Mexico is fundamental to our goal of crushing the cartels." A Western Union representative said the agreement reflected the commitment of the company to finding solutions to "border issues." "Assisting law enforcement in its efforts to combat illegal activity serves the public interest on both sides of the border and helps protect those who use our services," an executive vice president of the company said.

Under the settlement, Western Union agreed to pay $50 million to law-enforcement agencies to aid the investigation and prosecution of money laundering, arms sales, people trafficking, and other related criminal activities along the southwest border of the United States. Western Union also agreed to pay $19 million to enhance its anti-money-laundering program, $4 million to appoint a watchdog to oversee the program, and $21 million to cover the costs of the investigations in Arizona.

Taking $50 million from Western Union was like taking a single hair from a Persian cat. This company—a subsidiary of First Data Corporation—whose international headquarters are located in New Jersey, owns 3,500 banks in 240 countries and moves more than $5 billion annually. In Southeast Asia, India and Africa, their financial services are the ideal way for traffickers in women and girls to transfer money derived from sex tourism and forced prostitution on a daily basis.

The terrorist attacks of September 11, 2001 represent a landmark in the fight against terrorism, and they have also prompted the adoption of policies against money laundering on a worldwide scale. As a result of the attacks, the United Nations Security Council unanimously approved Resolution 1373, urging countries to "find ways of intensifying and accelerating the exchange of operational information." Moreover, the United Nations emphasized that these actions should focus on the "close connection between international terrorism and transnational organized crime, illicit drugs, money laundering" and other criminal activities. Likewise, the Financial Action Task Force (FATF), created at G-7 summit in 1989, offered its experience of fighting money laundering and terrorist financing. Undoubtedly, the industrialized nations of the G-7 are home to many of the banks that practically invented secret bank accounts.

Within the United Nations, there are people who fervently believe in the possibility of eradicating money laundering. But they are like small heroes, armed with bows and arrows, battling enormous financial dragons, owners of the crushing machine of unrestrained doctrinaire capitalism.

When the authorities close the door, the mafia opens a window, with the help of financial services companies. International anti-money-laundering agreements have the same weaknesses as the agreements against drug and people trafficking: domestic laws take precedence and often oppose international agreements. Corrupt judicial systems, politicians, and financial institutions impede transparency. It is difficult for some industries to survive without laundered revenue.

Money laundering takes place within the financial system but it also occurs through non-financial channels that operate only in cash as a way of avoiding detection. On a worldwide scale, law-enforcement authorities know that they must regularly check the activities of certain bank drafts and certain businesses that can be used to launder money. In Mexico, for example, since 2006, real-estate agents, lawyers, notaries, and accountants, among others, are required to report to the Mexican Federal Tax Administration any compensation received in cash (in national or foreign currency), or in gold or silver, if it exceeds $10,000. These professionals have been incorporated into the regulatory system to prevent, detect, and combat money-laundering activities. This rule also extends to those activities known internationally as "gatekeeping": casinos, dealers in metal and precious stones, art dealers, auction houses, pawnshops, and charitable organizations must also report suspicious activities.

The obligation to report income has been extended to notaries, lawyers and accountants because they are in a unique position to identify criminals. Lawyers and accountants are particularly sensitive to this issue because they claim it threatens their duty of confidentiality to their clients, who can always seek legal loopholes to defend themselves.

Drugs and Women: The World Market

From Costa Rica to the United States, from Russia to Japan, from Vietnam to Qatar, I heard the same reasoning: the sex trade is not about pleasure; it's about money.

Globalization has helped to open up a great market in which there is unlimited supply and demand. Following the same business model as drug trafficking, the human slave trade will continue to grow and perhaps outstrip the sale of narcotics, simply because there are entire communities and countries that are economically dependent on sex tourism, people trafficking, and the sex trade.

Besides using the same trade routes, there are many parallels between drug trafficking and trafficking in women and children. For decades, drug-traffickers have been involved in the sex trade through bars, cheap restaurants, brothels, and casinos, as well as providing protection to certain groups. However, the principal similarity between the two lies in the type of local economy they promote.

In many countries, people wonder who can convince a lower-middle-class teenager to study hard, if studying will only get him a job with a company that pays between $3 and $11 an hour, whereas selling crack or heroin can earn him between $100 to $2000 per week. The answer is nobody.

The drug trade is sustained by the exporters who promote consumption, the addicts who provide market stability, drug pushers on the look-out for new users, as well as banks and companies willing to launder dirty money so that it becomes a part of the economy's flow of legal money. In the sex trade something similar takes place. According to the *Global Report on Trafficking in Persons* published by the United Nations Office on Drugs and Crime in 2009, which covers 155 countries, 79 percent of trafficking is for the purpose of sexual exploitation. Every day more women in situations of poverty, hunger, and inequality are entering the sex trade.

The Hollywood Madam

In 1987, Heidi Fleiss, a twenty-two-year-old from California, met Madam Alex, a sixty-year-old woman from the Philippines who had amassed a fortune from illegal prostitution, and was considered the most powerful madam in California.

Alex hired Heidi to work as a prostitute, but after a short time, Heidi became her assistant. In 1990, the two women went their separate ways, and Fleiss came to run the most successful prostitution ring in the southern United States. For one night with one of her "special girls," Fleiss would charge up to $10,000. Her girls would receive a 40 percent commission for each job.

Fleiss was registered with the US Internal Revenue Service as a real-estate agent. In 1992, on her tax return, she declared $33,000 in income, even though she bought Michael Douglas' house for $1.6 million. Law-enforcement authorities knew about her business, but Fleiss was untouchable. Arresting her would have meant opening Pandora's box. Names of actors, businessmen, and powerful politicians would be revealed. Naturally, the madam had a solid network of political and police protection. In 1995, the FBI and a local sheriff arrested her after she had hired various prostitutes and asked them to carry cocaine. Fleiss was sentenced to three years in prison for money laundering and tax evasion.

She was admired by pimps and madams all over the world for her ability to launder millions of dollars obtained from her illegal business. Bank accounts were opened under relatives' names. She reinvested money in real estate, and bank loans allowed her to manage her finances so that, upon entering prison, she was able to declare herself bankrupt. Within two months of leaving jail, she was driving a Porsche and living in a mansion. She has always argued that her family had savings to support her.

Fleiss earned another few million dollars from selling the rights for the movie about her life to an American cable network. Years later, she became the madam of a legal brothel in Nevada, near Las Vegas. She is credited with making prostitution glamorous to women between the ages of eighteen and twenty-five in the United States. Heidi Fleiss became not only an expert money launderer but also the voice of the new generation working in the sex trade.

Launderers for Traffickers

"Smurf" is a nickname coined by a Florida police officer for the managers who visit ten or fifteen medium-sized banks every day to deposit small sums of cash, until the money, earned from clients of prostitution, is successfully recycled. "They appear to be small and inoffensive [amounts of money], but they are a threat to the financial world," states a federal agent.

The casinos function like banks: they exchange money from various countries, cash and write cashiers' checks for their clients, and provide safety deposit boxes. A trafficker can deposit his earnings in a Las Vegas casino, and a few weeks later withdraw them in Naga World in Cambodia, before moving the money to London. By law, casinos are required to report any suspicious clients.

Money can be and frequently is laundered through lotteries. The launderers have bloodhounds who contact lottery winners, whose winning ticket they exchange for cash. Many lotteries pay the prize money in installments, dividing it into monthly payments deposited in a bank account. By buying the winning ticket, criminals can have a bank account into which money flows legally, while the original winner of the lottery puts his money under the mattress.

Law-enforcement authorities in all of the countries I have visited assured me that they know for certain how much money is produced by the sex-slave industry, yet they cannot trace the money or arrest its owners. Why? The answer, given to me by M. Alvarez, an Interpol agent, is that it is very complicated to distinguish between money from prostitution—which despite being illegal, isn't criminalized—and money from sexual slavery, which is a crime in some countries.

The only way to control money laundering and freeze the profits from trafficking in order to stop the slave trade would be to have the same legal requirements for money transfers through-out the world, so that senders and recipients would have to prove their identity and hence the original source of the money. More than 500,000 transfers of funds totaling a trillion dollars take place each day. Recording and vetting them—especially the small transactions—would prove impossible, and no country would want to invest more money than it can confiscate from abuses of the system. In addition, as I have already stated, there are regions and whole industries that depend on the criminal activity and the hidden movement of money being made from it.

IO

The Pimp Profession

The pimp synthesizes elements of the patriarchal culture that suggest that there are power mechanisms embedded in both the male and the female body, which are used by the pimp himself in a broader context of socio-economic and historical structures that favor these types of practices.

—Oscar Montiel Torres, *Human Trafficking*

Millions of people believe that prostitution is the world's oldest profession, but if we chose to hear what the people in the trade have to say, the oldest profession is that of procurer, pimp, hustler, or trafficker. The Mexican terms for those who manipulate, manage, train, exploit, and control women in the sex trade are *padrote* and *madrota*, the feminine equivalent. They imply a kind of foster father or mother who "educates and protects" adult women and girls in prostitution rings. *Padrote* is derived from the colloquial verb *padrotear*, meaning to cheat and steal money from someone.

In Mexico, the southern part of the state of Tlaxcala is known for its high number of *padrotes*, who recruit, place, and sell women for sexual exploitation in the country's capital, in nearby provinces, and even in the United States. In many respects, their activities in this region—as well as on the border of Guatemala and Mexico—are astonishingly similar to those in the rural areas of Cambodia, Thailand, and Vietnam, which I visited for this investigation. While laws against sexual exploitation advance globally, the similarities between pimps or traffickers who operate in rural areas have created a dominant culture that spans social groups and ethnicities.

In *Human Trafficking: Pimps, Initiation, and Modus Operandi* (2007), a fascinating study of the philosophy of traffickers, Oscar Montiel Torres explains the profession through the voices of pimps in Mexico. With his permission, I am presenting a summary of his findings.

How to Become a Pimp

Being an apprentice to a pimp is one way to gain knowledge about the sex trade. The aspiring pimp seeks out someone established and experienced to adopt him. If the pimp accepts, he will then share his knowledge about prostitution, strategies to get women and introduce them to prostitution and, above all, how to exercise power over the female body. The following is one man's account of the process he followed to become a pimp through apprenticeship:

> Before, I worked selling ice-cream, from sunrise to sunset—if they were selling well, that is. If it rained . . . I didn't make a cent, and I had to support my family, my wife and two little girls. Those days, I remember sometimes reaching the point of banging my head against the ice-cream cart. And I began to think: My God! What can I do to get out of this lousy situation? Then I made the decision to find some friends of "La Meca" to help me out. I had known them since we were kids, when we would hang out with the gang. One of them agreed to take me on, and he is one of the best because he became a good godfather to me and he gave me good advice. I am who I am today thanks to him, because without his support I would still be as fucked as before.

The pimp justifies his choice of profession through the economic hardships he faced and his eagerness to overcome them for his family. His way out was to find a pimp who would help him by sharing his knowledge of the profession. He became the apprentice of one of his childhood friends, a buddy who was good to him.

After finding a godfather, the learning process begins. There are many ways to learn to be a pimp, and the way you learn depends on the pimp you select. The basics include: how to dress; the way to convince women to work as prostitutes and hand over the money they make to their pimp; how to keep them "eating out of your hand," in other words, "under control."

A pimp is not a husband, because he does not seek a relationship based on marriage or any other family bond. Instead he aims to exert his power and dominate women. Pimps do not fall in love, but the women do. The women think that they are in a love relationship, but the pimps are only interested in a relationship of exploitation.

Learning to become a pimp within the family is another form of initiation. The men of the family, usually related by blood or marriage, teach another how to be a pimp. During my research, I found the same patterns as those described by Montiel Torres: in Cambodia, Thailand, China, Vietnam, South Africa, Brazil, and Guatemala, to name several countries, there are families that for three or four generations have dedicated themselves to the sexual exploitation of women and girls. This family tradition often includes boyfriends, husbands, grandfathers, uncles, and cousins, and even sons who "manage" their mothers.

In Spain, at the Colectivo Hetaira, an organization that defends prostitutes' rights, some women explain that a prostitute's word often counts for nothing and police officers sometimes arrest the prostitutes' partners—their companions, not their pimps. This same allegation is made by many women who work as prostitutes on the streets of Mexico, Guatemala, Venezuela, and Colombia, who were apparently initiated into the business through "family tradition." It is a very complicated issue, given that experts and police officers regularly ask: "How can we distinguish a pimp from a family member who doesn't exploit the woman but does live from the money made from her work as a prostitute?" This is a valid question, not because these women are unable to express themselves or are liars, but because coercion may come into it; many rescued victims have confessed that they worked under threat of death and that their pimp had instructed them to say he was a husband, partner, or uncle.

Traffickers are familiar with the latest technology, and they always aim to stay one step ahead of law-enforcement authorities. They are fully aware that it is no longer so easy to threaten women and that there is too much publicity about sexual exploitation, so they have sought new strategies. For example, we find pimps using social networking sites to contact clients and send young women as escorts for two or three days to a wide range of cities.

Montiel Torres interviewed one such trafficker, nicknamed "Santísima Verga" ("Holy Dick"): "In this game, as in any other, if you want to be the best, you have to learn the rules well and you have to be up to date with the latest technology to be able to compete and be at the cutting edge." Talking about how he became a pimp, he says: "It's like an apprenticeship between a teacher and a student. To learn the trade, you have to choose a good teacher who will guide and teach you the best way." One of the rules followed by all traffickers is to "kill the emotion. If you have a tender heart, you're not cut out for this."

Internalization of Domination

Pimps have developed time-honored ways of making women fall in love with them; they use these strategies to recruit women for sex work. This objective is achieved through training, discipline, and domination. To expand on this point,

Montiel Torres quotes Pierre Bourdieu from his book *Masculine Domination* (2001):

> The work of transformation of bodies which is both sexually differentiated and sexually differentiating and which is performed partly through the effects of mimetic suggestion, partly through explicit injunctions and partly through the whole symbolic construction of the view of the biological body (and in particular the sexual act, conceived as an act of domination, possession), produces systematically differentiated and differentiating habits. The masculinization of the male body and the feminization of the female body, immense and in a sense interminable tasks which, perhaps now more than ever, always demand a considerable expenditure of time and effort, induce a somatization of the relation of domination, which is thus naturalized. It is through the training of the body that the most fundamental dispositions are imposed, those which make a person both *inclined* and *able* to enter into the social games most favorable to the development of manliness: politics, business, science, etc.

Montiel warns that "domination" of the female body— repressing passions and disorderly behavior—aims to convert it into a body *of* and *for* others. Developing social and gender relations that favor masculine activities and making them feel "natural" requires immense effort. When pimps look for "merchandise" for sex work, the internalization of domination has already occurred. It is a historical process in which men and women have taken part by developing an understanding of "being a man" and of "being a woman." This understanding, already embedded in the beliefs and outlook of individuals, is the pimps' turf.

Being a "Smooth Talker"

You have to have charisma, good looks, and, above all, the ability to sweet-talk a woman into falling in love—a pimp needs to be a "smooth talker" to be able to chat up and seduce the girls. Pimps have to have all of this, plus the latest car to drive around schools, parks, factories, or places where young people usually congregate. When a girl allows the pimp to get close to her, he uses all his skills to convince her that they have a romantic relationship. Once he succeeds in making the girl fall in love, the pimp's ability is put to the test, because a "good pimp . . . shouldn't take more than two weeks to convince the girl to work as a prostitute." Persuading her should take as little time as possible so that she does not have time to find out the true profession of her new boyfriend or his plans for her. A pimp called Compa also makes the following recommendations:

> No, man, when you go looking for "merchandise," it's hard, but once you've got her, you have to be clever. Smarter than the women, cos they are quite intelligent, sometimes more so than men, but you can't let them think this. You can't even let them take a breath. Because if you take too long, they start with the questions. That is when you have to do your smooth talking. Like this one time I was going out with a good-looking girl who fell in love really fast; this is when you turn on the charm to persuade the girls. I told her that she was the best thing that had ever happened to me, that I wanted to give her many luxuries, give her a good home, and buy us the latest car. You have to make her share in your ideas and get her used to the good life; this is the first step . . .
>
> After the girl agrees to live with you, you have to start working on her. You have to convince her that her future is somewhere else. For example, you have to tell her that you are a salesman and that there are good opportunities for selling your clothes, or whatever, in Guadalajara. This is how

you get her to leave the places she knows. Since these girls are fifteen or sixteen, they still don't know much about the world. So when they get to a new place, they don't even know how to get around town, and you start making her depend on you for everything.

Compa expands on the steps in the girl's initiation:

You leave her in the room you've taken her to. Meanwhile, you go out, apparently to work. But, no, really you are going out with your friends that are in this city and you have fun or you can continue to look for merchandise. When you get back, you tell her that it all went to hell; that you didn't think it was going to be so hard. Again you use your smooth talk so that she will fall for it and accept being a prostitute. Within a week, you stop carrying cash; there's not enough to eat; but you have to continue persuading the girl: "No, my love, I think we're fucked, but I don't want to go back home a failure." As long as the girl believes your lies, you're doing well. The girls even tell you that they are willing to work to help out, but to start with you refuse, and you tell them that you are the man and that it is your job to take care of them. After a week, you come home with a story that you ran into a friend and you told him your problems, and you say to the girl, "What do you think, my love? I ran into Rolas. Things are going well for him. He's making loads of money. Do you think his wife is working as a prostitute?" You don't propose anything. You just describe how well things are going for your friend. Again, smooth talking, you say, "No, my love. What a person has to do to get out of poverty!" And you keep up the story that all is going to hell for you. After a fortnight, with the financial situation becoming intolerable, you tell her that you can't take it anymore and that you don't know what else to do. There are times when the girls suggest it themselves and say to you, "Listen, my love, could your friend help us out so I could work where his wife works?" If this happens, you've done it.

"You've done it" is a key moment. It is the point where the pimp's smooth talking has got results: the woman "is willing to do anything for love." Without resorting to physical violence, he has convinced the woman to work in the sex trade: this is one of the distinguishing characteristics of a pimp. However, there are times when women are not so easily convinced, and the pimps have to be more cunning, as Compa explains:

On one occasion, a friend had the woman, but she wouldn't loosen up. She didn't want to work. Then my friend asked for advice . . . and we decided to play a trick on her. It went like this: my friend told her, "My love, you see; now we're fucked. I have to pay the money I borrowed and I have to sell my car." I pretend I'm the one he owes money to. In the morning, he and his woman go to a car dealership in Puebla to sell his car. Then another friend arrives and offers him 100,000 pesos for his car, but the car cost 150,000 pesos. And his woman says, "No, my love. How can you going to sell the car for less than it's worth?" He says, "I know, honey. But what can we do? If I don't pay what I owe, they'll put me in jail." When they get home, they collect up their money and set off for my house, intending to pay off the debt. That did it. As my friend later told me, his woman said, "Fine, my darling, I don't want to see you sad; don't worry. I'm going to work as you say, but only until you get back the car you just sold. Then, that's it." But after women see how easy it is to make money, it's hard for them to leave the business. My friend told me that once they got the money to buy the car, he told his woman, "Fine, now that we have the car, you can stop working." And the woman said, "No, my love. Once we get a house. Then that's it." And so the woman carried on working the streets.

Some men pretend to be the "uncles" of pimps to ask for a village girl's hand in marriage, or to "ask for forgiveness" after she has been seduced. However, once the woman realizes that she has been deceived, what can you do? This is Compa's answer:

> Sometimes the girls say, "You are a jerk; you tricked me." But you have to be smart and tell them that you are not making them do anything, remind them that they wanted to help you. When you have fights, sometimes the woman wants to be a smartass. When she returns from work, she throws the money at you and says, "Take the money. Let's see what you make for me to eat." You should stay calm and use reverse psychology and say, "You think that because of your money, you can tell me what to do? If you're not happy with me, there's your money. I don't need it. Besides, you work because you want to. It would be best for me to return to my home, so you don't spend all your time criticizing me." Once the girls see that you are serious about leaving, they say, "No, my love. I'm sorry. It's just that I had a hard day at work." But you have to keep up your game and stay mad until she humbles herself before you. That is, you have to make it clear that you don't need her in your life.

In *Disposable People: New Slavery in the Global Economy* (1999), Kevin Bales confirms that in Thailand, "the new slavery appropriates the economic value of individuals while keeping them under complete coercive control—but without asserting ownership or accepting responsibility for their survival . . . The slave is a commodity, added to the production process when needed, but no longer carrying a high capital cost." In the case of sex slaves, pimps earn enormous sums from exercising power over the girl to ensure her docility and subordination. Women simply become marketable, exchangeable, and disposable commodities.

Antonio Salas' book, *The Year I Trafficked Women* (2004), is also revealing. With a hidden camera, this Spanish journalist pretended to be a sex trafficker for a year in order to piece together the puzzle of the sex trade in Spain. His investigation took him from the shadiest places where prostitutes offer their services to bars, hotels, and massage parlors, and he documented high-level prostitution through catalogues. Salas highlights how the pimps use diverse strategies to ensnare women, including marriage, false offers of employment, debt, witchcraft, and so on. Without pimps and traffickers, one would not be able to understand forced prostitution. Salas states: "Prostitutes are no more than the tip of the huge iceberg that is the sex industry, a business of colossal dimensions."

The Old Violence Revisited

During this investigation I have often asked myself why there is such an increase in the number of women and girls in the sex trade worldwide. I have already discussed this in the chapter on clients. Both Victor Malarek and Montiel Torres show, through the voices of the suppliers and the consumers of sexual exploitation, one common element that we should not ignore: a backlash of women's liberation. Challenging the traditional paradigms of masculinity, something that had never happened before, has angered millions of men. In almost all cultures there are sexist values that have remained unchanged. They have reinforced patriarchal relationships that require obedience and use violence to exercise control over women.

Oscar Montiel provides a key to understanding the behavior of traffickers who sexually exploit adults and children. What he says could explain how the young male tuk-tuk drivers in Cambodia can take clients to have sex with their little sisters and cousins or how young men, barely teenagers, negotiate the price of girls who are four or five years old with investigators who pose as clients before hidden cameras, as seen on You Tube.

> Males, individually and collectively, have historically domi-
> nated women in rural and indigenous communities, and
> hence there are cultural practices that give the men sexual
> monopoly over women: "kidnapping a bride," "buying a
> bride," or polygamy. One possible explanation for the in-
> crease and endurance of pimping in these communities is that
> men have adapted the "traditional" cultural means of control-
> ling women's bodies to suit the sex trade, which is promoted
> as a profession and a way of life.
>
> Being a pimp is part of a process of learning and adopting a
> particular construction of masculinity that can be understood
> as a privilege provided by the patriarchal system. The control
> that men exert over women's bodies suggests that the pimp-
> prostitute relationship is based on an imbalance of power
> founded on gender differences.

After studying hundreds of traffickers and clients of prostitution, Victor concluded:

> If we really want to do something about prostitution, we
> should recognize the role of clients (johns), and they have
> to assume responsibility for their actions. If prostitution can
> be understood as a result of opportunities and decisions, the
> opportunities always belong to the client who chooses to pay
> a woman for sex. The clients "choose" to go with a "work-
> ing girl" instead of investing in an interpersonal relationship.
> They choose to go to sex tourism destinations in impover-
> ished countries because they feel disillusioned or frightened
> of Western women. They decide not to look at the painful
> reality of those women and girls who have to put their bodies

up for rent. They impose their will on extremely vulnerable women.

The clients are the ones who in reality have the opportunity to choose, and they are the ones who win if prostitution is legalized . . . Society must confront the deterioration of masculinity and the destructive characteristic of male behavior. Prostitution seriously limits the possibility of creating relationships of equality, respect, and honesty between men and women in every aspect of life. It teaches men and boys to believe that women and girls are sexual objects for their use, instead of human beings that are equal to them.

The same mechanisms that lead to domestic or intrafamilial violence are at work in the way the daily lives of women who are forced into prostitution are appropriated and controlled. According to the United Nations Development Fund for Women, six out of nine women suffer domestic violence, physical, sexual, psychological, or economic, at the hands of a husband, boyfriend, or lover. Like battered women, those coerced into the sex trade through familial or affectionate relationships, will deny that they suffer any violence unless they are offered real alternatives.

Exploitation and discrimination by clients, traffickers, police officers, and society in general leaves such a mark on some women that once they escape slavery they become strong and successful campaigners for the abolition of prostitution. Among them is Norma Hotaling, founder of SAGE (Standing Against Global Exploitation), based in San Francisco. Norma, whom I met a few years before she died of pancreatic cancer, succeeded in prosecuting pimps who exploited girls and young women. She was also responsible for the first program to educate clients who had been arrested for their participation in prostitution. However, one of the most serious complaints made by adult women in the sex trade is that abolitionist groups interfere in their lives to the point of organizing police raids in which the prostitutes are abused, blamed, deported, and, on many occasions, raped and imprisoned.

In countries where there are laws against domestic and familial violence, the police usually arrest the aggressor and not the battered woman. So why do they arrest women who practice prostitution? And why do pimps and clients remain free in 90 percent of cases? The answer is clear: this happens almost everywhere in the world because of discrimination against women and acceptance of men's sexual promiscuity; the way the laws on trafficking for sexual exploitation are drafted; the prejudices and doublespeak underlying such laws; and the policy guidelines followed to enforce them.

A Religious Crusade

In a 2008 report from the United States Department of State, former US Secretary of State Condoleeza Rice declared that the abolition of slavery was "the great moral imperative of our day." This fueled the debate between those who want to abolish prostitution and those who want to regulate the sex trade. There was no way to sit on the fence. According to President Bush's cabinet, on this issue, "you are with God or with the devil." In 2009, Hillary Clinton, who succeeded Rice, toned down the argument. The Obama administration admitted that the topic of human trafficking hasn't been fully covered and the way in which it *has* been covered—in a language almost unilaterally imposed by Washington—needed to be revised.

Before slavery was abolished in the United States, the legal discussion focused on whether a slave could be considered a whole person or just three fifths of a person; meanwhile the slave traders, owners, and exploiters were invisible to the world, as were the laws created to protect their interests. Something similar is occurring today with authorities' doublespeak about prostitution. For example, in the United States it is a crime to be a client of a prostitute; however, thousands of nightclubs, massage parlors, and escort services advertise in the most prestigious newspapers and they are granted government licenses, accept credit cards and cross the line between legality and illegality.

Many people involved in the global debate about people trafficking and prostitution do not know what laws exist, what they say, and what and whom they protect. This is one of the reasons why there are more misinformed discussions—full of religious and moral sentiment about sexual freedom—than serious debates about Western cross-cultural influences and the role played by federal and state laws, as well as international treaties ratified by the majority of nations.

The majority of activists I have interviewed around the world are clear that people cannot—or do not want to—see the connection between trafficking and prostitution. Those running the sex trade are the big winners of this social confusion and in-action: as long as people continue to defend prostitution as part of a liberal philosophy, without getting to the bottom of the issue of trafficking, the slave owners—such as the group that manages successful sex shops in Cartagena, Colombia, which has financed the defense of prostitutes' rights—will continue to make millions of dollars each year. In 1998, the Colombian police arrested twenty-nine pimps and rescued 370 boys and girls between the ages of twelve and sixteen who were subjected to forced prostitution and child pornography by these businessmen.

Laws and Agreements
Of the 175 nations investigated in 2009, the Protection Project, a human-rights institute based at the Johns Hopkins University School of Advanced International Studies in Washington, DC, provides the following statistics:

- fifty-nine countries have a comprehensive anti-trafficking act

- seventy-six countries have anti-trafficking criminal provisions
- thirteen countries have an anti-trafficking draft law
- six countries have anti-trafficking provisions in their immigration and other laws
- six countries have an anti-trafficking law or provision relating only to children
- seventeen countries have no anti-trafficking laws (but they do prohibit prostitution)

Let us look at some of these laws. The most crucial came into existence after World War II. In 1949, the UN Convention for the Suppression of the Traffic in Persons and of the Exploitation of Prostitution of Others was created. Of the 430 women and 312 men I interviewed, nine out of ten people I asked about its existence had never heard of it. As early as 1949, the eradication of prostitution, was being discussed, although without reference to clients and pimps. There was no mention of the prostitution market specially created and supported by the Japanese and US military forces, even though these were the most notable and scandalous of several cases.

This convention is a legally binding agreement that proclaims "prostitution and the accompanying evil of the traffic in persons for the purpose of prostitution are incompatible with the dignity and worth of the human person and endanger the welfare of the individual, the family, and the community." The convention includes the following key provisions:

Article 1

The Parties to the present Convention agree to punish any person who, to gratify the passions of another:

1. Procures, entices or leads away, for purposes of prostitution, another person, even with the consent of that person;

2. Exploits the prostitution of another person, even with the consent of that person.

Article 2

The Parties to the present Convention further agree to punish any person who:

1. Keeps or manages, or knowingly finances or takes part in the financing of a brothel;
2. Knowingly lets or rents a building or other place or any part thereof for the purpose of the prostitution of others.

Article 6

Each Party to the present Convention agrees to take all the necessary measures to repeal or abolish any existing law, regulation or administrative provision by virtue of which persons who engage in or are suspected of engaging in prostitution are subject either to special registration or to the possession of a special document or to any exceptional requirements for supervision or notification.

Article 16

The Parties to the present Convention agree to take or to encourage, through their public and private educational, health, social, economic and other related services, measures for the prevention of prostitution and for the rehabilitation and social adjustment of the victims of prostitution and of the offences referred to in the present Convention.

Article 17

The Parties to the present Convention undertake, in connection with immigration and emigration, to adopt or maintain such measures as are required, in terms of their obligations under the present Convention, to check the traffic in persons of either sex for the purpose of prostitution.

In particular they undertake:

1. To make such regulations as are necessary for the protection of immigrants or emigrants, and in particular, women and children, both at the place of arrival and departure and while en route;
2. To arrange for appropriate publicity warning the public of the dangers of the aforesaid traffic;
3. To take appropriate measures to ensure supervision of railway stations, airports, seaports and en route, and of other public places, in order to prevent international traffic in persons for the purpose of prostitution;

Article 20

The Parties to the present Convention shall, if they have not already done so, take the necessary measures for the supervision of employment agencies in order to prevent persons seeking employment, in particular women and children, from being exposed to the danger of prostitution. Other agreements and laws include:

- Convention on the Rights of the Child (CRC)
- Convention on the Elimination of All Forms of Discrimination Against Women (CEDAW)
- Inter-American Convention on the Prevention, Punishment, and Eradication of Violence Against Women, 1994 (Belém do Pará Convention)
- Optional Protocol to the Convention on the Rights of the Child on the sale of children, child prostitution and child pornography, 2000
- Convention on Transnational Organized Crime, 2000
- International Convention on the Protection of the Rights of All Migrant Workers and Members of Their Families
- American Convention on Human Rights (Pact of San José)
- Abolition of Forced Labour Convention, 1957 (No. 105)
- Worst Forms of Child Labour Convention, 1999 (No. 182)

- Palermo Protocols: two protocols to the Convention against Transnational Organized Crime, adopted by the United Nations in 2000, which consist of the Protocol to Prevent, Suppress and Punish Trafficking in Persons, especially Women and Children (also referred to as the "Trafficking Protocol"), and the Protocol against the Smuggling of Migrants by Land, Sea and Air
- Beijing Declaration and Platform for Action, Fourth Conference on Women, Beijing, 1995, adopted by the representatives of 189 countries

It should be noted that the follow-up meeting to the Beijing Conference, also known as Beijing Plus 10, took place at UN headquarters in New York in 2005. During the Beijing Plus 10 sessions, Resolution 49/2 "Eliminating demand for trafficked women and girls or all forms of exploitation" was adopted. The resolution emphasizes the increase in trafficking on a global scale, especially for the purposes of sexual exploitation, which disproportionately affects women and girls. It also expresses concern that the exploitation of women in international pro-stitution and trafficking networks has become one of the major focuses of transnational organized crime. It calls upon govern-ments to adopt, strengthen, and enforce legislative measures and other educational, social, and cultural measures, including bilateral and multilateral cooperation, to deter exploiters and eliminate demand. It recommends that countries include people-trafficking laws in the criminal code, foster judicial cooperation, and implement the UN Convention Against Transnational Organized Crime and its Protocol to Prevent, Suppress and Punish Trafficking in Persons, Especially Women and Children.

Point 2 of the resolution calls upon governments and civil society to "take appropriate measures to raise public awareness of the issue of trafficking in persons, particularly in women and girls, including addressing the demand side of the problem, publicizing laws, regulations and penalties relating to this issue and emphasizing that trafficking is a crime, in order to eliminate the demand for trafficked women and girls, including by sex tourists."

Point 3 encourages governments to "intensify collaboration with NGOs in order to develop and implement comprehensive programs, including help lines and programs to provide shelter for victims or potential victims of trafficking and effective counseling and training for the social and economic reintegration of the victims into society."

Point 4 exhorts the business sector, particularly the tourism industry and Internet providers, to "develop or adhere to codes of conduct, with a view to preventing trafficking in persons and protecting the victims of such traffic, especially with regard to commercial sexual exploitation, and promoting their rights, dignity and security, including through collaboration with governments and NGOs."

Now, despite the existence of all of these international legal instruments and political agreements, often the pressure applied by the United Nations and the US Department of State threatens to polarize society on the issue of the sex trade, while those who continue to lose out are the victims of slavery.

II

The Mafia and Globalization

After investigating mafias and their members' behavior, I came to understand that human trafficking is not a static criminal enterprise. It is constantly evolving, just like globalization. When friends learned that I was writing this book, they often asked: Is the mafia really involved in trafficking? We humans lead our lives based on perceptions, not realities: most people imagine the mafia as it is portrayed in television series such as *The Sopranos*. If we read in the newspaper that the Camorra killed seven police officers in Italy, we don't really give it much thought. However, if we see Tony Soprano in therapy discussing the reasons for his insomnia and the need to kill his enemies, it seems real and close. Seeing a mobster's humanity is disturbing, but it is also seductive. Soprano kills and extorts. He commits crimes and launders money, but he is also a good father and a loving husband, even though he is unfaithful.

Among the women I interviewed, there were some former wives of big-shot mafiosi: four were married to drug traffickers and three to international traffickers who own bars in major cities. They saw the human side of these men, and they felt loved by and attracted to them. As we have seen in the chapter on pimps, there are men who exploit the art of seduction and emotional manipulation.

The fictional, romanticized depiction of the mafia, which some people find attractive, does not help us understand how the mafia really works. What the mafia sells is unlimited power and the allure of money. In this superficial world where everything is for sale, what young people want is not only lots of fast money in large quantities—which is never "easy" money—but also the glamour that the mafia can offer them. Thus, casino owners in Cambodia, the United Kingdom, and Nevada in the USA, as well as the owners of elegant brothel-bars in Mexico, Colombia, and Spain, reach out to the wealthy classes, make donations to political campaigns, and invest in people's wellbeing. When a deputy of the most powerful Mexican cartels, Joaquín "el Chapo" Guzmán, was arrested, he stated that the boss had forbidden any kidnappings in order to maintain social peace. Several Mexican drug traffickers control entire towns where they pave roads, build churches and schools, and recruit young drug dealers.

Politicians prohibit abortion and businessmen invest money to legalize prostitution in the ghettos "out of sight of good women." They want to keep these other women hidden, because they are slaves that must be controlled.

At the same time the sex industry is being modernized, glo-balized, and marketed in politically correct terms. The mafia will always try to convince us that we are free when, as consumers, we enslave others, and that women are free because they can choose whether they want to be their clients' slaves. The left and postmodern feminists are not the only ones to buy this argument. Hiding behind the clergy's gown and the crucifix, the right, who enjoy high-level prostitution, also support it.

Riding Along Politics

Why has globalization left Thailand, Cambodia and some Latin American countries suffering from inequality that favors organized crime? At the end of the 1980s and during the 1990s, many developing countries came under strong pressure to integrate into international business and financial networks.

Globalization has allowed the mafias to hide in its interstices. It has also made the enlightened middle class believe that we are in a connected world where we share common interests. This false perception makes it impossible to counter the racism, classism, and sexism propounded by neoliberal politicians for many years. The mafia clearly gets it: their strength comes from deep injustice and the legal and information gaps generated by capitalism.

Mafiosi enter open-ended economic agreements with ambitious politicians who need to improve their standing to avoid being punished by Washington. These agreements and the constant social pressure against human trafficking have created a new generation of politically correct pimps and traffickers with a new way of doing things.

In Thailand, some NGOs insist that the mafia donate money to victims' shelters. The Thai government gives support to more than 200 shelters for illegal immigrants and victims of violence. It was impossible for me to visit them, since journalists are not welcome to snoop into a problem that the government wants to hide from the international community. According to AFESIP, most victims are women under the age of thirty from Vietnam, Indonesia, Russia, Burma, China, and Uzbekistan. Some local experts say that when traffickers decide to get rid of the old, over-used victims, they alert the police who then carry out a raid to take these victims and deport or "repatriate" them.

This is the exact pattern seen in Turkey, Mexico, Guatemala, the Philippines, Singapore, Colombia, Brazil, and the United States: the mafias know that, even if Washington and the United Nations issue recommendations, in the judicial systems the burden of proof falls on the victim; she is the one who has to prove that she was enslaved, which is often a difficult, if not impossible, task.

New Times, New Strategies

These days, many traffickers start out by giving money to their victims and, little by little, ensnare them through indebtedness— the classic human-trafficking practice of debt bondage. The traffickers tend to use physical violence less often, although victims' initiation into sex slavery continues to be carried out in the same violent way throughout the world. In recent years, in Mexico, Colombia, the United States, Guatemala, and Thailand, it has become common practice to give the drug Ecstasy to young women who dance in clubs and karaoke bars. "You are a slut and an addict," an Argentine trafficker told a Cuban slave in Mexico. "You think that the police are going to believe you or me, a successful businessman?" In his office he has a photograph of himself posing with a governor of the state of Quintana Roo and a famous Mexican journalist, chatting over a glass of wine.

The group of ex-military men known as the Zetas currently controls the distribution of illegal adult and child pornography in Mexico and Guatemala. A source, who lived with one of the group's leaders in southeast Mexico, says that the software for sending the porn videos via computer comes from Singapore. In order to avoid detection, the group uses servers in Holland and other Nordic countries, where pornography is legal.

More proof that the mafias keep up with new technology is that they use military-grade satellite telephones, as an Arizona police captain discovered when he arrested Jean Succar Kuri, a known trafficker of girls from Mexico, El Salvador, and the United States, who operated out of Cancún. The telephones were provided by a Hungarian who acts as a representative for the Russian mafia in Mexico and Guatemala.

Some journalists, together with the international police, carried out undercover investigations in Thailand—the world's school for people trafficking—for several years. This led the mafias to tighten their security procedures, and they now require that clients "become a member" before being allowed to enter the brothels run under the guise of karaoke bars. Members sign up through the Internet, so the mafia obtains their credit card information and e-mail addresses.

According to the British and Spanish cyber police, the mafias' use of technology competes with and often outstrips that of the law-enforcement agencies. To prove this, several years ago, I opened an account in a chat room for clients seeking sex. Initially, I did this through my personal computer, which has good anti-virus software. I registered as a man and in a week I received a friendly message that this space was not for me. At the bottom of the message were two attachments that served as a warning: one was a pornographic image infected with a virus, and the second was a tag with my IP address and my complete name. The IP address is the "digital fingerprint" of each personal computer and server. It takes expert technical knowledge to trace someone in this way, and doing so is also illegal. When authorities run a trace of this sort, they must have a court order, otherwise the evidence is inadmissible in court. Given the mafias' ability to trace me, for my subsequent computer searches for the so-called "whorists," "sexmaniacs," and "realmen," I used a good friend's laptop, and I never used my name.

What the Authorities Never Say
Today, mafia-linked traffickers have more power than ever before: the number of people arrested and sentenced for trafficking is lower than for all other crimes.

On the border between Malaysia and Singapore, many people buy girls to sell and torture. An AFESIP report reveals these unspeakable acts. It is suspected that these torture sessions are filmed as pornography, a type of light snuff. It was impossible for me to obtain any such video, but I was able to interview a young woman in a shelter who had deep scars on her body. Photographs of her appear on a web page as though she were a "sadomasochist prostitute." She was handed over to a "thirty-year-old North American" who paid $7,000 for her. The perpetrator kept his face covered by a black mask, but her face was uncovered. He filmed and took photos of her using cameras mounted on a tripod. Subsequently, the client paid the trafficker to "ensure that she was taken to a private clinic," so that nobody would investigate the lashes, puncture wounds, and cuts. The trafficker did take her to a clinic, and then afterwards gave her $200 and left her on the street in Malaysia. She felt grateful that he had not left her to die of an infection.

In Thailand, some young women who have escaped and been rescued from these "private porn" rings are allowed to stay in the rescue organizations' shelters only if they are natives. The organizations work hard to help victims to heal and feel safe. However, the legal system offers little recourse. "How can a victim file a lawsuit for pornography that was the product of torture, if she cannot prove that she didn't 'enjoy' it?" asks Anne, the psychologist of an association helping victims. "The law assumes that these women are free to be sadomasochists and that pornography is normal. How can you explain what is happening?" she complains, her eyes brimming with tears from physical and emotional exhaustion and anger.

The mafias know the answer: there is no way, because pornography represents a fantasy, a popular product. The new pornography, not the type in *Hustler* magazine or on the Playboy Channel, that is available free on the Internet or can be bought for $30 in Shanghai and less than $20 in Tokyo; it mostly belongs to traffickers who have invested in the new "pop slave culture." Jean, a young North American, spent two months in hospital with a head injury resulting from a punch she received while being raped in Tijuana. One year later her brother found a photograph of her on the pornographic web site www.deputaspormexico.com (translates as "whoringinmexico.com"). There are also websites such as www.slavefarm.com that are a shocking view of reality. The slavery pornography is here to stay. As long as it is protected as freedom of speech, it cannot be regulated or limited by anybody, except consumers and society.

At the Sands Expo Convention Center in Nevada, the sex industry holds an annual fair called the Adult Entertainment Expo (AEE), which attracts 22,000 people. During the 2009 fair, brothel owners attended a course on marketing and sales. At the end, two businessmen from Mexico, three from Singapore, a Colombian woman with operations in Tokyo, and one of the most powerful owners of massage parlors in New York and Chicago met in a suite where they exchanged business cards and closed deals to renew their operation routes and to "hire new girls." The source who was present told me that the Colombian woman proposed that they go into partnership to open a travel agency in Chicago with branches in each of their countries to facilitate the internationalization of their girls' shows.

Some of the courses on offer at AEE are: "Power and Influence: The Growing Presence of Women in the Adult Entertainment Industry," "Businesses Based on Technological Models: The Models you Should Know About," "Creating the Best Sales Teams: Sex Education for your Staff." One of the most popular courses is the workshop on legal issues by Arthur Schwartz, where respectable police officers and lawyers explain the new laws and how to abide by them. Meanwhile, in the halls, the real mafiosi agree on how to evade them. At the AEE, one can find fans of the sex industry who see it as an educational resource to liberate eroticism, along with national and international traffickers who take advantage of the environment of creative freedom while living off slavery. Anyone who dares to question the connection between the mafias and their connections to the mainstream sex industry will meet an onslaught of attacks from those who believe that this is just a fantasy, like snuff pornography with victims from Ciudad Juarez, Tijuana, and Thailand.

Why Only a Few Lawsuits?

Skeptics ask, if there are so many slaves in the sex trade, why are there so few lawsuits? Slavery is supposed to be a crime, but in general, due to sexism and classism, law-enforcement agencies do not see it this way. The head of the special police force in Bangkok assured me that it is difficult to do anything in this respect, "especially when the young women who are rescued want to return with their traffickers . . . I suppose they like it, poor things."

When the police rescue a victim upon receiving a complaint from tourists or embassy personnel who collaborate with rescue organizations, the traffickers go to the prison, identify themselves as relatives of the victim, and pay the victims' bail. A cleaning woman at the detention center told me that the police know the true identity of these men. In one week a trafficker nicknamed "the Dog" paid bail for nine "nieces," and the police never asked any questions.

With the increase of prevention campaigns, the traffickers give the slaves their own version of the rescue organizations' work, telling the women and girls the names of these organizations and warning that if they ask for help and tell the police that they are trafficking victims, they will be imprisoned for a year or longer without seeing their families and without being able to send money. The traffickers also make the threat that they will kill a family member if the slaves break the rules of the "contract."

In Cambodia, a twenty-six-year-old woman escaped and the caretaker ring of tuk-tuk drivers located her. The trafficker told her that if she wanted to buy her freedom she would have to bring him a girl from her town. Like thousands of other victims, she agreed to his request. The same pattern can be found in Mexico and Guatemala. Women's participation in trafficking rings is growing exponentially, not by coincidence. The mafias have done their job: they study the laws (a Filipino trafficker whom I interviewed knew the Palermo Protocols by heart) and they make deals with law–enforcement authorities.

The New Colonizers

According to local experts in Southeast Asia, regional treaties allowing the free movement of people without a passport have facilitated the work of traffickers who travel between Laos, Burma, Thailand, Cambodia, and Vietnam. However, almost no one mentions the Europeans who have colonized whole towns for the purposes of sexual and domestic exploitation of women and girls.

In 2007, a Swiss citizen married a Thai teenager in Pattaya, Thailand. He later took other Swiss men there and they all married local young women, who were then moved to Switzerland. Nobody filed a complaint; the facts were simply recorded in both countries' immigration records.

In northeastern Thailand, in the province of Surin, a British man who was living in Pattaya chose to marry an eleven-year-old girl in order to establish a link to the community. Later, he opened a restaurant and created what the locals call an "international community."

I could not get near it because the foreigners have complete control over the tuk-tuks, and "even the police are scared to go there," said the owner of a small hostel a few kilometers from the Brit's restaurant. They all know the story, and they think that the economy has improved due to the presence of the Europeans, whom they call *farang* ("whites"). The authorities feel grateful to these Europeans for their donations to schools and Buddhist temples, even though they have also created networks of pedophiles with access to sex slaves and domestic laborers. Right now, there are thousands of Europeans married to Thai women and girls who are living in domestic and sexual slavery. The majority of these men are Norwegian, German, British, French, Japanese, and Dutch.

Germany (where prostitution is legal) and Holland, are the countries that have expelled the most pedophiles. There are approximately 15,000 Dutch people registered as living in Thailand, many of them in Pattaya; but according to the Dutch government, there are in fact up to 50,000 nationals from the Netherlands. Some of them are retired men over the age of sixty with criminal records. The majority of the pedophiles who buy the services of girls and boys under the age of ten are from the United States, France, Norway, and Canada.

The mafiosi operate through travel agencies in Norway and Pattaya. The United States and Canada have a strategy to alert their governments when a citizen frequently travels alone to Thailand and Cambodia. To avoid customers being placed on this travel alert register, the travel agencies organize charter flights with stops en route in Qatar and Kazakhstan.

Globalization's Traps

In every place I have visited, from South America to Asia, Europe, and Africa, global migration is a contradictory phenomenon: thousands of people, excited by the promise of a better life, are seeking opportunities in other countries that have many jobs to offer but where discrimination, racism, and exclusion are the norm.

The capitalist basis of free-trade agreements encourages labor exploitation openly and strategically. In various places, I found businessmen who were convinced that being able to hire illegal immigrants on a temporary basis was directly related to the possibility of paying low wages without guaranteeing workers' benefits. Their reasoning is that the laborers come from poor countries, and, without work, they will die of starvation. Karen J. Hossfeld, in *Women of Color in US Society* (1994), quotes a businessman who owns a Silicon Valley assembly shop as saying: "When hiring an employee, I just look for three things: small, foreign, and female. You find those three things and you're pretty much automatically guaranteed the right kind of work force. These little foreign gals are grateful to be hired—very, very grateful—no matter what." To investigate the government's complicity, I interviewed migration officials responsible for approving temporary contracts for foreign workers. In Canada and the southern United States, there were many stories of people who had permits to be field hands. However, in Mexico I found the most remarkable example of how the institutional network is interrelated with exploitation and corruption.

A high-level government official working on immigration issues in the Office of the Secretary of the Interior told me that many permits are issued for Mexican border factories. He asked me not to publish his name, since the case he then talked about involved Kamel Nacif, who was known for using violence to take revenge on those who investigated him:

> I was in my office. In the morning, I received a phone call from the President of the Republic, Vicente Fox. He informed me that an important Lebanese businessman running factories would come to see me later to request a permit for temporary residency for about 200 Chinese people, who would work in his factories in various places throughout the country. His name is Kamel Nacif. The recommendation implied that preferential treatment was necessary. The president consider-ed him to be an exemplary businessman since he had opened clothing factories in southeastern, central, and northern Mexico, significantly increasing job opportunities in those regions. The name was familiar to me; Nacif was known as the "King of Jeans" because of his numerous jean factories in Mexico.
>
> A few hours later, Nacif arrived with three individuals holding briefcases. With an arrogant air, they entered my office to apply for the entry permits for the workers coming from China. Nacif placed a long list of names on my desk. I

glanced at it, and then politely explained that to process the permits it was necessary for them to fill out forms for each individual. I held out one of the forms. Nacif, clearly angry, his eyes bulging, told me that he was a friend of President Fox: "Fox didn't talk with you?" he spat out, full of contempt. I replied that I had indeed received a call from the president, but that I could not circumvent legal procedure; the most I could do, given the president's recommendation, was allow him to fill out the forms in my office rather than in the general public offices in the usual way. Despite my explanation, the businessman was still upset, threatening to call the president if I didn't facilitate the process. After a heated exchange of words, I suggested that his companions, apparently lawyers and an accountant, fill out the forms in my office.

Nacif ordered them to do so, and, seeing that his threats had no effect, he changed his tone. He said, "Look, sir, if you are worried that these Chinese people are going to escape, don't worry, because I'm going to have them locked up in a warehouse during the six months that they'll be working for me. They won't have a chance to leave, and we'll hold on to their papers. I assure you that none of them will escape and that we'll return them in one piece to China."

The fact that this man, the business partner and friend of governors and mayors in Mexico, felt free to describe the methods used by his company to traffic and subjugate Chinese workers shows the high-level of impunity and the deceit with which the protection networks operate. In 2006, a recorded conversation between Nacif and one of his business partners in the US—a man of French origin—came to light. The man recommended that Nacif provide a dining room for his workers. Nacif replied, "Let them starve to death." Workers who are "temporarily imported" from other countries become slaves to a system that treats them as objects, in complete disregard of any employment or human rights.

Union victories in most developing countries vanish under free-trade and global-market migration policies. From Vietnam to Nicaragua, from Mexico to central Asia, each time a group of exploited factory workers meets to create a union and demand their rights, they are confronted by a company that prefers to close before accepting local laws.

For example, in Toronto, Canada, on May 28, 2004, the former employees of Matamoros Garment and Tarrant Mexico testified in a public hearing before Canada's National Administrative Office (NAO), which is responsible for receiving and responding to labor grievances from countries that are part of the North American Free Trade Agreement. The NAO issued reports detailing the human-rights violations, but no penalty could be enforced directly against the company owners because both factories closed soon after the workers filed their complaints. Governments dare not demand that such companies improve their labor policies and there is no threat of legal sanction. They prefer to favor these businesses—regardless of labor conditions. This is because they help increase employment, and government officials do not want to risk that business owners take their business elsewhere.

NGOs have been leading the defense of labor rights for factory workers worldwide. Through strong campaigns and social networks, they have pressured certain brands and companies (such as Adidas, Tommy, Puma, Disney, etc.) to demand that their products being manufactured by cheap labor are not tainted by human exploitation and trafficking. Nevertheless, corporate mobility and free-trade agreements increase the amount of human trafficking and exploitation much faster than any organization can fight for human rights.

The Mafia and Poverty

The majority of organizations that rescue victims insist that a discussion of prostitution, must cover politics, poverty, inequality, racism, and exploitation.

On the World Day for Decent Work in October 2009, activists from twelve European countries denounced the low salaries paid to workers who make the garments sold in large retail stores. In this context, the European Campaign for Clean Clothes (translated from the Spanish: "Campaña Ropa Limpia") pressured the supermarket chains, such as Carrefour, Tesco, Aldi, or Lidl, to take into consideration the Asian Floor Wage Campaign. This is a proposal put forward by NGOs and Asian unions in response to the garment industry's miserably low salaries, perpetuated by competition within precarious and unfair labor markets. The average salary for a garment worker in Asia is $2 for an eight-hour day. The official requirement that workers spend a maximum of eight hours is systematically violated, and workers spend as many as fourteen hours in the factories, depending on the volume of work. It is true that prices in Bangladesh, India, and China are lower than in Europe and the United States; however, NGOs and unions calculate that a Bengali worker should be paid $8 per day to have the same purchasing power as an average worker in the European Union. The Asia Floor Wage Alliance organizations are not demanding that this wage be paid, but they have worked out a different comparison based on the World Bank's indicators of purchasing-power parity. They have used this system to calculate the wage that a worker needs to buy a package of basic products and services: $475 a month to achieve purchasing-power parity.

To receive a decent wage is an internationally recognized right, even though workers in the garment industry do not receive this in most cases. The workers who make the clothes for the international clothing chains are usually women who are living in extreme poverty. They often live in unhealthy housing, without running water, and they do not have enough money available to feed their families.

What is a decent wage for a young Thai woman who has to support a family? Clearly, the mafias offer much more than a minimum wage. They offer what governments are not willing to promise: riches, fairness, and the freedom to pursue them, although you may lose your life and emotional health and integrity in that pursuit. The trafficking mafias throughout the world understand that they are engaged in business and social politics: one of dehumanization, humiliation, and violence, but still politics in the end.

After this journey among the mafias, something became very clear to me: only the power of society and of NGOs can bring about a cultural shift, from the bottom up, from the roots. The change must recognize the wishes and desires of "other" people, and that, although they may be different from me, they are also human.

During the trial in which I came face to face with the traffickers of young girls in Mexico, it became clear to me that their power was not so real: they are not monsters; they are human beings with small souls. Their greatest power lies in our fear, and our power lies in our capacity to fight them and eliminate them from our streets, not by using the police, but by putting them out of business.

A new masculine revolution is necessary. We need a new generation of men, not warriors, not armed, not threatening divine punishment, not violent, but men who possess a strong sense of progress and justice. In the past few years, I have met scores of them. Male power must re-invent itself before the mafia and global society, which turns a blind eye, succeed in convincing girls that becoming a sex slave is the only way they will be able to study, eat, buy goods and services; before a new generation comes to believe that buying slaves is a sign of progress and modernity.

12

Shifting Numbers, Moral Panic, and the Debate

During this investigation, I met with traffickers, prostitutes and their clients, academics, pornography producers, porn stars, and feminists. The feminists often argue against organizations that seek to abolish prostitution and that rescue and protect women and girls subjected to sexual slavery. Their main argument is that the number of existing victims worldwide is frequently misquoted or exaggerated and that it is possible to differentiate clearly between voluntary prostitution and forced prostitution. Almost all those in favor of regulating prostitution agree that the statistics should be based on whether the person in question has freedom of movement and whether she views herself as enslaved.

There is a general consensus that commercial sexual exploitation is the most frequent and most documented type of human trafficking in the world (79 percent). The international sex industry depends on this type of trafficking. Forced labor is the second most common type of human trafficking at 18 percent. The remaining 3 percent consists of domestic slavery (one of the most under-documented activities), forced marriage (which in some countries is a religious custom) and organ extraction (carried out by the medical mafia and barely documented in countries with the highest incidence). Exploitation of children for begging and to serve as soldiers is not documented in detail.

In this book, I have tried to chart the various groups suffering different levels of exploitation. I tried to do it as honestly as I could after listening to hundreds of stories of rape, enslavement, murder, deception, humiliation, crime, and fear. Although my approach is objective, my sensitivity varied depending on the story of the person—victimizer or victim—as I looked into his or her eyes and observed gestures and emotions. I have tried to show the diversity of their experiences and visions of the world. For example, a French sociologist insisted that if the teenage girls in the Vietnamese villages I visited were coming and going from the brothels unaccompanied, they must be voluntary prostitutes. However, after eating and staying with them over the course of a couple of days in their communities, I witnessed the levels of domestic and sexual violence they suffered and the punishment they received from their parents if they did not bring money home "from the Dutchman." In my view, these girls are being exploited as slaves, but they are also enslaved by the cultural values of violence against women: they are victims of structural violence.

The debate on slavery and freedom of movement has become very heated. However, I believe that it has contributed to a deeper understanding of the issues. It has pushed everybody to ask more questions rather than believing that we can find answers that are all black or all white. I feel deeply grateful for having had the opportunity during these years to listen to specialists from "both camps" and to be listened to as well; this was my personal challenge, and it has allowed me to learn a great deal.

Before turning to the numbers, the doubts, and the arguments put forth in the global debate on the sex trade, I would like to consider some of its premises. It is important to have a look at the things that are left unsaid in this debate, things that make it difficult for people who do not want to engage in a pitched battle to stay on the sidelines of an issue that is vital to the citizens of the entire world. The traffickers' success thrives on this confusion. As they say, "the devil is in the detail."

Measuring: How and Where

The confusion created by the fact that trafficking is hard to quantify has contributed to the distortion of certain local realities. The problem with crime statistics lies in the way they are measured and the assessment techniques used to create credible results. For X number of crimes reported, there is the number Y that have never been reported; it is difficult to quantify Y, but that does not mean that Y does not exist. For example, "honor" crimes, such as rape and incest, continue to go unreported around the world, from Sweden to Nicaragua. For the most part, this is due to the embarrassment the victim may feel in making such a crime public, or to the humiliation she would undergo by testifying before third parties in an impersonal, mechanical way. For the victim, the rape is not a mechanical experience in the way that it is perceived by the police; rather, it is a complex and painful experience involving various forms of violence that are difficult to articulate before strangers, especially in a world where sexuality, violence, and taboos are intimately connected with a person's privacy. In most countries, it was not until the twentieth century that sexual violence began to be treated as a specialty. New judicial, clinical, therapeutic, and social paradigms and models of professional attention and intervention are being created in this new field.

In this book, I have explored the paradoxes of globalization, free markets, and their conflicting policies on freedom of movement. I have examined the defects, weaknesses, and contradictions of some international laws that do not apply in certain countries. I have also pointed out the problems of migratory movements of specific social groups that are rooted in poverty and the pursuit of freedom and hope. But none of these things makes the task of studying an issue as complicated as human trafficking any easier. It is necessary to create new analytical methods in order to document and unravel the distortions that generate errors when examining this issue. For example, of the 155 countries documented by the United Nations Office on Drugs and Crime, the countries that have laws on human trafficking tended to have police reports with a high incidence of women being arrested under the charge of trafficking in women and girls. Even though it is true that many women run brothels and that many victims become victimizers, there is a dangerous bias here. In many developing countries, prostitution is illegal, although it is permitted in "special areas," and, generally, women who are arrested are the weakest link in the chain of exploitation. On the one hand, the number of clients arrested continues to be absurdly low throughout the world; on the other hand, the most powerful men in the sex-slave industry have managed to remain invisible in official statistics.

The fact that the authorities still lack in-depth knowledge of organized crime is alarming. Most of the law-enforcement agencies that I interviewed in various countries concluded that drug cartels were not connected to trafficking in women and minors. However, from the border of Afghanistan to the trade routes of Colombia and Cuba, to Mexico and from there to the United States, the names and methods of the drug traffickers cropped up again and again in the protection of traffickers and those buying and selling slaves.

The solution will not be easy. To classify a businessman from Monterrey in Mexico, or a hotel owner from Punta Cana in the Dominican Republic, as traffickers, governments must prove that they promote prostitution, the purchase and sale of women and, in many cases, the "export and import" of people with immigration permits, plane tickets, and official visas. The US government, to cite one example, should classify all the strip and lap-dancing clubs in America using the same criteria it applies to those operating in Thailand, the Philippines, Suriname, or Mozambique. According to the United Nations Protocol to Prevent, Suppress, and Punish Trafficking in Persons, Especially Women and Children, 80 percent of women working in these businesses around the world are victims of trafficking. Thus, many of the clients, managers, and owners of the clubs should be classified as traffickers.

Several years ago, there was a campaign to stop violence against women that asked victims "not to allow themselves to be abused," while ignoring the role of the abusers. In 2000, the campaign focused on the aggressors and, instead of saying, "Every fifteen seconds a woman is abused," it said, "Every fifteen seconds a man chooses to abuse a woman." The current campaigns against human trafficking in Bolivia, Russia, and other countries use the slogan: "Don't let them fool you." Most victims around the world feel guilty for "letting themselves be fooled."

Cultural Diversity

One of the things I have learned during this investigation is that we cannot use the same yardstick to measure a post-war society such as Cambodia, which is still living with the social trauma of the genocide committed by the Khmer Rouge, and other societies such as Mexico, Guatemala, Pakistan, and Kenya. Although the incidence of extreme poverty may be similar and the child trafficking indicators almost identical, it is necessary to understand the socio-economic situation of the women and girls in each region, as well as the cultural perceptions of sexuality and violence. It is also important to take into account, in each case, how globalization and the assimilation of religious values have affected the sexual experiences of people of all ages. The voices of local and regional experts are important when seeking to corroborate what is happening. We must also find a common analytical language. Millions of clients have given us a valuable clue: they respond to racist sexual stereotypes. Along with pimps, clients should be studied thoroughly; with the implementation of laws against sexual exploitation, it is they who are responsible for great migratory movements, predominantly for sex tourism, to countries with weak judicial systems, where there are "loving and submissive women," as they themselves told me.

It is important to see how the racial and ethnic classification of victims affects the statistics collected in all countries, especially in the developed ones. The traffickers who supply the Spanish market obtain their victims primarily in Brazil, Suriname, Colombia, the Dominican Republic, and the Antilles. Nearly 50,000 women (black and Latin) are trafficked to Holland and Germany for the sex trade, which is legalized; because they are illegal immigrants, these victims are imprisoned and deported most often and they receive the worst treatment from the European Union. Susana Chiariotti, an Argentine attorney and researcher of trafficking in women, documented 3,000 Mexican women trafficked to Japan for sexual exploitation.

In any case, we must not forget the central role that the mafias play in this business. The large and small mafias take advantage of the confusion generated by this debate, and on many occasions they promote it through political and social lobbying to normalize human slavery. The Office of the United Nations on Drugs and Crime has to pressurize signatories to investigate businessmen involved in the sex trade and their networks of lawyers and administrators, who, as I corroborated in many cases, are also linked to other serious crimes such as drug trafficking and money laundering.

The Victim's Experience
What criteria should be used to determine whether a person is a victim of trafficking? In about twenty cases known around the world, victims of systematic rape have defended their captors in court. Interviews with trafficking victims should include questions to detect Stockholm Syndrome, or a simple questionnaire on familial violence suffered during childhood. If they have suffered from physical abuse in their early childhood, many victims assimilate sexual and psychological violence

as something natural, something they deserve due to their gender, race, nationality, or class, or, in some cases, all of these combined.

The personal stories are critical when it comes to measuring the impact of this social and criminal phenomenon. We need to understand fully how a Salvadoran girl who has been raped several times a day in a brothel has internalized her suffering emotionally and psychologically in order to survive. In the same way, it's important to understand how a six-year-old Brazilian girl has internalized her fear after being used, since she was four, to make child pornography; even though she does not like what they did to her, she believes this is what happens to all girls, because that is what the rapists have told her. We should also examine how priests or businessmen who pay to watch these videos in Mexico, Spain, or the United States completely ignore the fact that behind the porn video of this girl there is a criminal ring that has enslaved her. Likewise, we should listen to the female trafficker from the Philippines who uses liberal arguments to defend prostitution, but, by the end of the conversation, admits that she was sexually abused as a child, long before joining a brothel for Korean tourists in her native country. The fact that she has normalized her childhood abuse to the point of not feeling victimized, has allowed her to victimize, without any feelings of guilt, other girls and young women.

This is the only way for us to piece together the puzzle and understand that the more serious problem facing us is the normalization of violence, which makes it impossible for the victim to reclaim her right to live in a non-aggressive situation. Some prostitutes in Europe and the United States told me that accepting that they are victims of criminal activities feels like an insult, even worse than the humiliation of being beaten by a drunk client or anally raped. This is the logical conclusion of the liberal view of sexual violence as something isolated. This is why a Spanish prostitute in Barcelona can say, "I don't sell my body; I sell a specific sexual act, like a secretary sells her knowledge of how to write a letter."

Fina Sanz is an extraordinary Spanish psychologist, an expert in psycho-eroticism and creator of "re-encounter therapy," which has helped heal survivors of sexual violence throughout the world. She argues that sexual exploitation not only damages the body but it also damages the body's owner and the person as an emotional entity. In the context of prostitution and trafficking, the pimp, the client, and even the rapist view the sexual experience as an erotic act of sexual pleasure for themselves, not for the woman, and as a power trip, as they themselves have recognized.

For the woman I interviewed in Barcelona, selling a sexual act is the equivalent of preparing and selling a sandwich in a bar. However, for the client, penetrating a body, subjugating it, and treating it as an object, is definitely not the same as eating a sandwich. The latter is a mechanical act of nourishment, whereas the sale of sex has a socio-cultural weight that validates the right to buy people and abuse them for money. According to Sanz, "Eroticism can be considered a reproduction of socio-cultural values. It is lived through the body and understood as a sexual, sensitive, emotional, mental, spiritual and social totality that is experienced with pleasure." These are some of the nuances that are forgotten when discussing whether to regulate or abolish the sex trade, which feeds human trafficking. Prostitutes are socialized to believe that engaging in any discussion about psycho-sexual health means accepting a religious morality that would impede their sexual freedom.

If we count all the women in the world who belong to an association for prostitutes (or "sex workers," as some of them call themselves), they would number less than half a million people. Does this mean that, because they are in the minority, they do not have rights? Of course, they have rights. However, the debate becomes more complex if we consider that validating this minority's right to work in prostitution might mean promoting socio-cultural values and specific crimes that affect the majority.

Carmela, a former Mexican prostitute, who works to prevent violence in Miami, states:

> Before, women used to say, "My husband hits me because he loves me," because as girls we had been told that this meant love, until we came to understand that it meant the opposite. Now, it turns out that we should be saying, "The clients raped and humiliated me because I am free." This is monumentally stupid! To be free sexually is to decide not to be sexually exploited and to have sex with whom you choose, not to benefit an industry that promotes feminine indignity and normalizes violence.

Let's consider the debate about how pornography possibly damages a society. Catharine MacKinnon, the American feminist and activist, suggests that the more pornography is popularized and legitimized, the more violence against women is normalized, and the more society becomes desensitized to sexual exploitation. In addition, according to her, those who critique and analyze pornography and its socio-cultural effects are insulted and classified as enemies of freedom of expression. They are aggressively attacked. A significant number of therapists who support the abolition of prostitution argue that sexual exploitation for commercial purposes in all its forms is a violation of human rights. These factors are fundamental to understanding the sex trade and prostitution.

A philosopher at a top British university may pontificate about the freedom to prostitute one's self, but without considering the implications of his ideas for the prostitutes who suffer extreme sexual, racial, and gender violence at the hands of prostitution rings. This is structural violence with deep misogynist roots and consequences on an individual and collective scale.

At the other extreme, there are the Catholic and other Christian women who rescue young prostitutes. Normally, the rescuers have a hard time accepting sex as something healthy. Their abolitionist rage, steeped in their prejudices, fears, and orthodox values, shuts out any dialogue, even with the victims, who are almost always subjected to dogmatic religious lectures. This approach hides the complexities of the hyper-sexuality experienced by the victims in the context of severe post-traumatic stress.

Voices and Positions

Carolina Hernández, a Spanish woman who belongs to the Colectivo Hetaira, an organization of prostitutes seeking to defend their rights, states:

> To be a sex worker is something important. Work in the sex trade, as prostitution is called today, involves pimps, prostitutes, mafias, outcasts, etc., but people don't take into account that it is something that you freely choose, making your own decision. Yes, nobody forced the majority of my colleagues to work the streets; nobody tricked them into choosing this. The majority of the women on the streets are free to make their own choices. [. . .] This happens with Eastern European women: living with them, they have told me and I have seen that they need a male friend to take care of them, because there are men who want to take advantage of them. These men don't ask for anything in exchange; even though the women offer them gifts, the men often do not accept them. People call such men pimps, but it's not true. Many of these women have married these men and then left the streets. Our work is stigmatized by the police and neighbors, who accuse us of being surrounded by accomplices, drugs, and crime . . . But it isn't like that. All of this is wrong and ridiculous. [. . .] We must learn to live respectfully and in an educated way

so the sex workers become part of everyday life throughout the world.

Laura, aged twenty-seven, who was rescued from a trafficking ring in Navarra in northern Spain, tells a different story:

> They told me in Paraguay that I would be an exotic dancer in a top nightclub in Madrid and that, if there were clients, I could choose them myself. They brought me to Navarra and I had to endure sex with thirty men per day. It was terrible; my vulva was swollen. One guy bit my nipples and hurt me. Another guy wanted to suffocate me with his penis in my mouth and take photographs with his cell phone. Another one forced me to have anal sex and when I was crying he said it was because I liked it . . . I thought being a prostitute in Spain would be better. They told me that here the clients would show me respect, but it wasn't true. It's the same as in my country and in Panama, where they took me first: they pay to humiliate you.

Millions of women and girls in the poorest countries know their fate: more poverty and more hunger than their mothers suffered. The Vietnamese mothers and daughters I interviewed told me that every three months a Filipino woman named Star and two Japanese men—who claim to be her cousins—travel to the towns of Dong Tham, An Giang, and Kien Giang to recruit young people to work in Thailand, Hong Kong, Macao, and Cambodia as waitresses and prostitutes. When I asked the girls if they understood what it meant to be a prostitute in Cambodia, they just looked at each other in silence. Only one of them decided to speak up. Sixteen-year-old Bi'nh (her name means "peace") told me: "Star says that in the first year we could make loads of money and later return home to start a family business."

"Why for one year only?" I asked.

"Because the clients like virgins," she answered. While I was writing in my notebook, I looked back over the pages of interviews with the Cambodian police. According to them, 50,000 girls under eighteen are trafficked from Vietnam and are enslaved, extorted, starved, and sexually exploited. A girl under ten years old is given one euro for giving a European oral sex, but the trafficker charges 40 euros. According to some girls who were rescued, they have to have oral sex with fifteen to twenty clients each day. A trafficker can earn 600 euros each day from one girl. Supposing that they are exploited five days a week and using the lower number of clients, each minor generates 3,000 euros per week. The sexual exploitation of 50,000 Vietnamese girls in Cambodia provides the traffickers with 150,000,000 euros a week. This money is distributed among the owners and tenants of bars and hotels, taxi drivers and hotel bellhops, mafias that provide protection, and police officers who are paid to alert them to investigations being carried out by organizations defending children's rights. In addition, the profits support banks and local economies.

Lending her voice to feminists in favor of legalizing prostitution, the Mexican anthropologist Martha Lamas explains her reasoning:

> I am convinced that there is a market for sex work that some people choose for economic reasons, which involves the same violence that the capitalist system imposes on anyone selling their labor, and has nothing to do with trafficking.
>
> Exploitation is differentiated from slavery by the amount of freedom of movement permitted. Within capitalism, everything is exploitation. For me the main struggle is against all forms of exploitation. And I am convinced that the strategy should be not to "abolish" but to "regulate." I understand that within the sex trade there are distinct work conditions and that all workers should have rights and obligations: social

security, housing allowances, the possibility to unionize, taxation, etc.

I believe that it is necessary to differentiate between trafficking and work. It is essential to stop speaking about "prostitution" and redefine it as "work" when it is not forced labor. The clandestine activities should be brought to light and regulated, just as illegal drugs are.

There are no easy solutions that can be applied homogenously to the different groups of sex workers, but I am convinced that women who accept their situation and fight for recognition of their rights, including being able to work in this profession, should be supported and respected. They themselves understand that not all of them are victims and that they have chosen the lesser evil.

When we consider this argument, the big question is whether the traffickers, the mafias, and the clients, with their sexist and misogynistic perspectives, would be willing to respect women's rights: pay what each woman believes is fair, not exploit them, respect their choices, and not use violence against them. The statistics on violence against women and the number of women killed show that this is practically impossible, but this does not mean that women do not have the right to demand publicly the choice to make a living in the sex trade.

Martha Lamas states:

> The *a priori* victimization of those who work in the sex trade (not as a result of trafficking, but as an economic decision) does not seem correct to me. I believe that human beings have to be more cautious and respectful of differences. We feminists could try to define our own desires and needs (including psychological ones) and those of other women. If not, it is easy to fall into a type of "maternalism" with the intention of "saving them" from something from which they do not want

to be saved. This involves taking responsibility for their own acts, and, of course, their freedom to express themselves.

In *The Sexual Liberals and the Attack on Feminism* by Dorchen Leidholdt and Janice G. Raymond (1990), Catharine MacKinnon responds to this argument. She notes that in the past the women's movement

> understood that the choice to be beaten by one man for economic survival was not a real choice, despite the appearance of consent a marriage contract might provide . . . Yet now we are supposed to believe, in the name of feminism, that the choice to be sexually used by hundreds of men for economic survival must be affirmed as a real choice, and if the woman signs a contract to be a "model" there is no coercion there.

With respect to the number of women that practice prostitution either voluntarily or due to coercion, the Spanish activist Beatriz Gimeno Reinoso states:

> In debates of this nature I am usually against resorting to statistics, because these can always be manipulated; they are difficult to prove; they depend on many factors; and each group provides the ones they want. The figures do not convince anyone except those who are already convinced. Suffice to say that in the past few months the parties for legalization have declared that 5 percent of women are tricked, while the parties supporting abolition claim that only 5 percent of women are voluntarily involved. This is not a statistical problem; it is a social, ideological, and political problem: suffering is unique to each human being.

It is clear that the sex trade does not want to open a free market in which adult women who choose to sell sex by the hour or by the minute can do so healthily while also paying taxes, as suggested by Lamas. The business is structured to control and exploit. On the one hand, it provides men throughout the world with what women and girls refuse to give them for free—sex without rules, obedience, and subjugation. On the other hand, it enriches a few at the cost of many. It is naïve to believe that by legalizing prostitution, the mafias will stop engaging in the sexual exploitation of children, adolescents, and adults on a transnational level.

Around the world, sex tourism has generated a large market and a culture with certain values and norms, where adolescents and children are the commodities in increasing demand in a context of poverty. They have been dehumanized and objectified. Ultra-conservative groups can be blamed for mystifying and exploiting the moral panic over trafficking in order to expropriate women's bodies and give the rights over them back to government and religious groups. Between both worlds, women and children are the ones who are lost.

13

Conclusions

Should Prostitution be Legalized?

Today, many feminists consider the legalization of prostitution the best antidote to trafficking in women and minors for sexual exploitation. However, evidence shows that legalization would further open the door to the mafias and facilitate slavery. There is also a direct correlation between adult prostitution and sexual violence against girls at younger and younger ages. I hope that my trip to so many countries, and the testimonies I gathered about the heinous crimes against victims, will contribute to this debate.

It would be great if a solid set of laws could put an end to centuries of oppression and to so many stories of women and girls being dispossessed of their bodies. However, no country has made an effort to create real conditions for equality between the sexes. In a culture governed by misogynistic and patriarchal values, the female body is viewed as an object that can be bought, sold, used, and disposed of. Women are taught to follow certain rules, and men are instructed to uphold them without question.

In Islamic countries, prostitutes are punished with the death penalty. In Holland, Germany, and Switzerland, it is legal to work as a prostitute, run a brothel, and advertise such services. In the United States, except in the state of Nevada, prostitution is illegal, but, in reality, brothel owners are not pursued by law-enforcement agencies. In Spain, some ultra-right groups donate money to prostitutes' unions in order to keep alive the industry that enriches and strengthens them. At the same time, their political arm takes away women's sexual and reproductive rights. Mafias involved in prostitution run 4,000 brothels in Spain, bringing in 18 billion euros per year.

It is shocking to see the extent to which sexist violence has been normalized. Women who work as prostitutes cannot easily explain why they are able to detach their psychological identities from their bodies when dealing with clients who humiliate and assault them; they simply submit. Clients are also unable to explain what cultural and psychological mechanisms are at work that make it possible for them to separate their genitals from their emotions. Here is how "Thommo" explains it on his website, "Whorist": "I saw her little face in the Burmese brothel. Her mother charged me up front and told me that anal sex was prohibited. I see her and I want to put my penis in her mouth. We enter the room and she is scared, frightened; I like this because I can teach her . . . This way, the next time I visit, she will know to spread her legs." The man resists anally raping the girl only because there is a "strong, tall gorilla" guarding the door.

Those in favor of regulating prostitution say that we cannot see all adult female prostitutes as victims incapable of making their own decisions. They are right about this. However, we should take into consideration Somaly Mam's perspective:

> For postmodern feminists and prostitution's defenders, speaking of women's vulnerability is an insult. However, it is important to clarify that being vulnerable does not mean that we are weak or dumb; we are slaves because other people are unable to feel empathy for the situation in which society has placed us. Prostitution does not have anything to do with sophistication or freedom. It is believed that the practice of prostitution is based on an exchange of pleasure for money, but this is a distortion of the reality that hides women's helplessness.

After asking many prostitutes how they see themselves, I discovered that most of them do not view themselves as "whole." Many of them feel some power when carrying out small acts of revenge against their clients: they make fun of them—not to their faces—and they have a false sense of domination. Sometimes they are the greatest promoters of macho behavior and sexual stereotypes: "And what if I do? It's my choice," stated one of the women I interviewed. Violence against prostitutes is well documented and shows the absolute inequality that exists between them and their clients. Although they may be enslaved on a symbolic level, they are not necessarily victims of trafficking, unless a pimp is controlling them.

In childhood, things are very different. Many children who suffer sexual abuse and are obligated to work as prostitutes believe that "this is how life is, and I was born to do this," as they themselves told me. Many cities and towns have two or three generations of adult women and men who were victims of sexual exploitation and they now repeat what they have learned. Out there, in the global village, there is an army of adults convinced that it is normal to sexually enslave others and make a living from their bodies.

Those who want to simplify facts and provide "satisfactory" statistics can make a distinction between the adult women and the young girls who are being sexually exploited; however, in reality, it is practically impossible to differentiate between them. In the various pornography rings that I investigated, there were women aged twenty-two living alongside four-year-old girls. I also found some brothels where the prostitutes took care of each other's daughters; the girls witnessed everything as their mothers worked. In Tokyo, it is possible to find teenagers dressed like Lolitas on the streets, and, around the corner, you can find adult women dressed as geishas. In New York, there are also Thai masseuses in their twenties who, under their boss' supervision, train fourteen-year-old girls who have just arrived.

Those who argue that adult, adolescent, and child sexual exploitation are rigorously separated, because of the traffickers' indulgence or the prostitutes' free will, would be really surprised if they ever conducted extensive field studies.

When I hear arguments in favor of legalizing prostitution as a way to "give control over their bodies back to women," the lost look of the girls who never had the power to decide for themselves comes to my mind. Something tells me that passing laws to legitimize a despicable occupation in such an unequal world will end up favoring the victimizers and not the victims.

The Role of Men

Slavery—in particular sexual slavery—is an unresolved challenge for humanity in the twenty-first century. Its complexity is enormous.

To counter the prostitute's belief that her profession is the only option that the world has given her, we should fight for all women to have access to decent jobs, social security, and the right to housing and healthcare; to own their own bodies and their sexuality without having to sell themselves as merchandise in order to survive. But it is also imperative that men discover new ways of coexisting, in which pornography, violence, and sexism are not the only options for their erotic lives and their relationships with women and other men.

Few men are working to eliminate trafficking and violence against women; and not many of them express publicly the need for a transformation of masculinity, to make it less focused on the objectification of women. Meanwhile, the number of clients accessing child pornography and brothels where adolescents are enslaved is increasing. Clients are seeking ever-younger girls because they usually do not know how to defend themselves and it's easier to get them to cooperate and to work as prostitutes. However, as Victor Malarek states: "In the majority of investigations and reports on this tragedy, they, the principal consumers of prostitution, are unknown, and, in the end, they become the lost link."

Human trafficking is on the rise, due in part to the globalization of capitalism, free-trade agreements, and porous borders. However, the rise in demand for human beings can, above all, be attributed to deterioration in interpersonal relationships. The *Business Miscellany*, published by *The Economist* magazine recommends that high-level business executives follow the corporate etiquette of their hosts during business trips abroad, which may include going to brothels and strip clubs to close deals. Why is this "congregational prostitution," as it is known, never criticized? Making such recommendations—"When in Rome, do as the Romans do"—increases the demand for prostitutes.

What concrete measures can be taken in the face of this generalized phenomenon?

- Corporations that are willing to participate should create codes of ethics stating that no employee of the company shall close deals in establishments that promote prostitution, and no bills run up in nightclubs where prostitution is practiced will be accepted as "corporate expenses."
- Businesses, especially those in tourism, should offer an annual course for all their employees to understand the implications of human trafficking in their communities.
- Corporations should assign part of their taxes to organizations dedicated to educating boys about non-violent masculinity.
- Whoever chooses to consume pornography in print, television, or the Internet should bear in mind that it is probably providing resources to those who traffic in women, girls, and boys.
- The owners of newspapers, which often call for the end of sexual slavery on their front pages, should also refuse to

provide publicity or advertising for the sale of women and prostitution on their back pages.

Governments' Responsibilities

Despite being on a technologically hyper-connected planet, millions of slaves are invisible and their voices are unheard by society in general and by governments in particular. The majority of victims move—or are moved—from poor villages to more affluent cities, from countries with high unemployment to countries with more opportunities. In most cases, victims are unaware of their rights and they lack legal documents.

UNICEF calculates that 18 percent of children under the age of five in Latin America and the Caribbean have not been legally registered. In Brazil twenty-five million people do not have birth certificates. In recent years, three million newborns in Colombia have not been legally registered. In Mexico, in the indigenous areas of Chiapas, there are 25,000 boys and girls who do not have birth certificates. The percentage of people with no identification documents in sub-Saharan African countries is even greater that in Latin America.

A person without identification cannot have access to basic services, testify before the authorities, have formal employment, obtain credit, or receive an inheritance. If someone takes them to another city, they are unable to identify themselves fully, and their families cannot retrieve them. Those who "do not exist" because they lack papers understand that their captors control their lives and freedom. If they resist, they will be left on the streets, sent to prison, or returned to the poverty they were trying to leave behind, the poverty that originally led them to this place.

Millions of people are left without a way to identify themselves due to migration caused by wars—in Serbia, Cambodia, Burma, the Congo, Guatemala, El Salvador, and Nicaragua, among others. There are countless criminals ready to offer false documents—or real documents, illegally obtained—to these refugees in order to place them on the path to slavery. Women fleeing war, in a state of post-traumatic stress, sometimes find themselves trapped in European networks of mafias specializing in buying and selling slaves from countries where the violence has fractured or destroyed social networks. In wars, children are also sometimes enslaved so that they can be used as "cheap" and "expendable" recruits. In 2009 alone, in twelve countries armed government forces and their rebel enemies recruited thousands of child soldiers. Furthermore, the number of girl soldiers has also risen considerably, and many of these girls are used as sex slaves, as currently seen in the Democratic Republic of the Congo.

As long as those who impose their laws on the world deny any open discussion about how the sex industry operates, the slave market will continue to expand. What is for some a crime and for others a human tragedy turns out to be big business for a specific group of men who own companies that are listed on the New York Stock Exchange; who build and run five-star hotels; who buy airplanes and entertain politicians, police officials, military officials, businessmen, and religious leaders. The manager of a bar in Mexico that has been shut down three times for the prostitution of twelve and thirteen-year-old girls, but has been reopened thanks to his political connections, explains it like this: "This is a business, a business, a business . . . Stop screwing us."

The illegal trafficking of undocumented persons needs to be debated more honestly and internationally. Ambiguous laws and temporary work visas that provide workers with minimal rights should be revised. Those who find themselves working as prostitutes should not be considered criminals; instead those who buy prostitution and those who own establishments where trafficking is organized and encouraged should be penalized.

Over the last fifteen years, there has been great media interest in the issue of rescuing trafficking victims, especially those who have been exploited by sex-trade rings and by child abusers. However, in many places, the police tend to use trafficking to shock the public, and their righteous words do nothing more than horrify and disconnect people from an issue that is made to seem absolutely alien to them.

On various occasions, law-enforcement officials have manipulated the media and society in general by making their raids on brothels seem to be rescue missions to protect the victims' human rights; in reality, victims are arrested in these raids.

Some law-enforcement officials in countries such as the United States, Mexico, Spain, Turkey, France, South Africa, Colombia, and Japan treat victims as illegal immigrants and violate almost all of their rights. It is important to consider whether law-enforcement officials are acting based on double standards and sexist prejudices in order to project an image of effectiveness, or whether, after receiving good training, they are acting in a correct manner.

Even without the abolition of prostitution, those who want to regulate it and have signed the Palermo Protocols and other anti-slavery agreements can take various concrete steps to fight human trafficking. They include the following:

- Investigate the finances of brothels, bars, and modeling agencies suspected of money laundering.
- Undercover police should infiltrate companies producing pornography; a significant number of women and adolescent girls have been extorted to work for these companies.
- Maintain a register of law-enforcement officials who frequent brothels and strip clubs in their free time; their loyalty is almost always with the sex industry and not with their police force. Traffickers always seek to involve them as VIP clients in order to make them their accomplices.
- Create policies to prohibit and punish public officials who

frequent brothels. If a police officer, a military official, or a secretary of state were found taking drugs or drinking with a drug trafficker, he would be arrested immediately. Why is it, then, that the laws prohibiting pimping, procuring a prostitute, and trafficking are not applied in the same manner?

- Investigate and record the number and origin of child and teenage porn videos routinely found in the seized property of drug traffickers and illegal business throughout the world.

The Shelters' Fundamental Work

Most of the testimonies provided by people rescued from trafficking situations would not exist without the shelters that operate around the world. On the same sidewalk where crimes are committed, there are also safe havens where victims can sleep, eat, work, and eventually rebuild their lives. In these shelters, victims' stories are documented and their futures are reclaimed.

At a shelter in Guatemala, I found myself surrounded by forty-three girls between the ages of twelve and fourteen carrying their babies—conceived through rape—in their arms. These young girls had been rescued from brothels on the Mexican border. Some of the girls showed me their babies as if they were plastic dolls detached from their bodies and their emotions. Others caressed their babies as if they represented their inner child who grew up alone and abandoned. In Sri Lanka, I burned my fears on a bonfire along with Hindu women who were rebuilding their lives after twenty years of working in the sex trade. In Burkina Faso, I spent the night with three young girls who climbed on to my cot wanting to be hugged and to hear stories about little girls in Mexico. In Cuba, I listened to *jineteras,* as prostitutes are referred to there, seeking freedom from sexual slavery through poetry and music. In Japan, I witnessed the emotional intelligence of Filipino teenagers who wanted to be painters and never be forced to have sex again. In New York, I played basketball with seven Mexican teenagers who had been rescued after being sold by their siblings to brothels run by a mafia network. In Mexico, I helped a priest prepare sandwiches of *cochinita pibil* (slow-roasted pork, a specialty of Mexican cuisine) for twenty-three teenagers from Chiapas and El Salvador, who had been trafficked as slaves for manual labor. They worked twelve-hour shifts on construction sites, slept on a dirt floor, and were malnourished. In Barcelona, I spent a cold night listening to immigrant women from Africa dream of a happy life, a legal life. In France, I listened to seven Chinese teenagers, rescued from the Parisian mafia; they were planning to create a school for girls who would learn that being born female would not be a sin.

Every victim rescued from slavery who reclaims her human rights reminds me of the greatness of life and the importance of protecting human freedom and every person's right to follow her own compass and make her own path on this earthly adventure. This is what a good shelter can provide: it offers victims a chance to reflect on their lives, to learn, to choose, to forgive or not, and to move on. As a girl told me in Sweden: "The only thing you need is for another human being to look into your eyes and see you as an equal, to give you a mirror and offer a corner of peace where you can look at yourself and figure out who you are and where you want to go."

As long as human trafficking exists, these secure spaces will be essential, particularly in countries with high rates of sexual exploitation. (See the maps contained in *The Protection Project Review of The Trafficking in Persons Report*, July 2011.)* People who rescue victims and run shelters have become heroes. Unfortunately, society does not always do what it can to rehabilitate victims: we need collective, not individual heroism.

---

* www.protectionproject.org/wp-content/uploads/2011/07/TIP-Report-Review-2011.pdf

Only 133 countries have shelters and hostels for victims trafficked for sexual or labor purposes. In fifty-three of these countries, the shelters are run by NGOs, and 82 percent of them are directed by women. In thirty-six countries, local governments establish and maintain shelters. Governments collaborate with civil society in only twenty-nine countries to provide joint funding for shelters: the NGOs contribute 30 to 60 percent of funding and the government provides the rest. In four countries, the government prohibits the contribution of public resources to NGOs, which can only collaborate with international organizations by taking great political and diplomatic precautions. In Turkey, for example, the government runs the brothels, and victims' organizations are not allowed to accept public donations. In seventeen countries, the government not only refuses to collaborate with private organizations that rescue victims but also goes after human-rights activists, as noted by the John Hopkins University's Protection Project in 2009. Throughout the world, there are seven times more shelters for abused animals than for victims of slave trafficking.

Resources are fundamental for any private organization shouldering the costs of providing services and basic necessities to hundreds of people in crisis situations. These organizations rely on full-time specialists in the fields of mental and physical health; they need paramedics, medicine, security, transport, secretarial and administrative assistance, accounting services, and maintenance of buildings with thirty to forty rooms. The victims receive three meals per day; many of them suffer serious health problems related to malnourishment, and, in some cases, addictions induced by traffickers. Medicines and nutritional supplements can cost a great deal, especially for organizations operating in developing countries where a culture of humanitarian assistance and private donations does not exist. Most developing countries lack effective policies to encourage collaboration between the government and civil society. For example, in Mexico and Guatemala, in order to receive public resources, NGOs must be registered with the government and vetted for transparency and accountability; they have to pay 30 percent tax, which is higher than the tax rate on for-profit businesses.

In general terms, there are basically four types of shelters for victims of trafficking. Their mission is to provide housing, therapy, and legal and immigration assistance, but they differ in terms of professional standards. Some shelters apply integrated models and follow an operation manual with ethical principles, while others started in an improvised manner and barely function. Some shelters have been established in order to evangelize people in vulnerable situations.

Shelters for survivors of forced prostitution founded and directed by feminists

These shelters have been created based on the founders' experience. Most of them took radical positions to start with, which gradually developed into integrated models that are of great benefit to survivors. They have shown their ability to work together with government agencies to prevent women working as prostitutes being treated as criminals. Some of these organizations have not welcomed the new anti-trafficking laws because they realize that subjecting victims to insufferable interrogations and trials where they have the burden of proof turns out to be another form of re-victimization. They often document cases exhaustively and decide whether to turn the information over to Interpol or another agency to continue the investigation.

Numerous shelters, including the most well-known ones, have serious economic problems because the demand for their services has overwhelmed their resources. The specialists who work in these organizations usually receive very low wages and little or no benefits. The average duration of a victim's stay ranges from six months to three or four years, depending on the victim's age and specific problems. Providing therapy, food, housing, medical assistance, education, social services, and job training costs approximately $45 per day in a developing country and $200–300 in a developed one.

Some of the model organizations of this type are Somaly Mam's in Cambodia, Casa de las Mercedes in Mexico, and the Girls Educational & Mentoring Services (GEMS) in New York.

Shelters Run by International Organizations
Institutions such as the International Organization for Migration (IOM) have had great impact on countries and regions by increasing the scope of charitable organizations' operations. Like the United Nations Refugee Agency (UNHCR), in some countries the IOM runs shelters to rescue all types of immigrants subjected to trafficking and abuse. My interviews with various trafficking survivors have revealed that the IOM and the International Labour Organization (ILO) have played a critical role in supporting and protecting local organizations by providing theoretical, statistical, and methodological assistance.

The great weakness of these organizations is that they must proceed with caution and diplomacy under corrupt and abusive governments, even though their intervention saves lives and helps victims of trafficking for forced labor, sex, and organ donation. These organizations have been able to intervene in some very conservative countries that are not tolerant of women's liberation. They may have to keep a low profile and sometimes work under a different name that has nothing to do with human trafficking. Their budgets are assured, but their effectiveness depends, in large part, on who heads the local and regional offices, because these organizations are large bureaucracies that move at a slow pace. They have also become a very useful umbrella for human-rights activists in countries governed by dictators or where civil and social movements are outlawed.

Shelters Run by Religious Groups
The most powerful organizations in the world dealing with issues of trafficking are run by the Christian church. Caritas is a Catholic institution, and then there are Muslim organizations that have been set up in the last decade to help Muslim girls and boys in vulnerable situations in order to indoctrinate them.

Some organizations, such as Hagar in Cambodia, provide extraordinary assistance: their therapists are respectful of the girls' beliefs. However, others, such as the international network of the Iglesia Restaurada de los Perfectos, headed by the powerful millionaire Jorge Erdely, have been caught trafficking in children rescued in Asia and Latin America for illegal adoption by families within the church.

The orthodox religious communities represent a growing problem on a global scale, except in the cases of victims seeking shelter within their own religious group. In thirteen countries, mainly in Africa, religious leaders use their position to recruit trafficking victims for their own exploitation purposes. I interviewed various trafficking victims rescued from Koranic schools in Senegal, Mozambique, Iran, Iraq, Afghanistan, Uzbekistan, and Kirgizstan, where they were used as beggars to provide for their teachers. During my travels, I found hundreds of girls in small churches, including Protestant and Catholic ones, in Vietnam, Thailand, the Philippines, and Mexico. These churches' primary mission was to catechize the girls, instilling fear and punishment. The result of this type of effort to rescue victims is devastating: the guilt, sexism, and idea of sex as taboo are re-instilled in the minds of these girls and women, making them more vulnerable than ever.

Some of the girls I talked with had been trafficked twice. The IOM rescued them from a marabout, an isolated ascetic Muslim community, where the girls said that they were learning "to serve Allah and to obey their masters and the men of Islam." The testimony of a Muslim activist reveals that in the marabouts the girls are taught to obey and subsequently marry adult men and become slaves of servile marriages.

Extremists are not really interested in abolishing forced prostitution because they need it as an excuse so they can rescue girls and women. In some places, Catholic priests and Protestant preachers who have opened shelters for minors have molested the victims. In February 2010, Pope Benedict XVI had to travel to Ireland to ask for forgiveness for seventy years of Catholic priests' sexual abuse of boys and girls in religious schools and orphanages. Of course, these are individual incidences: not all Catholic priests are child molesters. One example of a good priest comes to mind: in the state of Chihuahua, Mexico, Father Antonio Urrutia has undertaken extraordinary and respectful work with prostitutes in the so-called "bilateral corridor" between the United States and Mexico.

Temporary Shelters Before Repatriation

Some governments have opened these types of shelters. In various US cities, these shelters retain victims for two weeks before they are repatriated. In order to obtain a humanitarian visa based on having been trafficked, they must prove that they are victims. Task forces need to be deployed to actively investigate traffickers.

Defenders of Human Rights in a Hostile Environment

As we have already seen, countries with the most corrupt governments and the lowest levels of democracy are the ones where human trafficking is growing exponentially. Of the 175 countries investigated by the Protection Project in 2009, sixty-seven showed the complicity of their government officials in regularly committing or covering up criminal activity.

Government officials' corruption has been well documented.*
Despite international agreements and laws signed by governments, the lack of transparency in these nations provides
favorable conditions for police corruption and weak criminal
justice systems.

The charitable organizations that attempt to reproduce international models, such as those provided by US, Spanish, and
British task forces, often run into a brick wall because the
governments do not allow them any real or direct participation.
Time and time again, from Colombia to the Philippines, I have
found defenders of victims' rights being threatened and pursued
by the police, who should be their allies. Human Rights Watch
provides extensive documentation of this fact.

The mafioso advising the finance minister in Cambodia,
the Japanese police chief allied with the Yakuza, and the
Mexican judge sold to the Arellano Félix cartel, which controls
prostitution in Tijuana and on the border, are all part of the web
surrounding the charitable organizations that provide assistance
to trafficking victims. As a result, many shelters are at a great
disadvantage, with few resources, paying unsustainable taxes,
and under pressure from their donors to prove that their work is
having an impact on a large population.

As a prerequisite for funding, many international foundations
and governments insist that NGOs develop business models with
professional standards of excellence that show their operations
are self-sustaining. This absurd capitalist model requires that
victims' organizations become social enterprises that generate
profits in weak economies and under failed development
policies. The outlook is therefore not too encouraging: small
charities do not have their own resources, and the employees
of these organizations must be prepared to risk their lives in

---

* See the map entitled "Corruption Related to Human Trafficking",
www.protectionproject.org/wp-content/uploads/2011/07/TIP-Report-
Review-2011.pdf

an environment of corrupt police and weak institutions. In some countries where laws against slavery and exploitation have been passed, they are not implemented, because this would mean sacrificing the large amounts of money that the sex trade contributes to the economy.

And Nevertheless . . .

As I wrote this book, I stopped hundreds of times to look at the photographs, the drawings, and the small keepsakes that victims gave me when I visited them and listened to their stories: a pair of earrings made of wire and bits of wood that a girl in Guatemala made for me; a drawing by Dany, a boy used for child pornography in Arizona, who told me that he wanted to marry me when he grew up because I love baseball and Harry Potter.

Sometimes after transcribing dozens of interviews, I had to stop writing. I was overcome by waves of emotion. I was assailed by chills, hunger, lack of appetite, thirst, insomnia, and dreams. I gave vent to my indignation in deep sighs and conversations with myself: What more can be said about this? How to speak of these stories without making it an obscene exaltation of pain? At such moments, what came to mind was the warmth of the Uzbekistani girls' hands as they patted my skin on a cold night, and the smiles and amazement of the Afghan soldiers when I gave them a bag of cookies, which they accepted as though it were a kilo of gold dust.

Sometimes I would look at the computer screen and feel sick and tired. Then I would go out into the garden and play with my dogs, trying to rid myself of the burning questions: where is evolution taking us? Why is the human race incapable of using its power to alleviate suffering?

I returned to my notes and recordings and I read my journal: I was left astonished by people's ability to reconstruct the facts, narrate their experiences, and extract new meaning in order to confront their pain and suffering. I felt alarmed by the ways in which societies normalize one of the most fundamental forms of violence: colonizing a body in exchange for a few coins for food is a modern, subtle, and effective form of exterminating the right to love and enjoy sex for millions of women and girls.

As I was working on this investigation, I received constant threats from criminal networks, which meant I constantly had to seek emotional balance and inner peace. I could not allow myself to get caught up in the overwhelming current of anger and fear that surrounds certain businesses, nor in the desperate claims of organizations defending trafficking victims, which sometimes resort to exaggerating statistics to attract society's attention.

I understand that emotional fatigue, being burnt out from empathy, is something that must be addressed. It is impossible not to feel indignant and not to suffer when listening to hundreds of horrifying stories of systematic rapes of girls, women, and men who cannot stop crying and keep asking, "But why me?"

I found that many of the people who work to help victims are in different stages of burnout: police officers, investigators, legislators, journalists, human-rights lawyers, men and women involved in politics who dared to raise their voices only to be met by insults.

Many of the radicals who form public opinion consider any person who dares to question the damage caused by pornography, prostitution, and clients of the sex trade to be backward, ignorant, conservative, prudish, frigid, or homosexual. A Guatemalan delegate who was debating the prohibition of prostitution when I was visiting Guatemala City was given an anonymous note warning her that if she meddled in the prostitution business she would die being raped "by sticks and machos" in order to cure her of her frigidity. Amazingly, she knew that the note had come from a high-ranking military official who controlled the sexual exploitation of adolescents.

The problem is that it is difficult to defend people's freedom and autonomy in an environment of hatred and constant insults. I learned from the most rabid abolitionists who belonged to religious groups and from the most intolerant proponents of regulation, that resentment and the need to control other people's lives, along with the inability to empathize with others' pain, can limit or destroy dialogue and fuel fanaticism. The Mexican poet Octavio Paz once said that the great moral and spiritual flaw of liberal democracies is their emotional insensitivity. Society's on-going task is to reinvent love and eroticism without violence.

A decade ago, my work as a human-rights advocate led me to establish a high-security shelter. There, women, girls, and boys begin the process of healing from different forms of violence. This experience has profoundly marked my life: I learned that victims are the only experts on their own cases. They are the ones, with the help of appropriate support and therapy, who find the path to emotional healing and follow it toward a different destiny. I discovered that in order to become a survivor it is necessary to be free. Only in this way can a person choose to leave the pain behind. Only in this way can girls and boys rescued from slavery wake up one day with the confidence that to be alive among humans has new meaning. They are reborn before our eyes to teach us how to reinvent a soul. For this to happen, the person who accompanies them on this journey must have complete respect for the victims' self-determination. Their greatest enemies are the clients of the slave market and their greatest allies could be millions of men willing to question slavery from the ethical standpoint of otherness.

Glossary

This section provides a glossary of the terms, definitions, and basic concepts used in this book. I have chosen the words I consider essential to reach a common understanding between readers and all the people to whom I give a voice. In different countries, various local terms are used to explain the same phenomenon. Where possible, I have given the legal terminology from the international treaties and conventions signed by the majority of the countries I visited.

Abolition of prostitution: a movement that proposes to repeal laws, rules, or customs that promote or support prostitution because they violate human rights. The term "abolitionism" derives from the movement to abolish slavery and considers that every person is a "subject" with legal rights, not an "object."

Acquired Defenselessness Syndrome: a psychological condition in which victims come to believe that they have no control over the situation in which they find themselves, and that anything they do is useless. Their victimizer uses a cycle of intimidating acts to show that he exercises control over their life; this is often done through a rewards and punishment system. As a result, victims remain passive when faced with an uncomfortable or harmful situation.

Battered Women Syndrome: this includes three syndromes that develop from long-term psychological, physical, and emotional violence: **Stockholm Syndrome**, **Acquired Defenselessness Syndrome**, and **Post-Traumatic Stress Syndrome**. Battered Women Syndrome does not connote that the woman is ill, but that she shows trauma from violence. She can overcome these traumas once she has left the adverse situation.

Commercial sexual exploitation: the sexual abuse of women and children, giving financial advantages to one or several of the parties involved in the sexual activity. The most common forms of sexual exploitation that involve human trafficking are prostitution, sex tourism, and pornography.

Domestic violence: generally understood as a series of discreet acts of violence, in reality it is a system of power and control that the aggressor establishes and maintains over a partner, spouse, ex-spouse, or child. Isolation, intimidation, and threats, plus emotional, economic, and sexual abuse, are interrelated strategies that the man employs to subjugate his victims. The women and children who suffer domestic violence learn to accept coercive control and they are the most vulnerable when confronting traffickers.

Forced or coerced labor: work or services demanded of an individual under the threat of a penalty, which the individual engages in against his or her will.

Illegal human trafficking: transporting persons and facilitating their illegal entry into a country where they are not a citizen or permanent resident, for the purpose of obtaining, directly or indirectly, a financial or material benefit. Unlike traffickers, smugglers lose control of the victims once they arrive at their destination or when payment is received.

Mafia: a special type of organized-crime syndicate, which originated in Italy; the term is now applied worldwide to any group with similar characteristics irrespective of national boundaries. Some of the most important mafias include the Chinese Triads and the Japanese Yakuza, Russian organized groups from the former Soviet Union, the Italian mafia, the Turkish mafia and the South American cartels.

Money laundering: the conversion or transfer of money obtained from criminal acts to hide or disguise its illegal origin, thereby making the proceeds of crime appear legitimate.

Moral panic: the term coined by American anthropologists Carole Vance and Gayle Rubin to describe the accumulated fears relating to public morality and security. This type of fear tends to unite social movements on a large scale in response to general anxieties generated by sexual issues.

Pimp or madam: the intermediary between a client and a person subjected to sexual slavery or prostitution. Also known as a manager, sugar daddy, godfather, godmother, mack, hustler, panderer, etc.

Post-Traumatic Stress Syndrome: a set of symptoms that may appear after surviving war, torture, disasters, accidents, terrorist attacks, or slavery situations. A person forced into prostitution who has suffered abuse may suffer from this condition. The victim has flashbacks, relives the nightmare, and develops phobias. Other symptoms include difficulty concentrating, irritability, eating disorders, recurrent suicide attempts, self-mutilation, and personality disorders.

Prostitution: engaging in sexual relations with other persons in exchange for money; from the Latin *prostituere*, which means "to exhibit, as for sale." The use of the term "prostitution" is controversial: there are groups that seek to replace it with "sex work." Others argue against this because all over the world trafficking for sexual purposes and prostitution involves coercion. In this book, I use the word "prostitution." See abolition of prostitution and state regulation of prostitution.

Slavery: the ownership of a person, who, under the control or dominion of another, loses the ability to control his or her life, liberty, and fortune.

State regulation of prostitution: a movement seeking to control and organize prostitution in accordance with rules issued by the government, covering taxation, social security, retirement, etc. Such regulation considers prostitution as legitimate employment where the body is the tool used by a sex worker.

Stockholm Syndrome: describes the behavior of kidnapped or enslaved victims who, over time, become sympathetic to their captors. Sometimes these women end up in affectionate or romantic relationships with their captors. In the majority of cases, traffickers encourage this behavior in their victims; as a result, once these victims have escaped or been released, they often don't press charges.

Survivors: people who remember violent acts without being paralyzed. With emotional and therapeutic support, survivors can regain control of their life, and acknowledge their emotions and thoughts about crimes perpetrated against them, while also being able to look to the future and find hope.

Traffickers: those involved in trafficking in persons. They may include organized criminal groups; family members (fathers, mothers, uncles, aunts, siblings, grandparents, etc); persons with authority over others (bosses, employers, public officials, community leaders, or priests); businessmen (owners, managers, and operators of businesses in the sex industry, such as motels, hotels, lap-dancing or strip clubs, massage parlors, bars, restaurants, and other establishments that act as a cover for forced prostitution.)

Trafficking for sexual purposes: the practice of transporting persons in and out of their own country to sexually exploit them through the of use of force, coercion, manipulation, deception, abuse of authority, family pressure, familial or community violence, economic deprivation, and other conditions of inequality. Some writers call this "forced prostitution."

Trafficking in persons: the recruitment, transportation, transfer, harboring or receipt of persons through the threat or use of force or other forms of coercion, to give one person control over another for the purpose of exploitation.

Victims: women or children who, whether held captive by their traffickers or not, suffer all the symptoms of Battered Women Syndrome and cannot find the means to get away from the deep suffering they are experiencing.

Violence against women or girls: all acts of violence against the female sex that can result in physical, sexual, or psychological harm or suffering for the woman or girl, including threats, coercion, and deprivation of freedom, whether in public or in private.

Appendix

What Needs to be Done

Eradicating trafficking in women and children for the purposes of sexual slavery is a tremendously complex mission. The most important thing is to begin with specific goals that will allow political leaders and relevant social groups to define clearly the challenges and possible solutions. Admitting that human trafficking is a part of the global commercial sex industry is an essential starting point. Likewise, it is important to understand that this business receives different levels of protection from government officials and from members of organized-crime groups who couldn't care less about philosophical debates about their activities.

It is essential to know the risk factors for potential victims:

- Poverty and extreme poverty
- Lack of sex education
- Lack of love education
- Lack of opportunities for education, employment, etc.
- Encouragement of prostitution within the family or social circle
- Transferring women and children from less developed countries to developed ones
- Problems of addiction, isolation, and discrimination
- Having a history of sexual or physical abuse as a child

We should also be aware of the consequences of sexual exploitation:

- Sexually transmitted diseases and infections
- Trauma caused by violent sexual relations with men
- Isolation of women and children, far from their families, who are involved in a relationship of dependence with pimps and brothel owners
- Victims' difficulty in asking for help, due to their illegal immigration status, use of fake documents, and working as prostitutes
- Rejection by family and social groups after victims are deported and return to their homes
- Victims' difficulty in reclaiming ownership of their own bodies

What Can I Do?

- Contribute a percentage of your salary to organizations that rescue girls from slavery and that offer them opportunities to study and be free (see www.lydiacacho.net for a list of such organizations.)
- Support professional soccer, tennis, basketball programs that promote non-violent and non-sexist masculinity for boys.
- Do not give money to children who beg in the streets, because traffickers are usually controlling them. It is preferable to donate to a local organization that offers them education and opportunities.
- Speak openly about eroticism and sexuality with our children; help them to understand the power they have through owning their bodies and emotions; speak with them about the importance of equality, as well as the harm of violence against human beings.

- Refuse to consume products manufactured by slave labor (see www.oit.org.)
- Participate in movements protesting against human slavery in your country.
- Travel as a responsible tourist; ensure that the hotel you choose has a policy against human trafficking, particularly against child sex tourism (a list of recommended establishments can be found at www.ecpat.org.uk and www.savethechildren.org.)
- Do not generalize: millions of men are not willing to enslave or sexually exploit women or minors; ask these men in your community to take a stand on this issue.
- Write to newspapers, magazines, and conferences that cover issues on human slavery; participate in prevention campaigns.
- If you are willing to commit to this cause, ask for material from campaigns against human trafficking and distribute it in your children's schools.
- Consume products that help to prevent trafficking in children; The Body Shop and Oxfam, for example, have products sold in aid of eradicating child slavery.
- Remember that you hold the power to participate in social transformation; choose: there are millions of people in the world who have no opportunity to do so.

Some of the Myths and Realities of Child Abuse

In 1998, a group of pedophiles met, first in person and later on the Internet, to create International Boy Love Day (IBLD) to be celebrated on June 24. According to them, this date would be used "to reclaim the rights of adult males to have sexual relationships with young boys." The campaign spread via the Internet and in each country—from Holland, Belgium, Egypt, and South Africa to Argentina, Mexico, Canada, and the United States—pedophiles lit blue candles.

The reactions to IBLD were immediate. One part of society decided to distance itself because it considered the issue unpleasant; other groups of young people, particularly in Europe, in an effort to defend their progressive ideas, argued that every person has a right to express his political, sexual, and ideological beliefs. However, various civil society organizations working to defend human rights analyzed the negative consequences of forcing boys into slavery in order to pleasure non-conformist, powerful adults.

On May 30, 2006, a group of pedophiles formed a political party called the Party for Neighborly Love, Freedom, and Diversity (PNVD) and registered it with the Dutch authorities. Based on movements to legalize prostitution, this group invoked the constitutional freedoms of thought and expression to defend children's rights. The PNVD said that its members included important Dutch politicians, businessmen, fathers with families, teachers, priests, and "all types of free men who have chosen to express their sexuality and erotic lives through relationships with boys and girls." In its manifesto, the PNVD demanded that the age of sexual consent be lowered to twelve and that bestiality, child pornography, and all forms of sexual acts performed on minors should be legalized.

Each day, more men from developed countries such as Spain, Norway, the United States, Canada, Australia, England, and Germany, join this type of movement.

Pederasts or Pedophiles
Pederast comes from the Greek *paiderastos*, from *paidos*, meaning "boy" and *erastos* meaning "lover." Pederasty is defined as engaging in sexual relations with minors. In contrast, pedophilia refers to an adult's sexual attraction to minors.

Freud and Lacan laid the ground for the current psychiatric and psychological view of those who commit child abuse as people who are sick or suffering from some pathology caused by a traumatic situation. Some researchers—without solid evidence—believe that pedophiles are responding to a childhood trauma of sexual abuse. There are also scientists, such as R. J. Kelly and R. Lusk, who point out that the pedophile's sexual activation could have its origin in childhood memory, given that the first sexual awakenings normally occur with other small children. According to the theory of social learning, pedophiles may have been sexually activated at this moment, and for this reason they are only aroused by the physical conditions of boys and girls, by the lack of pubic hair or by small genitals. These experts fail to explain that pedophiles can be found in positions of responsibility, trust, and power toward their victims. It has been shown, on the other hand, that the majority of pederasts are men and women who function socially in a normal way; they are even capable of having responsibilities in all aspects of their lives.

Child-Abuse Experts

The clinical psychologist Jorge Garaventa, one of the most recognized child-abuse experts in Latin America, states that "physical and sexual abuse of a child occurs in an unequal situation where the adult holds the power and uses his superiority to get pleasure from his victim who is destroyed and subjugated." Garaventa explains that "sexual abuse by an adult of a minor, as in the case of rape, does not come from a sexual impulse or necessity; instead it is an act of power and submission expressed through an eroticized act."

Against the old view of pederasty as an incontrollable pathology, various experts in new areas of humanistic psychology who deal with sexually abused minors state that those who commit these acts should not be considered a product of their culture, since there is a definitive subjective moment when, with or without pain, every person chooses his path. It is true that in Greek and Roman culture, pederasty was socially acceptable and that centuries of patriarchal domination has cloaked this form of violence in silence. It is essential to question received wisdom and listen to the experts who are leading theoretical thinking and effective treatment for victims.

Healing the Pedophiles?

Not a single scientific study proves that psychiatric treatment for pedophilia works in the long term. Imprisonment has not proven to be effective: many of the most publicized cases in the United States and in Australia involved men who acted with more violence and fury after having served prison sentences for sexual crimes. Some countries have resorted to chemical castration to deactivate the part of the brain that controls the sex drive. However, it has not yet been proved that controlling libidinal impulses inhibit aggression towards minors.

While pedophiles form a political party and bolster the sexual abuse networks, joined by some "normal men," it is calculated that only one out of thirty-six cases of rape is reported. UNICEF reports that around 1.2 million children are being subjected to sexual exploitation on the planet. Imagine what might happen if this movement is not stopped, a movement that aims to normalize the raping of minors.

Acknowledgements

This book is journey, a search, a reunion with the human race and its complexities. Every word in it distills the breath, the impulse, and the vital energy of hundreds of people who listened to me, spoke to me, believed in me, and even protected me in dangerous moments.

Together we have tried to unravel the issue of modern-day slavery in its multifaceted forms. It would not have been possible without my sister Myriam's nurturing and loving care, nor without the endless support of my brothers José, Alfredo, and Paco, as well as my father Óscar and his smiling partner Olga.

I would like to thank Lía, my other sister, who took care of me when I was sick and when I was happy; to María Guadarrama, my doctor, who helped me reduce my stress levels; to Nubia and Ángela, who listened to me, gave me feedback and made me laugh; to my colleagues at the CIAM refuge in Cancún, who are tireless peace makers, giving their attention daily to women, and children.

To my colleagues and teachers, from whom I learned and with whom I argued; your words and your works allowed me to take this project forward. To Melissa Farley, Kathryn Farr, Alicia Leal, Marta Lamas, Montse Boix, and Marcela Lagarde. To Mónica Díaz de Rivera, who read these pages with interest and patiently corrected errors; to Malú Micher; to Cecilia Loría, who died before seeing the book finished; to the incredible and tenacious Tere Ulloa; to the remarkable Norma Hotaling;

to Rafaela Herrera, for making me understand the power of restorative justice; to my colleague Marco Lara Klahr, for his advice and friendship; to Sanjuana Martínez, Lucía Lagunes, the CIMAC team, and Paka Díaz Caracuel, friends and teachers in this investigation; to Zlatko Zigic and Marinka Franulovik, for their support during my trip to central Asia and their friendship ever since; their work in the region for the IOM has a huge impact on many people.

To Roberto Saviano, Victor Malarek, Ricardo Rocha, and Javier Solórzano, four colleagues who made me feel I was not alone during difficult times; to Somaly Mam and her team in Cambodia; to the women of ECPAT in Thailand, who gave me a hug when I most needed it; to Debby Tucker; to Sue Hannah of Australia; to Maki Kubota and Ritsuko Kudo, the fantastic colleagues who accompanied me on my field trips at night in Japan; to Daniel Garret; to the women at the Asian Woman Center in Tokyo; to Michiko Kaida, who works in Thailand helping all Asian children; to Doctor Jean Nady Sigmond; to the good and coherent Mark Lagon; to the patient Claudia Hill from the US Federal Bureau of Prisons; to Elina, my Croatian friend who helped me disguise myself and survive among traffickers; to Sonia K., who taught me to pronounce Russian words and understand the mafia's mindset; to John Perkins, who helped me understand how the mafia's businessmen think; to Alberto Islas, for not letting me lose sight of the Mexican drug cartels and their networks; to Victoria Thian of Kyrgyzstan; to M.M. of Italy, who taught me how to restore one's happiness; to Stephanie Urdang of South Africa; to Philo Nikonya, my sister in Kenya; to Malalai Joya, for her strength of character and determination to transform Afghanistan, her native land; to Bermet Moldovaeva of Kyrgyzstan, Madhu Bala Nath of India, and the doctor Charlotte Faty of Senegal, all guides and experts; to my dear teacher Chivy Sock in Los Angeles; to Jurgen of France and Bangkok, for taking the risk of showing me the route used by the regional mafias; to Maria Shriver, Mariane Pearl, and Carmen Aristegui, for their honesty and compassion.

To the agents of Interpol, SIEDO, the extinct KGB, ICE, and the FBI, whose names I cannot reveal, but whose frankness was extremely helpful to me; to my dear Fernando Espinosa, Francesc Relea, and Fran Sevilla; to my emotional and financial supporters, Alicia Luna and my brothers and sisters at the Fundación LC; to Bertha Navarro and Luis Mandoki; to Cristina del Valle and the Platform for Women Artists Against Gender Violence, who bring together willpower and hope; to Minister Bibania Aido and to Nuria Varela, for their tenacity and openness; to Eve Ensler, for reminding me that I am an emotional creature and that this is marvelous; to my teacher Jean Shinoda Bolen.

To Lino and Ms Carmen, who made sure that I was protected and well fed during many nights spent in front of the computer; to Karla, for looking after me, with cheerful professionalism; to Leda and Pita, who gave me kindness, joy, and good tequila on those ill-fated nights.

A special thanks to Eduardo Suárez, my brotherly friend who withstood long hours of one-sided conversation in an effort to help me understand the rhythm of my words, for his careful reading and tenacious criticism. To Cristóbal Pera and the editorial team at Random House Mondadori, who believed in my work from the beginning.

To Darío, Cynthia, Mario, and all the legal team of Article 19, I thank you for vindicating my right and freedom to express myself. One may get used to living under threat, but it is more bearable when one is supported by a legal team that does not yield to the mafia's corruption and impunity.

To Anna Politkovskaya, with whom I laughed and cried before she was assassinated; we never thought that they would kill her, but we knew that it was worth it to risk our lives for our ideals.

And, of course, to Jorge, for vindicating a masculinity that is sweet, loving, playful, and hopeful.

About the Author

LYDIA CACHO is an internationally admired Mexican journalist-campaigner. She is a columnist on *El Universal*, a prominent feminist activist against violence, and teaches workshops on how to help trafficking victims. She has been named UNESCO World Press Freedom Hero and received the PEN International Writer of Courage award 2010.